Twenty-First-Century Symbolism
Verlaine, Baudelaire, Mallarmé

Contemporary French and Francophone Cultures, 83

Contemporary French and Francophone Cultures

This series aims to provide a forum for new research on modern and contemporary French and francophone cultures and writing. The books published in *Contemporary French and Francophone Cultures* reflect a wide variety of critical practices and theoretical approaches, in harmony with the intellectual, cultural and social developments which have taken place over the past few decades. All manifestations of contemporary French and francophone culture and expression are considered, including literature, cinema, popular culture, theory. The volumes in the series will participate in the wider debate on key aspects of contemporary culture.

Recent titles in the series:

NIKOLAJ LÜBECKER

Twenty-First-Century Symbolism

Verlaine, Baudelaire, Mallarmé

LIVERPOOL UNIVERSITY PRESS

First published 2022 by
Liverpool University Press
4 Cambridge Street
Liverpool
L69 7ZU

This paperback edition published 2024

British Library Cataloguing-in-Publication data
A British Library CIP record is available

ISBN 978-1-80207-012-5 hardback
ISBN 978-1-83553-732-9 softback

Cover Illustration: Broodthaers, Marcel (1924–1976), *Un coup de dés jamais n'abolira le hasard* (A throw of the dice will never abolish chance, by Stéphane Mallarmé, 1897), 1969. Mechanical engraving and paint on twelve aluminum plates, plate (each): 12 3/4 × 19 9/16 × 1/8 in. (32.4 × 49.7 × 0.3 cm). Publisher: Wide White Space Gallery, Antwerp, Galerie Michael Werner, Cologne. Digital image © 2022, The Museum of Modern Art, New York/ Scala, Florence. DACS, London.

Typeset by Carnegie Book Production, Lancaster

Contents

Acknowledgements

I would like to thank the many friends and colleagues who invited me to explore this material at conferences, in workshops, at seminars, in reading groups and over a drink; I would also like to thank the editors of – and readers for – the various journals in which earlier versions of this material were published: Patrick Bray, Jørgen Bruhn, Petr Budrin, Christopher Bush, Maddy Chalmers, Dominique Combe, Andrew Counter, Corry Cropper, Martin Crowley, Lisa Downing, Reidar Due, Elizabeth Emery, Ann E. Fernald, Daniel Finch-Race, Daisy Gudmunsen, André Guyaux, Mairéad Hanrahan, Chloe Johnson and her colleagues at Liverpool University Press, Sarah Jones, Marie-Chantal Killeen, Diana Knight, Julia Kristeva, Patrick Labarthe, Michael Lucey, Marie Lübecker, Ian Maclachlan, Johanna Malt, Bertrand Marchal, Emily McLaughlin, Martina Morab, Ben Morgan, Ève Morisi, Barry Murnane, Jennifer Oliver, Roger Pearson, Kriss Ravetto-Biagioli, Daniele Rugo, Debarati Sanyal, Douglas Smith, Francesco Sticchi, Michael Syrotinski, Emilija Talijan, Jessica Tanner, McNeil Taylor, Gemma Tidman, David Uhrig, Seth Whidden, Emma Wilson, Alastair Wright, Panayiotis Xenophontos, Jennifer Yee, two very helpful anonymous reviewers, St John's College, and, most of all, Julie.

Earlier versions of some of these arguments were previously published as:

- 'Mallarmé's Instruments: The Production of the *Individu-Livre*', *French Studies* 73:3 (2019), pp. 367–83;
- 'Mallarmé's Digital Demon', *Paragraph* 43:2 (2020), pp. 140–58; and
- 'Twenty-First Century Baudelaire?, Affectivity and Ecology in "Le Crépuscule du soir"', *Modernism/modernity* 27:4 (2020), pp. 689–704.

I am grateful for permission to draw on this material.

A Note on Translations

I have mostly drawn on published English translations. With complicated poets like Verlaine, Baudelaire, and Mallarmé, it is tempting to adjust translations to highlight those aspects that suit my reading. I have (mostly) refrained from doing this – partly out of respect for the wonderful job done by excellent scholars and translators such as Barbara Johnson, Rosemary Lloyd, and others, partly because any adjustments were likely to leave out other important dimensions of the original texts (and produce numerous explanatory footnotes). When the original French sentences translate almost directly into English, I have not provided a translation; when I do not reference a published translation, I am responsible.

A Note on the Cover

The cover presents the Belgian avant-garde artist Marcel Broodthaers's variation on the penultimate page of Stéphane Mallarmé's *Un coup de dés jamais n'abolira le hasard*. Mallarmé's poem is from 1897, Broodthaers's work from 1969. As is evident, Broodthaers has put black bars over Mallarmé's words. The gesture is simple, the work polysemic. Does it prolong Mallarmé's poetics of negation, with Broodthaers embracing the Mallarmean dictum 'La Destruction fut ma Béatrice' ['Destruction was my Beatrice'], playfully turning negation against the poet himself? Do the redactions point to the well-known ideas about the poet's secrecy and hermeticism? If I have chosen to put Broodthaers on the cover, it is not to emphasise negation and secrecy; rather, I like to think that his gesture brings out the poem's pulse – an outlandish, cosmic Morse code. What Mallarmé has to do with coding and cosmic communication will hopefully be clearer by the end of this book.

Introduction

Twenty-First-Century Symbolism

At the beginning of *Sur Racine* (1963), Roland Barthes characterized the seventeenth-century dramatist as being particularly available for a wide range of theoretical approaches, and he suggested that contemporary critics should take advantage of this availability. He also reminded his fellow critics of the historical nature of their own work, encouraging them to embrace this historicity and make sure that Racine became part of the contemporary world's conversation with itself. Barthes puts these ideas in the following terms:

> [E]ssayons sur Racine [...] tous les langages que notre siècle nous suggère; notre réponse ne sera jamais qu'éphémère, et c'est pour cela qu'elle peut être entière; dogmatiques et cependant responsables, nous n'avons pas à l'abriter derrière une 'vérité' de Racine, que notre temps serait seul (par quelle présomption?) à découvrir; il nous suffira que notre réponse à Racine engage, bien au-delà de nous-mêmes, tout le langage à travers lequel notre monde se parle à lui-même et qui est une part essentielle de l'histoire qu'il se donne. (1993, 987)

> [Let us test on Racine [...] all the languages our century suggests. Our answer will never be anything but ephemeral, which is why it can be complete. Dogmatic yet responsible, we need not shelter our answer behind a 'true' Racine whom our age alone (by what presumption?) has discovered; it will be enough if our answer to Racine engages, beyond ourselves, the entire language by which our world expresses itself and which is an essential part of the history it calls its own. (1983a, x)]

As is well known, not everyone agreed with this suggestion to read Racine using contemporary vocabularies, in partisan ways, giving up on the idea of a 'true' reading, and thereby becoming more responsible. The Sorbonne-based Racine specialist Raymond Picard reacted with *Nouvelle critique ou nouvelle imposture* (1965), accusing Barthes of many sins, not least that of dehistoricizing Racine. Barthes responded with *Critique et vérité* (1966), opting for a mix of polemic and trivialization, arguing that it is only logical that 'un pays reprenne ainsi périodiquement les objets de son passé et les décrive de nouveau pour savoir *ce qu'il peut en faire*: ce sont là, ce devraient être des procédures régulières d'évaluation' (1999, 9) ['a country should periodically review in this way the things which come down from its past and describe them anew in order to find out *what it can do with them*: such activities are and ought to be normal assessment procedures' (2007, 1)].[1]

This book takes its cue from Barthes and considers *what we can do with* Verlaine, Baudelaire, and Mallarmé today. How do these authors speak to the present? How does our present invite us to re-read their texts? Formulated in this manner, these questions are likely to set off alarm bells. For instance, readers may object that it is reductive to look for something like the contemporary use value of these three poets, because it invites an instrumental approach to literature whose limitations have already been pointed out by many thinkers – the three poets and Roland Barthes included. Furthermore, these guiding questions are politically suspect (not least in a book about three dead white European men): the singular term 'present' necessarily simplifies a much more complex set of circumstances, violently excluding many relevant aspects of our contemporary situations. It is therefore appropriate to begin by setting out which specific version of the 'present' this book will be referring to. To reuse the terms of Roland Barthes: which twenty-first-century languages will be tried out on Verlaine, Baudelaire, and Mallarmé?

Since the end of the 1990s, a plethora of new theoretical approaches has emerged in literary studies as well as in the humanities and social sciences more widely. Labels such as 'affect theory', 'new materialism', 'object-oriented ontology', 'animal studies', 'ecocriticism', 'post-humanism', 'cyborg theory', and 'speculative realism' have been coined. Even if this proliferation of labels also testifies to well-known logics of fashion and the marketable, it is difficult to deny that collectively these approaches speak to important mutations in current scholarship (and in our world more widely). In 2015, Richard Grusin attempted to bring this diverse set of theoretical formations together under the umbrella term 'the

---

1   Unless otherwise noted, emphases are (as here) in the original.

nonhuman turn' (Grusin, 2015). For reasons that will soon become clear, I will avoid the term 'nonhuman' and instead prioritize the no doubt less elegant term 'non-anthropocentric'. However, although Grusin's term does not appeal to me, his effort to bring out what these writings have in common is still very helpful. He saw them as responses to some of the key societal challenges facing us today – above all, the global climate crisis and the rapid developments in (bio)technological sciences. In other words, these various theoretical approaches aim to reconsider the place of the human being in a world where ecological and technological developments prompt us to push the questioning of the human in ways other than those pursued from the 1960s to the '90s.

To explain this change of emphasis, we may borrow from Rosi Braidotti's overview of contemporary scholarship in *Posthuman Knowledge* (2019). Here, Braidotti first refers to the 1960–90s critique of European Humanism, a critique carried out in the name of 'sexualized and racialized others claiming social justice and rejecting exclusion, marginalization and symbolic disqualification' (9). She quotes Edward Said's observation that it is possible to critique Humanism in the name of Humanism, and she observes that 'these critiques are as essential to the Western project of modernity as to the modernist project of emancipation' (9). But towards the end of the twentieth century, she continues, the debates around Humanism and anti-Humanism so typical of the postmodern moment increasingly found themselves upstaged by the need to include considerations of the place of human beings in a wider planetary ecology. In Braidotti's terms, the critique of Humanism gave ground to a critique of anthropocentrism that

> enacts a double shift. Firstly, it requires an understanding of ourselves as members of a species, and not just of a culture or polity. Secondly, it demands accountability for the disastrous planetary consequences of our species' supremacy and the violent rule of sovereign Anthropos. (10)

Of course, this does not mean that there are no continuities between contemporary post-anthropocentric theory and what preceded it, and it certainly does not mean that the problems that gave rise to a critique of European Humanism are a thing of the past.[2] However, a shift has taken place, and post-anthropocentric theory therefore insists that the critique of European Humanism can no longer be carried out in the name of any

---

2 In this paragraph, I am using the term favoured by Braidotti: 'post-anthropocentric'.

new and improved form of Humanism. It can, however, learn from the cultures that European Humanism repressed during the years of colonial expansion – cultures that contributed much less to what Braidotti called 'the violent rule of sovereign Anthropos' than did our own Western cultures.

Let me bring these wide-ranging debates closer to the texts studied here. If we return to Barthes, it is well known that the texts mentioned above – *Sur Racine* and *Critique et vérité* – were part of his polemic against biographical criticism in the 1960s. Barthes's critique is also expressed in texts like *S/Z* (1970) and *Le Plaisir du texte* (1973), but in terms of public impact it arguably culminated in the famous article on 'La Mort de l'auteur' (1967). All these texts trouble conventional ideas about the author and the human subject more widely, and they have therefore often been associated with postmodern anti-Humanism. However, they never sought to challenge anthropocentrism. It is thus characteristic that when Barthes drafts Mallarmé (Valéry, Proust, Surrealism and modern linguistics) into his battle against the figure of the author, it is to argue that the death of the author must pave the way for 'la naissance du lecteur' (1984, 69) ['the birth of the reader' (1977b, 148)]. As we shall see in Chapter 5, Barthes is right: an important aspect of Mallarmé's poetics does indeed consist in giving initiative to the reader. However, there is also a speculative dimension in Mallarmé's work, which suggests that the poet offers a more radical challenge to the human perspective: 'Impersonnifié, le volume, autant qu'on s'en sépare comme auteur, ne réclame approche de lecteur. Tel, sache, entre les accessoires humains, il a lieu tout seul: fait, étant' (2003, 217) ['Impersonified, the volume, to the extent that one separates from it as author, does not demand a reader, either. As such, please note, among human accessories, it takes place all by itself: finished, it exists' (2007, 219)]. Mallarmé therefore speaks to a contemporary situation where we are required to think at the limits of the species and the Anthropos. And, as this book will seek to demonstrate, so do Verlaine and Baudelaire.[3] Indeed, in many (although not all) of their texts, the three poets push their readers toward the non-anthropocentric ontologies that emerged at the turn of the twenty-first century.

---

3   It can be argued that Barthes, too, had already begun to move beyond the critique of Humanism and towards post-anthropocentric thought by the end of the 1970s. In my first chapter on Verlaine, such an argument will be outlined through a reading of Barthes's texts on haiku-poetry.

I am conscious that some readers will be sceptical about exposing Verlaine, Baudelaire, and Mallarmé to what may appear to be the latest fashions in critical theory. Baudelaire and Mallarmé obviously had a very different relation to *la dernière mode*, but the sceptical reader might nevertheless be relieved to hear that the following pages will focus on the situation these new critical idioms are responding to, rather than the idioms themselves. The multitude of labels (of which I have mentioned only a few) are unlikely to stick around in the long term, but they are responding to a situation – of ecological crisis and intensified technological mediations – that it would be irresponsible to think of in terms of fashion. So even though I do engage some of these newer theoretical idioms (not least affect theory, ecocriticism, technology studies, and certain theories about cognition and embodiment), the thrust of my argument will be situated at a level that most of these schools share, that of a non-anthropocentric ontology and its concomitant conceptualization of individuation.[4] What matters to me is the very broad question of how the three poets can contribute to a thinking about the place of human beings in the contemporary world. As Braidotti puts it, 'we need a subject position worthy of our times' (2019, 41) – this volume goes via Verlaine, Baudelaire, and Mallarmé in an attempt to carve out such a subject position.

It is my conviction that the climate crisis and the emergence of multiple technological innovations (two developments that must be thought together) now force us to think differently about ourselves and our relation to the world. These developments therefore also impact on the ways in which we read literature and write criticism. I believe that we must think of ourselves as more intimately connected to the world than has previously been our habit; or more accurately, that we can no longer continue to ignore our intimate entanglement in the world. This conviction is one I share with many critics in the schools mentioned above.[5] It is not an exclusively new position, and throughout this book I will show that the 'contemporary critical landscape' relies on many earlier critical, artistic, and philosophical discourses. For instance, I will

---

4 'Individuation' will be a key term throughout this volume, and it will therefore be presented in detail in Chapter 1. For the purposes of this introduction, 'an always ongoing process of subject formation' will do as an explanation.

5 This is obviously not the only possible way of responding to the current crises. Other critics have argued that the answer to the climate crisis lies in more Cartesianism, stronger subject–object distinctions, and more dialectics. See, for instance, Slavoj Žižek (2008) and Adrian Johnston (2014).

seek to demonstrate that the late work of Maurice Merleau-Ponty, the writings of Gilbert Simondon, and a number of cybernetics-inspired texts from the 1960s and 1970s can prove useful for a contemporary re-reading of well-known poetic texts by Verlaine, Baudelaire, and Mallarmé.

Pitching my argument at the level of ontology and individuation explains why this is not a book about late-nineteenth-century nature writing or the many technological inventions that made of that period the first example of a technologically mediated network society (due to inventions such as the telegraph, photography, railways, cinema, etc.). Many books on these topics already exist, and they form part of the background of my arguments, but I am primarily concerned with how the chosen poets write their way out of an anthropocentric worldview. Indeed, my argument is that reading Verlaine, Baudelaire, and Mallarmé can be seen as a practice in non-anthropocentric ontology, and that this is a crucial exercise in the current situation. So, while my ambition is to deliver new readings of Verlaine, Baudelaire, and Mallarmé, arguing for the poets' continued relevance today, showing that their curiosities and sensitivities were far more wide-ranging (and less anthropocentric) than often said, I also hope some readers will begin to rethink notions of subjectivity, perhaps even approaching the ecological conception of individuation that I argue is in line with current socio-political (and scientific) developments. This is a book about the ongoing importance of French symbolist writing for our understanding of ourselves.

'Symbolist' may seem like a misnomer. To begin with, it is not the label most commonly applied to Baudelaire. He is more frequently described as the canonical poet of modernity (by Walter Benjamin, and his numerous followers) or as a site of conflict between romantic and modern tendencies (see for instance Pichois [2005] and Metzidakis [2017]). Furthermore, symbolism is associated with one of the most tedious manifestos of the literary avant-gardes, written by Jean Moréas, a writer now exclusively read by specialist scholars of late-nineteenth-century French literature. Verlaine famously spoke about symbolism as 'cymbalisme', drawing attention to Moréas's talent for beating his own drum. In his poem to Mallarmé in *Dedicaces* (1890), Verlaine took care to rid the work of his friend of the label 'symbolisme' (and his own work of that of 'decadence' [Verlaine, 1962, 557]). In the twentieth century, the term continued to have bad press. Philippe Sollers hit a typical note when he argued against classifying Mallarmé as a symbolist:

> 'Symboliste' est devenu péjoratif, s'agissant de la littérature, et à juste
> titre, évoquant aussitôt un aspect désuet, renfermé, idéalisant, littéraire

dans le plus mauvais sens du mot, un aspect de décadentisme esthétique, bref ce que beaucoup, par une sorte de malentendu volontaire, s'acharnent encore à retrouver chez Mallarmé en détachant de ses poèmes des fragments où ces défauts sont visibles. (1968, 68)[6]

[When it comes to literature, 'symbolist' has with good reason taken on a pejorative meaning, immediately evoking the literary in the worst sense of the word: an obsolete, constricting, idealizing element, an aesthetic decadentism, in short precisely what some, by a sort of willful misunderstanding, still attempt to impose on Mallarmé by isolating fragments of his poems in which these shortcomings may be found. (1983, 65–66, translation modified)]

If I have nevertheless decided to go with this unappealing term, it is not so much because of the alluring idea of an -ism that no one wants to be part of (a loser-ism), but partly by default – after all, this term has been used for all three poets (Marchal, 1993) and no other term could obviously replace it – and partly in a more affirmative spirit: although I share Sollers's aversion to the containment-capacities of certain -isms, I believe it is time to take a closer look at some of the tendencies that have been associated with the so-called idealism, detachment, and political conservatism of symbolism. This approach will be introduced in the opening chapter on Verlaine and then articulated most clearly in relation to Baudelaire, about whom I will argue that those aspects of his work that sociologically inclined readers have tended to either criticize or marginalize (the 'pastoral' dimensions, as Marshall Berman [2010] called them) deserve renewed attention, because they challenge our anthropocentric habits more effectively than the better-known image of Baudelaire as the poet of modernity. And with this last sentence, I have begun to anticipate the arguments of the six coming chapters…

Individuation and Practice: Verlaine, Baudelaire, Mallarmé

Twenty-First-Century Symbolism opens with two chapters devoted to Verlaine. To answer the guiding question – what can we make of these poets today? – chapters 1 and 2 read four of Verlaine's most

---

6   It is of course possible to nuance this presentation of symbolism – for instance, by paying attention to the differences between French and Belgian symbolism, and to the differences between symbolist poetry, prose, and theatre (see McGuinness, 2016).

famous early poems, three well-known critical texts about Verlaine, and a series of recent (and less recent) philosophical texts that engage with the question of individuation. Here, as elsewhere in the book, the two chapters are interconnected but can also be read independently. The first chapter presents a more optimistic Verlaine, the second a more pessimistic Verlaine, as well as an attempt to bring these two sides together without offering a synthesis. Each of these elements – close readings, extensive discussions of selected critical readings and philosophical intertexts, and the non-synthetic constellation of lighter and darker texts – can also be found in the chapters on Baudelaire and Mallarmé.[7]

The Verlaine chapters aim to demonstrate that his poetry – not all of it, but the most famous portions of it – relies on a thoroughly ecological conception of individuation. To explain what this means, I first consider Roland Barthes's writings on haiku-poetry, making the case that Verlaine is as close as we have to a late-nineteenth-century French haiku-poet. Barthes's writings on haikus allow me to introduce the key concept of *individuation.* Taking a few steps back in time, I then go from Barthes's notion of individuation to his source of inspiration, Gilles Deleuze, and back to one of Deleuze's forerunners, Gilbert Simondon. Simondon will be a recurring reference in the volume more generally. These first two chapters argue that Verlaine's understanding of individuation can be elucidated via Simondon's writings on the topic.

The analysis of individuation leads to a second key idea presented in the opening chapters: Verlaine understands poetry to be a *practice.* More specifically, poetry is a practice that allows the reader to sense the co-emergence and entwinement of the mental and the environmental. Because the poems push this process of imbrication so hard, Verlaine frequently 'casts anthropocentricity in doubt' (238), as Clive Scott presciently wrote in 1988. In this manner, Verlaine's poetry orients us towards what today is theorized as affects and 'nonconscious cognition' (Hayles, 2017). I argue that Verlaine is the French affect-poet par excellence, and I draw on recent developments in affect theory to give to

---

7 I should say from the outset that in the first four chapters, the distinction between optimistic and pessimistic writings will largely remain practical, operational. The fact that Verlaine and Baudelaire write about both their painful and pleasurable experiences of entanglement will not inspire any normative considerations about which texts are the best or most productive. In chapters 5 and 6, this distinction between optimism and pessimism will be addressed more explicitly.

this statement a more precise signification than we have previously been able to lend it.

The chapters on Baudelaire continue the examination of the two central themes in my readings of Verlaine: individuation and poetry as practice. Chapter 3, the darker of the two chapters on Baudelaire, reads the prose version of 'Le Crépuscule du soir' from *Le Spleen de Paris* – and a limited number of texts associated with affect theory and new materialism. It engages closely with Baudelaire's poem, attempting to demonstrate how Baudelaire's linguistic work pushes us to think non-anthropocentrically. The chapter also steps back to clarify how an affective reading of Baudelaire differs from (and resonates with) well-known interpretations by Georges Poulet (1961), Jacques Rancière (2014a), and Ross Chambers (2015). By the end of the chapter, we will have seen that 'Le Crépuscule du soir' invites us to think human beings as dynamic mediations of their environments. And we will have broached the question of how such processes of environmental becoming relate to the important socio-political explorations also found in Baudelaire's work.

Chapter 4 turns to Baudelaire's art historical writings. More specifically, we shall examine how the theorization of colour perception allows Baudelaire to escape a world of subject–object dualisms and present a more process-relational ontology. To explain what this means, I draw on a wide range of thinkers (including Maurice Merleau-Ponty [1997], theories of embodied cognition [Varela, Thompson, and Rosch (2017)], and Gilles Deleuze [1994]), before I read Baudelaire in conjunction with Joachim Gasquet's conversations with Paul Cézanne (which took place in the late 1890s). Through this dialogue with Cézanne, Baudelaire emerges as an ecological, almost new materialist poet. At the end of the chapter, I then return to the well-known idea of Baudelaire as a poet of modernity, the city, and the capitalist transformations of late-nineteenth-century France. I explain how this particular Baudelaire can be placed in relation to the ecological, new materialist poet, and, as indicated above, I argue that whereas sociologically oriented readers of Baudelaire have marginalized his interest in topics such as colour and nature, often considering these to be among the more romantic and conservative aspects of his writings, we can now see how these themes disturb the anthropocentrism that many sociological readings (inadvertently) reinforce. In other words, today Baudelaire's speculative metaphysics may be as least as challenging for our contemporary capitalist culture as his more familiar texts about Parisian crowds.

What would Stéphane Mallarmé be doing today, if he had been born in the early twenty-first century? It is possible he would have been brought up on gaming and coding; maybe he would have been fascinated by the ways in which technical devices mediate and transform our subjectivities, and perhaps he would have been thinking about which devices – which forms of play and mediation – we should develop to create a better society. If this proposition of *Mallarmé as a game designer* seems less fanciful at the end of my final two chapters, I will be delighted.[8] My ambition in chapters 5 and 6 is to demonstrate how the kind of individuation we find in Mallarmé's writings resembles the one we find in twentieth- and twenty-first-century media environments. In order to bring this argument home, my final chapter reads Mallarmé's writings alongside twentieth-century cybernetics and twenty-first-century media theory.

First, however, Chapter 5 introduces key aspects of Mallarmé's poetics, picking up on the themes developed through the readings of Verlaine and Baudelaire. I investigate what Mallarmé means when he speaks about writing and reading as a 'practice', and I demonstrate that Mallarmé's 'Livre' relies upon an understanding of individuation that overlaps with the one we encountered in the work of Gilbert Simondon (Chapter 1). This chapter mainly draws on later texts by Mallarmé, where the poet expresses an optimistic view of the interactions between books, poets, readers, and the universe – a form of optimism frequently found in the more utopian versions of contemporary media theory.

The final chapter moves back in time to focus on the early prose poem 'Le Démon de l'analogie'. This poem presents a more dystopian worldview, one which is equally widespread in contemporary media theory. Why reverse the chronology and move from late to early texts, from optimism to pessimism, from utopianism to dystopianism? Why deny the reader of this volume a happy ending? The final part of the chapter nullifies these questions, demonstrating instead the synchronous nature of the two tendencies: all throughout his life, Mallarmé's work hosts ambiguities that also characterize twentieth- and twenty-first-century relations to media and technology. In short, for Mallarmé too, media are a 'pharmakon', both remedy and poison.[9]

---

8   Such speculations about Mallarmé and informatics can also be found in Marshall McLuhan (2001 [1964]), Vilém Flusser (2011b [1985]), and Bernard Stiegler and Ars Industrialis (2006). We shall return to Flusser, Stiegler, and Ars Industrialis in Chapter 6 (see also Bakken, 2018, 230).

9   The term 'pharmacology' is associated with Plato, and it can mean both

At times my arguments may seem to be in the grips of a 'démon de l'analogie'. This is particularly the case in the last chapter, which compares Mallarmé's poetics to twentieth-century cybernetics; but earlier in the volume I also suggest that Verlaine (almost) writes haiku, and (anachronistically) that Baudelaire can be understood through Cézanne's reflections on colour. Cybernetics was criticized precisely for being analogical thinking, built on comparisons such as those between brains and computers, biological and technological systems. Norbert Wiener, the key figure of cybernetics, responded to this criticism by embracing it, suggesting that analogy is simply the way in which we think: meaning is never intrinsic, it is constituted relationally, we think via comparisons. Mallarmé would have agreed (which is why you do not want a demon messing with your analogies). Nevertheless, the danger of analogical thinking is that it may overlook differences, and become blind to the elements a comparison marginalizes (for instance, the brain–computer analogy of first-generation cybernetics went hand in hand with a marginalization of the question of embodiment). In this book, I pursue analogies across different borders – national (Japan and France), disciplinary (cybernetics and poetry), and historical (the 1870s and the early 2000s). I believe these comparisons are worth the risk, and that not taking this risk comes with other forms of danger. I also believe that our current Anthropocene moment – as Timothy Clark (2015) has argued – blows open our usual perspectives, time scales, and well-established ideas about what constitutes a relevant context (see also Felski, 2015). Nevertheless, the issue of *temporal* border crossing perhaps deserves a few more introductory comments.

Like its main title, the subtitle of this book disturbs our historical habits. Going by date of birth, it should have read 'Baudelaire, Mallarmé, Verlaine'. However, I begin with Verlaine because the selected poems

cure and poison. This ambiguity was famously analysed in Jacques Derrida's 'La Pharmacie de Platon' (in *La Dissémination*, 1972) and it has been brought into media and technology studies by Bernard Stiegler and others to highlight the enormous potential – constructive and destructive – of technological innovations. Mallarmé is no stranger to this logic of the blurred lines between poison and cure. When composing *Igitur* in November 1869, he writes to his friend Henri Cazalis: 'C'est un conte, par lequel je veux terrasser le vieux monstre de l'Impuissance, son sujet, du reste, afin de me cloîtrer dans mon grand labeur déjà réétudié. S'il est fait (le conte) je suis guéri; *similia similibus*' (1998, 748) ['It is a tale by which I want to defeat the old monster of Impotence, which, by the way, is its topic, already revised yet again. If I complete it (the tale), I'll be cured: *similia similibus*' (1988, 89–90)].

so clearly work on our understanding of what 'individuation' means. Breaking our chronological habits allows my argument to move from the ontological with Verlaine to the ontological/sociological in the Baudelaire chapters.[10] More generally, however, I am content to propose an achronological subtitle because it clearly signals that this book does not offer a historicist study of the three poets. I will not write much about French society in the nineteenth century, and my main question is not how these poets placed themselves in their historical moment. There is already a tremendous amount of scholarship on this question, much of it very helpful for understanding the poetry.[11] Sometimes this scholarship also explains why we should remain interested in placing the poets in their historical context today; sometimes it takes for granted that such an endeavour continues to deserve our time and energy. Very rarely is the relation to the present the main focus of a study. This book tips the balance from the historical context to the contemporary situation more than most books on late-nineteenth-century literature.[12] I want to stress that these poets do not belong in the filing cabinet labelled 'mid- to late-nineteenth-century French literature', that twenty-first-century readers are caught up in their texts in ways more intricate and intimate than we initially think. This argument is not about denying strangeness and difference by claiming proximity to the past, but about histories being ongoing, and therefore not allowing us to step back and look from a safe distance.

10   This does not mean that Verlaine's poetry is unanchored from its socio-political context.

11   I have myself contributed to this kind of scholarship (see Lübecker, 2002, 107–207).

12   With this comes a sometimes-unorthodox set of references and footnotes. I have been inspired by contemporary media theory, process philosophy, eco-theory, affect theory, and many other texts; even if I have also benefitted from more historically oriented studies of the three authors, my footnotes prioritize the theoretical references as they speak more clearly to the analysis of our contemporary situation. Of course, I write to engage readers with an interest in nineteenth-century French poetry, and throughout these chapters I therefore also spend many pages locating my arguments in relation to a few important critical voices in this field, both classical (Jean-Pierre Richard, Georges Poulet) and contemporary (Arnaud Bernadet, Clive Scott, Anna Arnar, Jacques Rancière), but I am afraid that the adjustment of perspective that I am trying to perform has meant that many other critics and literary historians (some of whom write about the contemporary importance of these poets) have not found their way into the following pages.

Let me restate this argument whilst using the conceptual framework of *Twenty-First-Century Symbolism*. As mentioned, it is becoming increasingly common to think that we cannot (and never could) separate ourselves from the environments with which we evolve. We are spatially constituted to such an extent that we no longer feel comfortable speaking about *environments*, as if these were spaces *surrounding* us. But this ecological understanding of our always ongoing subject constitution has a temporal dimension also. We are not only mediations of space, but also ongoing mediations of time. The Anthropocene subject is a chronotope, unfolding and modulating both space and time. In this regard, my approach to literary history can be said to draw on writers such as Proust and Bergson. Indeed, what might happen if we reconceive literary history in a Proustian mode, relying on a Bergsonian conception of time?

Rather than considering the past as a distant historical object, Proust and Bergson emphasize its constant mutations and the ways in which these participate in the ongoing, creative production of the present and future. As Georges Poulet demonstrated, Proustian retrospection quickly becomes prospection, generating a story which the narrator of *Le Temps retrouvé* describes as being 'en perpétuel devenir' (Poulet, 1990, 12) ['in perpetual becoming']. Focusing on Bergson, Leon Ter Schure (2019) similarly explains how the philosopher makes history part of a process of becoming:

> Bergson does not just state that, like Hegel's owl of Minerva, only afterwards is the meaning of an era unveiled, nor that every epoch holds its own unique *interpretation* of 'the' past as some fixed entity in time. He goes further than this. Within duration, the past is constantly reworked. With a new reality truly comes the creation of a truth about the past, which means that the historical past is not given but actually *changes* within duration. (141)

Ultimately, this book is about such ongoing processes of becoming, including the argument that the poetry of Verlaine, Baudelaire, and Mallarmé can be particularly helpful when shaping the present.

Let me finish this introduction with a remark about my use of 'particularly' in the previous sentence. I am convinced that the works of Verlaine, Baudelaire, and Mallarmé are (as Barthes might say) 'particularly available' to our present. As has often been argued, these writers were all involved in a profound investigation of what literature, individuation, and matter might mean. They were busy rethinking the relations between – and near-indistinguishability of – language, subjectivity, the natural, and the social world. Certain key notions and famous phrases from the mid- to late nineteenth century very obviously speak to the contemporary moment. Rather than dismissing the cliché of the Verlainian 'je-ne-sais-quoi' or Mallarmé's 'l'air ou le chant sous le texte' (2003, 234) ['the melody beneath the text' (2007, 236)], we may thus rethink these well-known symbolist ideas in terms of affectivity and nonconscious cognition. Likewise, we can revisit Baudelaire's 'Correspondances' from an ecological perspective and 'Une Charogne' with new materialism, or we can associate the critique of representation that runs through the three poets' works with contemporary non-representational theory. As suggested, I shall pursue some of these endeavours over the six coming chapters, and I therefore hope that the claim about the poets' 'particular availability' will finally seem justified to readers. However, I do not want to labour this point. I am sure that many other poets and writers, from many other periods and cultures, are also due for a re-reading. In our current critical times, a lot can and should be done with the things that come down from our past.

CHAPTER ONE

Haiku-Verlaine

Unlike Baudelaire and Mallarmé, Paul Verlaine has never been a central reference for general critical or philosophical debates. Of course, he is well known, but he remains much less studied than Baudelaire and Mallarmé, Rimbaud and Lautréamont, or earlier poets such as Nerval and Hugo. Among scholars of Verlaine this has sometimes inspired attempts to distance Verlaine from well-worn clichés about his impressionism, musicality, and his *je-ne-sais-quoi*, showing that his work is much more heterogeneous and unruly than the anthology pieces demonstrate (Bernadet, 2007, 15), or that Verlaine is closer to Rimbaud, more avant-garde and more politically radical than is often assumed (Murphy, in Verlaine, 2012). In relation to such arguments, the next couple of chapters may seem retrograde. They will not be radicalizing Verlaine's poetry, nor will they discuss the heterogeneity of his work (even though I do find Bernadet's arguments convincing). Rather, these chapters will go back to the best-known – or rather, most frequently studied – poems by Verlaine, and rethink the clichés about Verlaine's symbolism, musicality, and the 'chanson grise' (Verlaine, 1962, 326). My intention is to demonstrate how this poetry speaks to the present, why Verlaine is a contemporary poet. The answer to this question has little to do with radicality and originality, traits that tend to make a poet stand out. In fact, it has more to do with an ability to blend in. More accurately, Verlaine's poetry forces us to reconsider critically what terms like 'originality' and 'radicality' might mean. To some extent, I therefore agree with Jean-Pierre Richard's famous suggestion (discussed in Chapter 2) that it is Verlaine's *fadeur* (blandness) that makes him interesting. It allows him to write poetry that disturbs our hermeneutic habits, and it fundamentally (radically?) challenges conventional conceptions of subjectivity, proposing new relations between human beings and their worlds. With this *fadeur*, Verlaine draws close to contemporary ecological and affective understandings of individuation, offering an ontology so flat that even Richard's sophisticated phenomenological analysis struggles to grasp it. I will argue that it is this understanding of subjectivity – rather than attempts to bring Verlaine closer to a more activist (but also more well-known) subject position – that holds the greatest potential today.

As hereby suggested, the poems prioritized in the following chapters rely upon an understanding of subjectivity that no longer presents a strong distinction between individual and environment. It is this conception of subjectivity – of individuation – that will be at the heart of the next two chapters. Verlaine's understanding of individuation is not new: it resonates with different forms of ancient philosophy and with the writings of Spinoza, for instance. But it has become increasingly prominent over the last 20 years (which have seen multiple re-readings of thinkers like Lucretius and Spinoza). Two contemporary and occasionally overlapping versions of this philosophy of individuation are found in ecocriticism and affect theory. These approaches therefore also play a part in the following analysis. One way to summarize the argument of these first chapters is to say that they seek to demonstrate that Verlaine is the late-nineteenth-century French affect-poet par excellence. With this comes a second claim: his poetry is fundamentally ecological. Neither of these claims should come as a surprise. Verlaine's interest in what lies just beyond the limits of representation, that which can only be suggested, has frequently been associated with the 'affective' in the broader sense of the term. However, with the development of affect theory over the last 20 years a new conceptual apparatus has become available, and this allows a more systematic account of what it means to call Verlaine's poetry affective. The second claim, that Verlaine writes ecological poetry, can be taken in a narrow sense: Verlaine explores the relations between human beings and their natural surroundings. This is true. But here ecology will be understood at a more ontological level (along the lines of Erich Hörl's [2017] notion of a 'general ecology'). The environment need not be natural; it can be urban, linguistic, or more broadly semiotic. What matters is Verlaine's exploration of how the environment (now taken in the broadest sense of the term) participates in the process of individuation.

As mentioned, these chapters do not offer a comprehensive analysis of Verlaine's work. The focus will be on a few poems by the character I call 'haiku-Verlaine'. This is the Verlaine that strikes me as contemporary. Verlaine did not write haikus and, considering how much *japonisme* was around at the end of the nineteenth century, he wasn't particularly Japanese. Nevertheless, the poems selected here present almost no narrative development, they prioritize environments or settings, and they explore mostly non-dramatic (or subtly dramatic) forms of entanglement between – and co-emergence of – environments and subjectivities. I will argue that the challenge of these poems is to get their 'gesture' – or *attaque* – right: to bring oneself in tune with the poetry and the universe that emerges in the verse. As with haikus, reading therefore becomes a special kind of *practice*. Verlaine's haiku-esque poetry is a *practice of ecological individuation*.

This argument will be developed in two interconnected chapters. The first delivers readings of two of Verlaine's more optimistic and erotic poems. These readings go hand in hand with a presentation of 'haiku-Verlaine'. In this first chapter, I draw extensively on Roland Barthes's theorization of the haiku (what he calls '« Mon » haïku' [2003, 53; 2011, 23]) and Gilbert Simondon's notion of individuation. In the second chapter, these initial readings and two additional analyses of more spleen-dominated poems are then situated in relation to some of the most interesting critical studies of Verlaine (by Richard, Scott, and Bernadet), and certain aspects of contemporary affect and eco-theory. Finally, a conclusion brings together the discretely ecstatic poetry and the more spleen-ridden verse, summing up how Verlaine's conception of poetry and individuation can be said to speak to the present.

Discrete Ecstasies

Let us begin, then, with an example of Verlaine's peaceful 'haiku'-poetry: 'La Lune blanche' from *La Bonne chanson* (1870, publ. 1872).

VI

La lune blanche
Luit dans les bois;
De chaque branche
Part une voix
Sous la ramée...

Ô bien-aimée.

L'étang reflète,
Profond miroir,

> La silhouette
> Du saule noir
> Où le vent pleure...
>
> Rêvons, c'est l'heure.
>
> Un vaste et tendre
> Apaisement
> Semble descendre
> Du firmament
> Que l'astre irise...
>
> C'est l'heure exquise.[1]

What is the structure of this poem? The rhyme scheme (ababcc) suggests that there are three stanzas, each containing six four-syllable lines. The mise-en-page blurs this three-stanza structure as the fifth line in each stanza ends with an ellipsis before a sixth, free-floating verse. The three suspended lines can be read as a direct address to the beloved: 'Ô bien-aimée/.../ Rêvons, c'est l'heure/.../ C'est l'heure exquise'. The poem thus permits a double reading (led by the rhyme scheme or by the mise-en-page), gently anticipating Mallarmé's more far-reaching challenge to linearity in *Un coup de dés jamais n'abolira le hasard* (1897). Both texts force the reader to keep several tracks going simultaneously; both authors spatialize time.

As the floating verses suggest, this is a love poem set at a privileged moment in time: 'l'heure exquise'. Whereas the suspended lines address the beloved, the five-line stanzas offer only discrete signs of human presence: we know that someone has been (and perhaps still is) watching and listening to a scene, and that this voice is now speaking about it. However, the poetic voice only comes close to appearing on one occasion, with 'semble' in the last stanza. Here the voice gently emerges through its hesitation. Otherwise, the stanzas paint a 'scene', giving the poem an image-like character.

Initially this image is in black and white. In the opening stanza, the landscape is lit up by the white light of the moon, and in the second stanza the light is reflected in the pond, producing the 'silhouette/ Du saule noir'. These chiaroscuro effects give depth to an image which

---

1   In the following readings of Verlaine's poetry, I will be referring only to the original French texts. In terms of vocabulary, syntax, rhymes, etc., the translations of Verlaine's verse are too far from the originals to be useful for close analysis.

stretches from the white moon in the sky to the dark depths of the pond. In the final stanza, colours subtly appear through the verb 'iriser', which typically refers to the colours of a rainbow or quartz; now the moon lights up the sky in a way that recalls a celestial phenomenon such as the northern lights.[2]

The discrete modulation of light, shadow, and colour goes hand in hand with a modulation of diegetic sound in the first two stanzas. First a voice goes out from every branch in the woods: 'Ô bien-aimée'. Perhaps the branches are hosting birds as they do in 'Birds in the Night', the final 'ariette' in *Romances sans paroles* ('parmi les ramures réelles/ se cachent les tourterelles'). In the second stanza, another sound is heard: we look into the mirror of the water and notice the dark willow tree 'où le vent pleure.../ Rêvons, c'est l'heure'. The verb 'pleure' evokes weeping willows; the tone is soft and slightly melancholic. But, the potentially negative associations of the verb 'pleure' should not dominate our reading: this is not a scene of despair and heartbreak. The last stanza is primarily one of appeasement (this four-syllable noun – 'apaisement' – *is* a line), building up to the naming of 'l'heure exquise' at the end of the poem. The overall effect is tender and ethereal: the light, the reflection, the voices... – nothing asserts itself too strongly in this peaceful scene.

The various movements in the poem are worth considering too: light plays in the forest, the surface of the lake reflects the willow tree, and peace 'seems to' descend from the sky as the firmament lights up. Together these descriptions create an expansive, multi-vectoral, almost elastic universe of wide horizons and fathomless depths ('profond miroir'). This expansiveness is 'vaste et tendre' rather than worrying and overwhelming. It goes hand in hand with an idea of precision conveyed by 'the exquisite hour' and the sharp contours of the black-and-white image. This interplay – or identity – between the precise and the indefinite is a staple of Verlaine's poetry (and will therefore be discussed later). Here it results from chiaroscuro effects, mirroring, and the succinctness of the poem and its lines. As mentioned, the structure of the poem supports this combination of the precise and the indefinite:

2   The third stanza speaks about the 'firmament/ Que l'astre irise...'. Although the moon isn't a star, I disagree with readers who think that Verlaine must be referring to some other celestial body: as the Larousse indicates, 'l'astre des nuits', 'l'astre nocturne' and 'l'astre d'argent' are all common literary expressions for the moon.

in each stanza, we have five short lines, which end with an ellipsis – then a sixth that threatens to drift off into space before it is reeled in by a feminine rhyme. In this manner the poem opens the 'stanzas' (Italian for 'room'), letting us feel the air. Suspended in the white space between the fifth and sixth line, between the nocturnal scenery and the address to the beloved, the poem and its reader hold their breath while moonlight floods the page.

Some of the most beautiful pages in Gaston Bachelard's *La Poétique de l'espace* are devoted to Baudelaire's 'immensité intime' (2012, 168) ['intimate immensity' (1994, 183)], and in particular to this poet's use of the term 'vaste'. Bachelard insists that the 'le mot *vaste* est une valeur vocale. C'est un mot *prononcé*, jamais seulement lu, jamais seulement vu' (179) ['the word *vast* is a vocal value. It is a word that is *pronounced*, never only read, never only seen' (196)]. And Bachelard also explains how Baudelaire uses vastness to ease distinctions between inner and outer: 'Pour Baudelaire, le destin poétique de l'homme est d'être le miroir de l'immensité, ou plus exactement encore, l'immensité vient prendre conscience d'elle-même en l'homme. Pour Baudelaire, l'homme est un être vaste' (178–79) ['For Baudelaire, man's poetic fate is to be the mirror of immensity; or even more exactly, immensity becomes conscious of itself, through man. Man for Baudelaire is a vast being' (196)]. It is precisely this experience of hosting the vastness of the universe that Verlaine's poem invites us to experience too – in the beautiful 'a' of 'vaste', in the remarkable 'espaces' between the fifth and sixth lines of each stanza.

Such an ethereal poem poses a challenge to the critic – precisely because there seems to be no challenge. Like other poems by Verlaine, 'La Lune blanche' is 'simple': the vocabulary is straightforward, the text never overloaded. For those reasons the professional critic might very well struggle: what is there to say? As Stanley Fish humorously suggested in 'How to Recognize a Poem When You See One', most of us feel more at ease with complexity and hermeneutical challenges:

> If your definition of poetry tells you that the language of poetry is complex, you will scrutinize the language of something identified as a poem in such a way as to bring out the complexity you know to be 'there'. You will, for example, be on the look-out for latent ambiguities; you will attend to the presence of alliterative and consonantal patterns (there will always be some), and you will try to make something of them (you will always succeed); you will search for meanings that subvert, or exist in a tension with the meanings that first present themselves; and

if these operations fail to produce the anticipated complexity, you will even propose a significance for the words that are *not* there, because, as everyone knows, everything about a poem, including its omissions, is significant. (1980, 327)

In the light of Fish's pronouncements, it is unsurprising that critics so often respond to Verlaine's simplicity with long and detailed commentaries, treating the texts as mysteries or riddles: riddles, for instance, about the poet's private life or about the ways in which he negotiates his place in literary history. Of course, it would be silly to deny that Verlaine's poetry is autobiographical, and critics may also want to write about the genre of the *clair de lune*. But the detective work that hermeneutical critics so often engage in (what is the poem *really* saying?) risks occluding the experience of clarity and simplicity it is so difficult to respond to.

A comparison with Baudelaire's 'Les Chats' can clarify this point. Baudelaire's sonnet is also about infinite spaces and a universe holding its breath. Like 'La Lune blanche', it is a seductive and softly erotic poem through which the reader travels. 'Les Chats' is wonderfully silent too, even more so than 'La Lune blanche'. However, a major difference is that Baudelaire plays up the enigmatic and mysterious aspects of his poem. His attraction to mystery and myth shows in the portrayal of the cats, who are 'sphinxes' holding the key to a secret that escapes us. With these references, Baudelaire appeals to the hermeneutic reader, offering a challenge, inviting us to decipher and speculate. Verlaine's poem, on the other hand, has no such mythical dimension. It does not claim to be in possession of a secret, and there are no 'prunelles mystiques' (Baudelaire, 1975, 66) ['mystic eyes'] at the end of the poem. It is less spectacular and much more difficult to speculate about.

A response to Verlaine therefore has to be tactful. Reading 'La Lune blanche', it seems inappropriate (to this particular commentator) to detail intersubjective relations or to look for various forms of symbolism. Yes, there is a 'bien-aimée', a hesitant poetic voice ('semble'), and an implicit 'nous' in 'Rêvons': this is a love poem. But this is not a poem that invites a psychological reading. Like the poems in his next collection, this is a 'romance sans paroles'; a text that brings language to a halt. Instead, Verlaine guides us into a silence that hides nothing but manifests itself directly on the page, in the white space separating the fifth and sixth lines of each stanza. The challenge is to place oneself in this gap, to linger with the ellipsis, and feel the weightlessness of this moment where the vastness of the universe tenderly opens before us: 'l'heure exquise'.

There is a poetic genre that presents similar challenges and therefore offers another entry point into Verlaine's poetry: the (Barthesian) haiku-poem. The next section will offer a close account of Barthes's theorization of the haiku, but first let me suspend three haikus as a response to the three ellipses (or, as the French call them, 'points de suspension') in 'La Lune blanche'. These haikus are all taken from a small collection that Barthes assembled for the students attending his 1978–79 seminar at the Collège de France. They were written by three classical masters, and they can be read as exercises in lowering the heart rate of the reader, allowing us to sense the transience of the world:

> Lune éblouissante,
> Pour reposer l'œil,
> Deux ou trois nuages, de temps en temps.
> (Bashō, 1644–94)

> Pas d'autre bruit
> Que l'averse d'été
> Dans le soir.
> (Issa, 1772–1858)

> Un bateau, on regarde la lune,
> Pipe tombée à l'eau,
> Rivière peu profonde.
> (Buson, 1716–84)
> > (in Barthes, 2003, 462–63)

> [Dazzling moon,
> Two or three clouds from time to time
> To repose the eyes.
> (Bashō, 1644–94)

> No other sound
> Than summer rain
> In the evening.
> (Issa, 1772–1858)

> The moon-viewing boat,
> I dropped my pipe,
> Into the river shallows.
> (Buson, 1716–84)
> > (in Barthes, 2011, 384, 387)]

Haiku-individuation

Barthes's fascination for haikus is visible in several texts, the two most important of which are *L'Empire des signes* (1970) and the late seminar *La Préparation du roman 1* (1978–79, posthumous). It is my contention that Barthes's theorization of the haiku resonates strongly with the Verlaine poems analysed in these first two chapters. This does not mean that Verlaine wrote haikus; rather, haiku is the horizon that some of his most famous early poetry tends towards. The Verlaine poems discussed here are short and condensed (although not quite to the extent haikus are); they are non-narrative, and pull away from psychology and personal pronouns (although not quite to the extent that haikus do); and they avoid abstraction by being situated and specific (although not quite to the extent that haikus are). In writing this, I agree with Roland Barthes. Verlaine is not a very important poet in Barthes's work, but in the late seminar he does play a role. His name appears on three occasions (four if we include a reference to 'Kaléidoscope'[3]), and he is presented as one of the few Western authors who comes close to the haiku. As Barthes makes clear, this is a view he shares with the linguist Maurice Coyaud, for whom Verlaine constitutes a notable exception to the logorrhoea of Western poetry.

Beginning with *L'Empire des signes*, there are two complementary ways to present Barthes's fascination for the haiku. The first has to do with the fact that haiku is *not* a Western form. A part of Barthes's analysis is therefore delivered in negative terms: haikus are *not* Western, because they are *not* aiming for complexity or richness of meaning. Instead, haikus insist on the right to be what poetry is *not* allowed to be in the West: 'futile, court, ordinaire' (2005, 94) ['trivial, short, ordinary' (1983b, 70)]. Therefore, the haiku also constitutes a problem for the Western way of reading:

> Déchiffrantes, formalisantes ou tautologiques, les voies d'interprétation, destinées chez nous à *percer* le sens, c'est-à-dire à le faire entrer par effraction [...] ne peuvent donc que manquer le haïku; car le travail de lecture qui y est attaché est de suspendre le langage, non de le provoquer. (98)

---

3   'Kaléidoscope' is of course the title of a Verlaine poem in *Jadis et naguère* (1962, 321–22). As we shall soon see, Barthes compares the individuating consciousness to a kaleidoscope; and – as we shall see in Chapter 4 – Baudelaire uses the same metaphor when describing the subjectivity produced through the experience of crowds (1976, 692).

> [Deciphering, normalizing, or tautological, the ways of interpretation, intended in the West to *pierce* meaning, i.e., to get into it by breaking and entering [...] cannot help failing the haiku; for the work of reading which is attached to it is to suspend language, not to provoke it. (72)]

It follows that haiku-poetry cannot be called symbolic (no sphinxes here) and that it resists the hermeneutic reader. Haikus also refuse to play any of the roles we usually give to literature ('instruire, exprimer, distraire' [113]) ['instruct, express, divert' (82)]. Instead, they perform a liberating, negative operation: 'ce qui est aboli, ce n'est pas le sens, c'est toute idée de finalité' (113) ['what is abolished is not meaning but any notion of finality' (82)]. Even the end of a haiku is not an end, for as Barthes reminds us, haikus are meant to be read twice and 'l'écho ne fait que tirer un trait sous la nullité du sens' (103) ['the echo merely draws a line under the nullity of meaning' (76)]. For all these reasons, the haiku represents an antidote to the view of poetry that Stanley Fish mocked in the passage cited above.

Promoting haikus at the expense of Western forms of writing and reading is not just an issue of what kind of poetry we prefer, it is also a question of subject understanding and politics. Barthes's theorization of the haiku in the 1970s connects to his ambition to escape Hegelian dialectics, hermeneutics, and what he calls 'la guerre de sens' (2002b, 517) ['war of meanings'].[4] Barthes is tired of what he perceives as the violence of dialectics (master–slave relations and the injunction to create oneself, to realize one's desire, through a struggle for recognition) and he seeks out alternative forms of coexistence, developing key concepts such as the non-vouloir-saisir and the neuter (in, for instance, *Fragments d'un discours amoureux* [1977a] and the late seminar on *Le Neutre* [1977–78]). As will be shown shortly, the horizon for Barthes's promotion of the haiku is the ambition to present a subject position that does not tie itself to the idea of an 'identity', a politics that evades the war of meanings, and a conception of literature that emphasizes the pleasures of participating in the pluralization of meaning.

The haiku can then be presented in more positive terms also. Barthes talks about a 'langage plat' (2005, 100) ['flat language' (1983b, 76)], and he emphasizes that haikus search for 'un moment où le langage cesse' (100) ['a moment when language ceases' (76)]. He goes on to specify

---

4   I have written in detail about Barthes's attempts to wrest himself free of Hegelian dialectics in Lübecker, 2009, 113–39.

that this 'cessation' – we can think of Verlaine's ellipses – must not be associated with a richness in signification: 'il ne s'agit pas d'arrêter le langage sur un silence lourd, plein, profond, mystique [...] ce qui est posé ne doit se développer ni dans le discours ni dans la fin du discours; ce qui est posé est *mat*' (100–101; we are approaching Richard's *fadeur*) ['it is not a question of halting language on a heavy, full, profound, mystical silence [...] what is posited must develop neither in discourse nor in the end of discourse: what is posited is *matte*' (74)]. This language is described as an 'a-langage', and Barthes highlights its liberating effect: 'cet état d'*a-langage* est une libération' (101) ['this state of *a-language* is a liberation (75)]. He then works his way to his famous one-word summary of haikus:

> le haïku s'amincit jusqu'à la pure et seule désignation. *C'est cela, c'est ainsi*, dit le haïku, *c'est tel*. Ou mieux encore: *Tel!* (115)

> [the haiku diminishes to the point of pure and sole designation. *It's that, it's thus*, says the haiku, *it's so*. Or better still: *so!* (83)]

This *Tel!* is contingent and never spectacular – it is not an event in the Western sense of the term; rather, the haiku offers an alternative to the Western metaphysics of the event.[5]

Nine years later, Barthes returns to the haiku in his penultimate seminar. Again, he criticizes Western writing and insists on the *Tel!*; he analyses the desire to reach a neuter through an experience of emptying out (*kenosis*) and thereby experience the kind of understanding the Japanese refer to as *Satori*. But in Barthes's later text, we also find a number of new ideas, and a more sustained engagement with the question of subjectivity. Much of the new material crystallizes around Barthes's engagement with the notion of *individuation*.

Barthes argues that in the moment of the *Tel!* (or 'c'est cela') the reader (or writer) experiences a *tilt* (Barthes uses the English word).

---

5   As the above quotations make clear, Barthes has to tread carefully when advancing his ideal of the haiku. The haiku's ability to avoid or derail discourse and symbolism quickly begins to resemble a new (revolutionary) discourse. In the above citations this danger is particularly manifest when Barthes described the haiku's 'a-langage' as a liberation, despite the fact that he wants to stay clear of any form of teleology. Of course, Barthes knows all too well how easily Westerners can make a flat language deep, how quickly the interruption of language can open the floodgates of commentary. Dialectics is a flexible machinery, and attempts to escape it are often drawn back into this machinery, positioned as antithesis.

This tilt results from a shift in intensity; it is an affective experience which Barthes places at the core of his idea of 'individuation'. He uses this last term a couple of times, before reluctantly addressing it in a more systematic, philosophical register. This happens over a few pages that are worth quoting in some detail. First, Barthes writes:

> J'ai parlé à plusieurs reprises d'*individuation* – de la Saison, du Temps qu'il fait, de l'Heure comme individuation. Je vais insister un peu sur cette notion. Philosophiquement, c'est une notion à laquelle le dernier Deleuze attache, je crois, beaucoup d'importance. Comme toujours, hélas, je la prendrai assez grossièrement, comme une *direction*. (2003, 77)[6]

> [I have spoken of *individuation* a number of times – of the Season, of the Weather, of the Times of Day as individuation. I shall dwell on this idea for a moment. Philosophically, it is, I think, an idea to which Deleuze attaches a great deal of importance (in his late work). Alas, as always, I'll be taking it fairly crudely, as a *direction*. (2011, 42)]

In this passage, Barthes invokes Deleuze as a theoretician of individuation. Over the subsequent pages his borrowings from Deleuze are substantial. He not only writes about 'individuation', he ties individuation to 'intensities' and to the very Deleuzian notion of 'affect' (a term he carefully separates from any kind of psychology [2003, 93–101; 2011, 55–69]). He also brings in Nietzsche, 'auteur deleuzien' (79), citing a posthumous passage in which the German philosopher presents his dynamic conception of the 'moi' – his idea of individuation:

> 'Le moi est une pluralité de forces quasi personnifiées dont tantôt l'une, tantôt l'autre se situe à l'avant-scène et prend l'aspect du moi; de cette place, il contemple les autres forces, comme un sujet contemple un objet

---

6   This desire to tie the notion of individuation to the rhythm of the seasons (and the day) is clearly circulating between Barthes, Deleuze, and Guattari in the late 1970s up to 1980. In *Mille Plateaux* (1980), Deleuze and Guattari examine the relation between human subject, season, time of day, and climate (see pp. 318–24 in particular). Rather than deterministic relations, they present logics of mutual participation. This leads Deleuze and Guattari towards a hyphenization that we will also encounter in the writings of Simondon and Bateson: 'Le climat, le vent, la saison, l'heure ne sont pas d'une autre nature que les choses, les bêtes ou les personnes qui les peuplent, les suivent, y dorment ou s'y réveillent. Et c'est d'une seule traite qu'il faut lire: la bête-chasse-à-cinq-heures' (1980, 321). ['Climate, wind, season, hour are not of another nature than the things, animals, or people that populate them, follow them, sleep and awaken within them. This should be read without a pause: the animal-stalks-at-five-o'clock' (1987, 289–90).]

qui lui est extérieur, un monde extérieur qui l'influence et le détermine. Le point de subjectivité est mobile.' (Nietzsche, in Barthes, 2003, 79)

['The Ego is a plurality of almost person-like forces, of which now this one, now that one stands in the foreground and assumes the aspect of the ego; from this vantage-point, it contemplates the other forces, as a subject contemplates an object exterior to himself, an influential and determining outside world. The point of the subject is mobile.' (2011, 44, transl. modified)]

In Nietzsche's passage there is an emphasis on mobility, intensity, and plurality. As one aspect of the 'moi' takes centre stage, others move into the background. Choosing between different metaphors, Barthes suggests that rather than an ever-changing river, subjectivity is a 'mutation discontinue' (79) comparable to what happens with the revolving movement (the 'tilt') of a kaleidoscope: abruptly, a new pattern emerges. This brings Barthes to a distinction between the 'individual' and the process of individuation:

On comprend mieux l'ambivalence (ou la dialectique) de l'individuation: elle est à la fois ce qui fortifie le sujet dans son individualité, son 'quant à moi' – ou du moins elle comporte ce risque, et surtout [celui] de complaire à l'image de la revendication individualiste – et aussi, à l'extrême contraire, ce qui défait le sujet, le multiplie, le pulvérise et en un sens l'absente → oscillation entre l'extrême impressionnisme et une sorte de tentation mystique de la dilution, de l'anéantissement de la conscience comme unitaire: très classique et ultra-moderne. (79)

[We now have a better understanding of the ambivalence (or the dialectic) of individuation: it's both that which strengthens the subject in his or her individuality, in his or her *'reserve'* ['*quant à soi*' (*sic*)] – or, at least, it contains this risk, and in particular [the risk] of looking like a claim for individualism – and, at the opposite extreme, it's that which undoes, multiplies, pulverizes, and in a sense absents the subject → oscillation between extreme impressionism and a kind of mystical leaning toward the dilution, the annihilation of consciousness as unitarian: very classical and ultramodern. (44)]

The unfinished nature of these seminar notes occasionally complicates their reading, but it is clear that Barthes distinguishes between two tendencies in the process of individuation. One of these leads to 'l'*individu* (sujet civique et psychologique)' (78) ['the *individual* (civic and psychological subject)' (43)] – a fossilized idea of individuality, which is a danger inherent in any process of individuation. The other tendency avoids this danger, remaining processual and fragmented.

This non-unifying process of individuation is described as being at the same time classical and ultra-modern; neither of these adjectives are explained, but in our context we could for instance link them to Bashō and Deleuze.

But the 'tilt' of a haiku is not just about the subject being shaken up or dynamized. Haiku-poetry inspires Barthes to emphasize how thoroughly situated and collective the process of individuation is. In the passage in which Barthes mentions Deleuze, he also reminds his students that he has already spoken about individuation 'de la Saison, du Temps qu'il fait, de l'Heure' (77) ['of the Season, of the Weather, of the Times of Day as individuation' (42)]. Indeed, in addition to the syllabic constraint (5-7-5), one of the key characteristics of the classic haiku is that it must be placed in our daily and yearly cycles. More generally, haikus bring a world into relief: they register the passing of a cloud, the rain on a leaf, the smell of a flower. They are alert to 'une *vibration* du monde' (63) ['a *vibration* of the world' (31)]. In the 'tilt' – in the experience of 'c'est cela' – we participate in this vibration. Individuation is therefore a moment where individual and environment are mutually implicated and co-evolve.

This environmental dimension is so important that Barthes slightly rewrites Bashō's definition of the haiku:

> la définition de Bashô: un haïku, 'c'est simplement ce qui arrive en tel lieu, à tel moment' (Coyaud). – Mais à vrai dire, pas tout à fait suffisant; je voudrais introduire une nuance: un haïku, c'est ce qui survient (contingence, micro-aventure) en tant que cela *entoure* le sujet – qui cependant n'existe, ne peut se dire sujet, que par cet entour fugitif et mobile (individuation ≠ individu). (89–90)

> [Basho's definition: a haiku 'is simply what happens in a given place, at a given moment' (Coyaud). – But in truth this isn't quite sufficient: I'd like to introduce a nuance: a haiku is what happens (contingency, microadventure), but only in that what happens *surrounds* the subject – who, moreover, only exists, and can only claim to be a subject, through this fleeting and mobile surrounding (individuation ≠ individual). (52)]

Clearly, it is important for Barthes to emphasize the ecological nature of the (always ongoing) production of subjectivity, the difference between individuation and individual. In an earlier passage, Barthes links haiku-individuation to the *Oikos* of ecology, playing up the manner in which the haiku draws us into – and makes us participate in – the crystallization of an environment:

Dans le haïku, il y a toujours quelque chose qui vous dit *où vous en êtes* de l'année, du ciel, du froid, de la lumière: 17 syllabes, mais vous n'êtes jamais séparé du cosmos sous sa forme immédiate: l'*Oikos*, l'atmosphère, le point de la course de la Terre autour du Soleil. (66)

[There's always something in the haiku to tell you *where you are in the year*, something about the sky, the cold, the light: seventeen syllables, but you're never separated from the cosmos in its immediate form: the *Oikos*, the atmosphere, the coordinates of the Earth's orbit around the Sun. (34)]

So, the haiku is both specific, situated – and cosmic. It brings readers into a particular situation and stretches them (reorders them) in such a manner that they connect to the world (or universe) as a whole. Barthes pushes this reading of the tilt beyond any form of speciesism, beyond any anthropocentrism: 'pureté de l'affect → or ici se produit une sorte de paradoxe: le plus humain (l'humanité en ce qu'elle a de plus déchirant) rejoint le moins humain: la plante, l'animal' (101) ['purity of affect → now, here a kind of paradox emerges: the most human (humanity at its most heartrending) rejoins the least human: plants, animals (61)].

When summing up Barthes's analysis of how the haiku participates in and reveals wider processes of individuation, it is therefore important to emphasize three interrelated elements. First, we have seen that Barthes presents the haiku as a place where affects (or intensities) register in a 'tilt'. Throughout his seminars he analyses the 'tilt' of the haiku, the manner in which it shakes the reader, bringing language and the process of signification to a halt with a liberating jolt (Barthes comes close to the photographic *punctum* here, and we shall return to the relation between haiku and photography in Chapter 2). He links this experience to the numerous expletives and exclamations that can be found in haiku-poetry (the so-called *Kireji*). These mark the interruption of language and the emergence of pure affectivity. He cites Bashō's famous pond-inspired haiku (1685), which in the French translation reads: 'Un vieux marécage/ Une grenouille y saute/ Oh! le bruit de l'eau'.[7] And he comments:

On a dit: peut-être le compte rendu d'un *satori*? Dans ce cas, le *Kireji* (*Oh!*): le moment du Satori, le passage à vide du langage → Chez nous? – Le plus proche du haïku: certaines inflexions de Verlaine: '*Oh* le bruit de la pluie...' (105)[8]

---

7   Or as Alan Ginsburg translated: 'The old pond/ a frog jumped in/ kerplunk!'
8   Barthes is misquoting Verlaine, conflating two hexasyllabic verses from 'Il pleure dans mon cœur': 'Ô bruit doux de la pluie' and 'Ô le chant de la pluie!' (Verlaine, 1962, 192).

[It's been said: perhaps an account of a *satori*? Here, the *Kireji* (*Oh!*): the moment of the Satori, the language passing into the void → in France? – What comes closest to the haiku: some of Verlaine's inflections: ('*Oh* the sound of the rain…') (64)]

Indeed, as Barthes rightly suggests, one of the more surprising aspects of Verlaine's 'chansons grises' is the high frequency of exclamation marks and expletives (Oh, Ah, Hélas,…) – not only in the famous ariette he quotes (studied in Chapter 2) but across the work more widely. A conventional Western interpretation of Verlaine's expletives would bring these back to the subject of enunciation, to the lyrical subject, and frequently to its subjective emotional state. But Barthes's theorization of the haiku precisely does not draw attention to any subjective experience of a lyrical subject. Reading Verlaine with Barthes, as I shall do again towards the end of this chapter, one of my points will therefore be that the French poet's 'kireji' similarly bring attention to the experience of participating in a certain crystallization in the environment, and not simply to a subjective emotion. As Barthes notes, this is the case with 'Oh le bruit doux de la pluie', and, as we shall later see, it is also the case in the opening poem of *Romances sans paroles* ('C'est l'extase…'): 'O le frêle et frais murmure!/ Cela gazouille et susurre'.

With these remarks, we have anticipated the second point: Barthes's analysis links affectivity and ecology. It links language, human being, and environment. The haiku is an environment that affords us the experience of participating in the movements of a cosmos – or rather, it gives us a chance to realize that we were always already participating. This is an entanglement so fundamental that our more dialectic vocabularies (which are keen to ascribe agency to the subject, the individual) struggle to map the relation between the human processes of individuation and environmental unfolding. Similarly, Verlaine's poetry brings us into the region where the impersonal takes over. In 'La Lune blanche' subjectivities and settings were suspended, and united, in the gaps between the fifth and sixth lines of the stanzas; and, as we shall examine in 'C'est l'extase…', a comparable ecological experience is offered by 'l'humble antienne'.

Third, and related to this second point, Barthes emphasizes that there is a strong practical dimension to the writing and reading of haikus. In many traditions, haiku is a spiritual practice. Haiku writers must abide by the principle of 'laisser venir ce qui vient' ['letting come what comes'], as Roger Munier (1978, vii) puts it, and then bring themselves in tune with the occurrence.[9] This practical dimension is also found in the poetry of Verlaine, Baudelaire, and Mallarmé, which thereby becomes what Mallarmé calls 'un instrument spirituel' (see Chapter 5). As readers, we play this spiritual instrument in order to mediate our relation to the affective, and through this practice we come to experience our ecological being. We are not only playing the poem–instrument, we are being played by it, opened up, so that we can find a place in relation to the universe and its subtle movements (tilts). This interplay between reader, poem, and universe is dynamic and non-anthropocentric: all three components are modified in this process; all three are implicated in a process of co-evolution. It is therefore not surprising that at the time of *Romances sans paroles* (16 May 1873), Verlaine announced to his friend Edmond Lepelletier that he was now planning 'un livre de poèmes (dans le sens *suivi* du mot), poèmes didactiques si tu veux, d'où l'*homme* sera complètement banni. Des paysages, des choses, malice des choses, bonté, etc., etc., des choses' (2005, 313–14) ['a book of poems (in the strict sense of the word), didactic if you prefer, from which *man* will be completely banned. Landscapes, things, malice of things [...], goodness of things, etc., etc. of things' (translation in Whidden, 2007, 78)].

To further explore this idea of individuation, let us now turn to one of its most substantial developments in twentieth-century philosophy: Gilbert Simondon's *L'Individuation à la lumière des notions de forme et d'information* (1964). I offer this presentation not only because Simondon played a very important role in Deleuze's (and Guattari's) engagement with individuation, but also to introduce a philosopher who will return regularly throughout this book. As we shall see later, Simondon's philosophy develops a number of themes that allow us to detail how the poetry of Verlaine, Baudelaire, and Mallarmé speaks to contemporary debates.

Individuation in Simondon

L'Individuation à la lumière des notions de forme et d'information develops an original take on the question of the individual. Simondon suggests that, if we want to understand what an individual is, the

9 In other traditions, as Barthes writes, this is too teleological a view of the haiku.

worst thing we can do is begin by considering the individual. If we begin with the individual – as has been customary in modern Western thought – and then seek to determine the individual's relation to other individuals, and to the world more widely, we will find ourselves in a dualist ontology: it will be 'the subject and the object', 'me and the other', inside and outside. But Simondon's ontology is not dualist, and he therefore aims for what he calls 'un retournement dans la recherche du principe d'individuation' (2013, 84) ['a complete change in the general approach to the principle governing individuation' (1992, 300)].[10]

To explain this change, he frequently draws inspiration from the ways in which crystals are formed (indeed, Simondon's book is not only about human individuation, but is divided into two main sections entitled 'L'individuation physique' ['Physical Individuation'] and 'L'individuation des êtres vivants' ['The Individuation of Living Beings']). To take one example, crystals can emerge from a salt-water solution. At some point, various factors, from the concentration of salt and the presence of germs to the temperature of the water, relate in such a manner that a process of crystallization sets in. This process continues as long as the relations are 'metastable' (i.e. in an intermediate energetic state before the crystal's state of least energy). In this case the crystal will carry on growing, from its outside, from its continuous interaction with the environment.

Simondon of course recognizes that there are important differences between non-organic and organic forms of individuation, but he nevertheless draws inspiration from this model of crystallization when he considers the field of psychic individuation (human individuation). He therefore theorizes an environment – which he calls the 'preindividual situation' – in which processes of individuation eventually form something like an individual. This individual will then participate in – and enable – other processes of individuation in the environment. The 'phasing' through which the process of individuation shapes itself is what he calls 'transduction'.

10   Although he is not a dualist, Simondon's philosophy is not exactly monist either. When developing his idea of communication, he explicitly distances himself from Spinozist monism, underlining that communication presupposes two unities that are both sufficiently open to enter into a relation and sufficiently distinct to not disappear when communicating (see Simondon, 2010, 24–26). Writing about Maurice Merleau-Ponty, Tom Sparrow (2015) uses the term 'post-dualist', a term that could apply to Simondon also.

It is important to understand that in this theory of individuation no single entity 'acts'. Rather an assemblage acts – and the individual is part of this assemblage. In Simondon's rather dense formulation:

> L'individu serait alors saisi comme une réalité relative, une certaine phase de l'être qui suppose avant elle une réalité préindividuelle, et qui, même après l'individuation, n'existe pas toute seule, car l'individuation n'épuise pas d'un seul coup les potentiels de la réalité préindividuelle, et d'autre part, ce que l'individuation fait apparaître n'est pas seulement l'individu mais le couple individu-milieu. (2010, 24–25)

> [Thus, the individual is to be understood as having a relative reality, occupying only a certain phase of the whole being in question – a phase that therefore carries the implication of a preceding preindividual state, and that, even after individuation, does not exist in isolation, since individuation does not exhaust in the single act of its appearance all the potentials embedded in the preindividual state. Individuation, moreover, not only brings the individual to light but also individual-milieu dyad. (1992, 300)]

As Simondon explains here, the 'individual' is never a finished entity. It will stimulate and participate in other processes of individuation in a continuous process of unfolding that in turn connects to collective processes of individuation (as we shall see in a moment). With Simondon, we are therefore always 'in the middle' (in both a temporal and a spatial sense) – always, as Verlaine might say with his preferred preposition, 'parmi' (etymologically: 'par le milieu'). Anne Sauvagnargues sums this up by saying that Simondon 'replaces an ontology of beings with an ontology of becomings' (2013, 58).

If Simondon has emerged as a key thinker of individuation over the last ten to fifteen years (and prior to that in the writings of Deleuze and Guattari), it is because passages such as the one just cited invite us to think individuation in what we would today call an Anthropocene way (and because he thinks our relation to technological environments in a similarly ecological way, as we shall see in Chapter 5). Simondon invites us to realize that our imbrication with the world is so fundamental that the individual must be reconfigured as what he called an 'individu-milieu'. The individual is an aspect of the environment; the individual is an environment.[11] As Miguel de Bestegui puts it:

---

11   Simondon is of course not the only thinker that has developed a subject position that we can consider 'Anthropocene-avant-la-lettre'. Alfred North

Instead of taking the individual as his point of departure, and asking how it became what it is, Simondon chooses to interrogate the reality that *results* in the individual as we know it. Where the word 'being' used to stand for a thing or a principle, it now stands for an operation. The shift, then, is from beings as things to being as event. (2013, 168)

Brian Massumi explains that for Simondon matter is 'a formtaking activity' (2013, 32). Human beings are part of that activity. That doesn't mean that Simondon's philosophy is 'nonhuman' (see Introduction). But it does mean that his ontology is a non-anthropocentric one – even as it allows for socio-political developments.[12]

If we move closer to Simondon's volume on individuation, we also find that it offers a theory of affectivity, which has played an important role in recent writings on affect (not least in those by Brian Massumi, as we shall see in Chapter 3). This theory is worth mentioning because, just like Deleuze and Barthes's theorizations of affect, it separates the affective out from the individual and the psychological. Simondon offers distinctions between affectivity, emotion, and action. Affectivity refers to the 'médiation entre le pré-individuel et l'individuel' (2013, 253), whereas emotion is more inter-individual. However, true to his environmental thinking, Simondon does not put in place a very strong dichotomy between affect and emotion. Rather, he proposes that '[l']affectivité peut donc être considérée comme fondement de l'émotivité' (247) ['affectivity can thus be considered as the foundation of emotivity']. We can think of the affective as the charge of the

Whitehead's 'superject' is another notion that has been rediscovered in recent years. Already in 1932, Jean Wahl explained: 'Il n'y a de sujet pour Whitehead que sur les bases d'un environnement, sur les bases d'activités préalables. Tout sujet est un résultat: tous sujet est un superjet' (2010, 123) ['For Whitehead the subject only exists on the basis of an environment, on the basis of already ongoing activities. Each subject is a result; each subject is a superject']. A third thinker (whom we shall return to in our last chapter) is Gregory Bateson. Just like Simondon, Deleuze, and Guattari, he uses hyphens to do away with any sharp distinction between subject and world; he writes about the 'flexible organism-in-its-environment' (2000, 457).

12   As suggested in my Introduction, it can be argued that Simondon's crystallization model speaks to the importance of time as well as the importance of space in the process of individuation. The crystal carries its history forward, and when new layers are added, they are sculpted in accordance with the ground laid by previous layers (as well as in relation to the new environments encountered).

pre-individual as this pre-individual becomes part of the individual-in-process. Next, he suggests that emotion 'implique présence du sujet à d'autres sujets' (247) ['implies the presence of the subject to other subjects']: it is formed through intersubjective relations. In this manner, we may say that Simondon's philosophy presents us with a set of 'tunings' – between pre-individual and individual (affective tuning) and between individual and collective (emotive tuning). In this transition from the affective to the emotive and eventually to action, we find a movement from something we might call unarticulated collectivity (the pre-individual) to articulated collectivity (the social), which presents the individual as a mediation between the pre-individual and the collective. And Simondon goes on to emphasize the importance of the collective: 'le sujet ne peut coïncider avec lui-même que dans l'individuation du collectif' (248) ['the subject can only coincide with itself in the individuation of the collective'].

With this in mind, let us consider a second Verlaine poem. As we turn to this poem – one of Verlaine's most frequently studied – I particularly wish to bring along from the previous pages the following ideas about ontology and individuation: Barthes's understanding of the haiku as practice and *oikos*, a practice through which we take part in a place or a setting; and Simondon's idea of individuation as environmental unfolding, stimulated by affects that pass through both environments and individuals (who are all modulated in that process), thereby opening us up towards collective and social mediations.

Verlainian Haiku

The opening ariette in *Romances sans paroles* was initially published in 1872 in a journal called *La Renaissance littéraire et artistique*. Here it appeared next to a long text by the art critic Philippe Burty called 'Japonisme'. This is a happy coincidence, for Verlaine's poem can indeed be read as a profound response to a certain version of *Japonisme*: the Barthesian version.

From the epigraph of this poem onwards, we are back in the gap that Verlaine carved out between the fifth and sixth lines in the stanzas of 'La Lune blanche':

I

Le vent dans la plaine
Suspend son haleine.

(Favart)

C'est l'extase langoureuse,
C'est la fatigue amoureuse,
C'est tous les frissons des bois
Parmi l'étreinte des brises,
C'est, vers les ramures grises,
Le chœur des petites voix.

O le frêle et frais murmure!
Cela gazouille et susurre,
Cela ressemble au cri doux
Que l'herbe agitée expire...
Tu dirais, sous l'eau qui vire,
Le roulis sourd des cailloux.

Cette âme qui se lamente
En cette plainte dormante
C'est la nôtre, n'est-ce pas?
La mienne, dis, et la tienne,
Dont s'exhale l'humble antienne
Par ce tiède soir, tout bas?

If the structure of 'La Lune blanche' was ambiguous, the one in 'C'est l'extase…' is clear: the poem contains three stanzas with six heptasyllabic lines. But first it presents a small epigraph that Rimbaud had brought to Verlaine's attention. This epigraph immediately introduces the theme of suspension and the trope of anthropomorphism. Both of these connect to 'La Lune blanche', where the suspension was visible in the mise-en-page, and the anthropomorphism particularly prominent in the description of sounds (such as 'le vent pleure'). The first stanza is then dominated by 'c'est' – which appears four times, offering something like a level zero of presence. What is present? An erotic, post-orgasmic sensation (or vibration) that seems to have seized (or 'tilted') both the landscape and the mind of the poet: this is another 'heure exquise'. Again, the poem is in a middle register: the setting is a 'bois', not a forest (forêt) or a garden (jardin); there is wind, but it is soft ('brise'); there is sound, but it is gentle and stems from multiple sources ('petites voix').

The second stanza continues to build this soft-spoken, vibrant universe. The generic 'c'est' is now replaced by the equally generic 'cela'.

We remain in the middle register, as the cry of the grass is 'doux'… and, in fact, only a comparison ('cela ressemble'). The 'roulis' of the stones is 'sourd', and a conditional makes clear that this is now just a *possible* comparison through which a 'you' gently makes its entrance ('tu dirais'). These (possible) comparisons take up four of the six lines in the stanza – making us drift from the description of a physical landscape in stanza one ('there is…') to the weaving together of this physical landscape with a mental landscape ('it is like…'). Still the universe speaks, and an ellipsis keeps everything suspended, unimposing.

Of course, it is also important to note (as *all* readers of this poem have done) that the stanza pushes from signification to sound. The first couple of lines clearly demonstrate how the poem not only refers to but also becomes a soundscape. The language thereby shifts from representation to performance, from being a system of arbitrary signs to being a system of motivated – onomatopoetic – signs: 'murmure', 'gazouille', 'susurre'. In this way, the second stanza brings two movements together: firstly, it operates through comparisons that take us from a landscape to (possible) impressions of a landscape, blurring the environmental into the mental; secondly, the stanza moves us from a language of representation to a more performative language that communicates by creating a soundscape, impressing itself on the reader. Taken together, these two movements gently challenge our usual distinctions between inner and outer, here and there, model and original. In this manner an entire representational system, a whole way of thinking the relation between humans and their surroundings, is disturbed. This world is not the well-known world of subjects, objects, and their representations. Instead, everything expresses itself, communicates, and impresses itself on the reader.

In the first couple of stanzas – in fact, right from the epigraph – we found an anthropomorphizing of nature as the wind held its breath and the grass gently cried; in the second stanza the poem made comparisons ('cela ressemble'), collapsing distinctions between inner and outer, drifting towards sound. In the last stanza, the entanglement of humans and nature is taken in a new direction as the poet wonders whether the sounds are those of 'our' shared soul too. '[L]a nôtre' refers to 'je' and 'tu', and (since it points back to the sounds of the soul as they emerge from the setting) it no doubt refers to the landscape as well. Throughout the three stanzas, the poem therefore goes from the establishment of a lively world to the gently posed possibility that the two lovers might be an inseparable part of this lively world. Indeed, and in a manner that brings us close to Simondon, 'C'est l'extase...' presents micro-vibrations that only gradually and never completely crystallize as human individuals. The two questions in Verlaine's final stanza mediate the relation between 'moi' et 'toi', and between 'us' and nature. But there are no answers to these questions. Instead, we remain suspended. It is precisely this suspension (this weakening of distinct identities) that brings home the entanglement of voices and landscape.

Just like 'La Lune blanche', the poem ends with the mediation of a tension. In 'La Lune blanche' the verb 'pleure' and the adjective 'noir' in the second stanza were softened as the final stanza opened towards a universe, 'vaste et tendre'; in 'C'est l'extase...', Verlaine introduces the verb 'se lamenter' and the noun 'plainte', but then carefully reduces any discord. The 'plainte' is not – as we might have expected – an expression of isolation or conflict, but instead holds the promise of a unification, a song shared by the lovers and the world: 'c'est la nôtre, n'est-ce pas?'

Previously we saw how Barthes summed up the operation of the haiku with 'c'est cela' (before further reducing his summary to the single word '*Tel!*').[13] 'C'est l'extase...' comes close. This can be illustrated via an exercise in reduction, invited by the minimalism of the poem. The first stanza essentially says *c'est* – repeating it four times, and at one point even isolating the word between commas. The second stanza emphasizes *cela* – this deictic word now opening two of the lines previously dominated by *c'est* (lines two and three). Reading the stanzas together gives us 'C'est... cela' – exactly the formula Barthes saw in the haiku. In this (haiku-)manner, Verlaine's poem effectively pares itself back in order to deictically point at an occurrence, a micro-event, a *tilt: l'extase.*[14] The third stanza, however, changes things slightly. If we were to reduce this stanza to a single recurring element (like 'c'est' and

---

13   In the 1978–79 seminar Barthes comments on a seventeenth-century haiku by Teishitsu, which Bashō described as the best ever written. Few poems are more forcefully deictic: '"Ça, Ça"/ C'est tout ce que j'ai pu dire/ Devant les fleurs du mont Yoshino' (2003, 125) ['"That, That"/ Was all I could say/ Before the blossoms of Mount Yoshino' (80)].

14   The 'micro-event', Barthes's 'micro-aventure', and Verlaine's general tendency towards the reduced (as in the diminutive *ariette*) must of course not be confused with a lack of ambition. 'Micro-' points to the precise and the localized – and therefore to a focal point with potentially wide-ranging consequences. The haiku is both 'micro' and cosmic. We find the same combination of the precise and the wide-ranging in Mallarmé's notion of 'L'action restreinte' (see Chapter 4) (and in Félix Guattari's [1989] idea about the wide-ranging effects of a micro-politics).

'cela'), it would have to be the question mark which appears twice in the final stanza. Summing up our condensed *ariette* we then have: 'c'est… cela… ?' On the one hand, as already argued, the question mark keeps the poem open, maintains a state of suspension, and thereby fits the haiku-aesthetic very well. On the other hand – and here we move away from the world of Barthesian haiku – the question mark turns the poem towards a 'tu' (and the reader), making it more dialogical. Readers may therefore be inclined to draw the poem into an intersubjective register, for instance by arguing that the poet is trying to seduce his interlocutor via the two questions in the final stanza. I would agree. But even if the poet tries to use 'notre âme' and the 'humble antienne' to seduce the 'tu', this does not mean that the poet is in control of the 'antienne'. Rather, the 'antienne' emanates from the world, from the situation.[15] Therefore, the poet is aiming for an encounter with the 'tu', which would take place in the environment of a song that will always exceed the intersubjective register. Or more forcefully: the poetic voice invites the lover (and reader) to participate in the ecstasy of the singing universe. The questions raised in the poem are therefore not rhetorical, the poet is not sure that the 'antienne' can become 'ours'. In this way, the poem evokes the erotic possibility of 'becoming-song' whilst giving the reader the chance to experience what this might mean. It is an experience that takes us beyond subjectivities: it is an ex-stase. This ex-stase (the experience of being outside of oneself) coincides with becoming part of the world (thereby also suggesting how rarely we are open to the world).

Before concluding this chapter, let me add one more remark about 'C'est l'extase…'. In pursuing a non-anthropocentric reading of the poem, I am distancing myself from the numerous critics who approach Verlaine's poetry biographically. Indeed, one of the most frequently debated questions about this poem has been whether Verlaine was writing to his wife Mathilde or to his lover Arthur Rimbaud. Although I am uninterested in the answer to this question, it is still worth noting how a biographical approach to Verlaine's collection relates to the reading offered here. In a very different and very good analysis of the poem, Russell S. King observes that unlike many of the later collections, *Romances sans paroles* allows for such debates about whether Verlaine was writing to a woman or a man. This is because Verlaine avoids

---

15 Interestingly, the word 'antienne' (antiphon) refers to a passage of the scriptures that would be sung twice – before a psalm, and after. Like the haiku, the 'antienne' echoes; it invites repetition and participation.

personal pronouns (or uses the indefinite person pronoun 'on'), opts for passive rather than active verb forms, prefers nominalizations, and therefore leaves the question of gender identity unresolved (indeed, as King points out, not until the seventh ariette can we say that the 'je' is masculine [1998–99, 125]). King's reading of Verlaine's ability to avoid any gendering leads him to associate Verlaine's collection with a form of bisexuality (which he theorizes with Luce Irigaray). I read this gender-indeterminacy differently, less anthropocentrically, instead placing eroticism and ecstasy on the side of the universe (and suggesting that poetry might then connect with this eroticism). I am thus proposing a kind of panpsychism that would include a strong erotic component too – a *paneroticism*. This is not as mysterious as it may sound: we all know that environments can be erotically charged, and that erotic energy depends on both human and environmental elements (such as music, odours, light, temperature, humidity, etc.).[16]

Conclusion

This first chapter on Verlaine has argued that 'La Lune blanche' and 'C'est l'extase…' conjure forth an ambiance that is erotic ('l'heure exquise', 'l'extase langoureuse'), vibrant, somewhat painful ('pleure', 'plainte', 'lamente'), but overall serene ('vaste et tendre', 'ce tiède soir'). The poems use a simple syntax; the end rhymes, internal rhymes, and other aural aspects are pleasing to the reader and invite repeated readings. In these re-readings, we modulate the sonorous aspects of the texts, participate in their vibratory movements; rather than moving deeper into a symbolic universe, semantics dissolve into sound. There is of course the level of the image also. We watch almost-empty landscapes at night, finding the unobtrusive presence of a poetic 'I' and (in the *ariette*) a poetic 'you'. It is possible (and common) to read for tensions

---

16   In so far as 'paneroticism' refers to a non-normative sexuality that operates outside the intersubjective relation, it points towards more radically non-relational forms of eroticism such as those theorized by Gilles Deleuze in his engagement with Michel Tournier's *Vendredi – ou les limbes du Pacifique* (1969, 350–72) and Leo Bersani in his reading of André Gide's *L'Immoraliste* (1996, 113–29). An investigation of Verlainian paneroticism lies outside the parameters of the present study, but I believe such a study could offer another way to make *Romances sans paroles* speak to the present.

and symbols, to try to recover the subjectivity and psychology of the poet, to detail intersubjective relations, but the present reading has emphasized how difficult it is to uphold such habits in these quasi-haikus which radically challenge our usual hermeneutical routines. Instead, they invite the reader to participate in a moment of suspension.

Through the two readings – and with reference to Barthes's and Simondon's theorizations of haikus and individuation – this chapter conveys the manner in which Verlaine's environments, through their affective vibrations, evoke and stimulate processes of ecological individuation. In Verlaine's haiku-poetry there are no sharp distinctions between environments and individuals, between individuals and other individuals. As mentioned, 'La Lune blanche' presents this entanglement graphically, with two tracks running in parallel – one of them unfolding a world, the other articulating an address to the loved person (and the reader). The point is that the two tracks operate simultaneously, meeting in the white moonlight between the fifth and sixth line in each stanza. In 'C'est l'extase…', Verlaine offers an environmental unfolding in stanzas one and two (C'est… cela…) and eventually a je-tu-landscape relation emerges through the formulation of two questions. The possibility of a more intimate resolution of the je-tu relation was always already intertwined with the possibility of joining in with the 'humble antienne', the song of the universe. In both poems, we sense movements, affects, and vibrations, but the poems break off before any distinct identities have emerged.

There is more to discover about these relations between worldly vibration, poetic voice, lover, and reader. Going forward I would like to emphasize that Verlaine's haikus constitute a practice through which we are invited to experience our entanglement with the universe. These poems bring us to the *Tel!*: this moment where place and time become active players that tilt the subject – poet, lover, and reader – to a new position. Philosophically, Verlaine's poetry thereby steps out of the dualisms that Barthes associates with the name of Hegel: subject–object, inner–outer.

The proposed reading runs somewhat counter to critical interpretations such as that of Steve Murphy, who is keen to save Verlaine's poetry from the clichés about impressionism (the clichés Sollers associates with symbolism [see Introduction]). In his critical edition of *Romances sans paroles*, Murphy insists on the significance of Verlaine's never-completed, pro-communard collection *Les Vaincus* (which Verlaine worked on between the two collections that I have chosen poems from,

La Bonne chanson and *Romances sans paroles*). Murphy argues that, if this collection has been marginalized in the scholarship on Verlaine, it is partly 'parce que le Verlaine des *Vaincus* est très différent de celui des autres recueils de l'époque et entre en contradiction avec l'image généralement propagée du poète – sa « petite musique », sa « fadeur », sa « chanson grise »' (Murphy in Verlaine, 2012, 27) ['because the Verlaine of *Les Vaincus* is very different from that of other collections from the same era and contradicts the image of the poet that was otherwise widespread – his "little music", his "blandness", his "grey song"']. Murphy's insistence on *Les Vaincus* is thus motivated by a desire to demonstrate that even a *seemingly* depoliticized collection such as *Romances sans paroles* has to be read in the context of Verlaine's attempts at positioning himself historically and politically. Murphy wants to move away from the idea of Verlaine and his 'petite musique', bringing him closer to an activist position. I share Murphy's desire to bring out the radical nature of Verlaine's poetry, but my argument has taken a very different route. I think attempts to keep Verlaine's poetry for a traditional left-wing politics run the risk of holding on to a conventional and (in relation to Verlaine's haiku-poetry) misleading understanding of subjectivity. Indeed, I have argued that Verlaine's most famous haiku-poetry invites us to let go of this subject, anticipating instead the theorizations of individuation that we find in the texts of Simondon and the late Barthes. I have thus attempted to show that Verlaine's 'petite musique' can help us bring out a subject position that is ecological and affective. This is what I call twenty-first-century symbolism. However, there is more to say about the question of Verlaine's contemporaneity. This is where we will be heading in the second chapter, where I will also seek to place my reading more fully in relation to other readings of Verlaine.

CHAPTER TWO

The Verlaine-Environment

This chapter continues the exploration of individuation in Verlaine's poetry, providing the reader with a larger framework with which to understand this notion. The first section examines an issue briefly mentioned in the previous chapter: the pictorial dimension of Verlaine's poetry. As is clear from the subheadings in Verlaine's early collections ('Eaux-fortes', 'Paysages tristes', 'Aquarelles', 'Paysages belges', etc.) his poetry looks to visual art as much as it looks to music. There is an implicit theory of the image in Verlaine's poetry. Analysing one of his spleen-haunted poems, 'L'Ombre des arbres', and continuing to build from the work of Roland Barthes and Gilbert Simondon, we shall explore how Verlaine's image is an active mediator, an interface. The second section then discusses how the present reading relates to three well-known and more wide-ranging readings of Verlaine's work by Jean-Pierre Richard, Clive Scott, and Arnaud Bernadet. These critics allow me to bring in other dimensions of Verlaine's work (such as his literary criticism), thereby widening the focus on Haiku-Verlaine. I will argue that there is a considerable overlap between my reading and the analyses of Richard, Scott, and Bernadet, but the comparison will also help to clarify how a Simondon-inspired reading stands out. This prepares the ground for a third section, which moves towards the contemporary context, explicitly addressing the key question: how does Verlaine speak to the present? At the end, the conclusions to the first two chapters will be summed up in a reading of Verlaine's most famous poem, Ariette III: 'Il pleure dans mon cœur'.

Verlaine and the Image

Let us begin with the final *ariette* in *Romances sans paroles*: 'L'Ombre des arbres'. Although it is set in a universe largely similar to the one we encountered in 'La Lune blanche', this poem conveys a more melancholic atmosphere. My ambition is to examine how the poem blurs the distinction between a physical and a mental landscape, and to determine what role the image plays in this blurring.

IX

> Le rossignol qui du haut d'une
> branche se regarde dedans croit
> être tombé dans la rivière. Il est
> au sommet d'un chêne et toutefois
> il a peur de se noyer.
>
> (Cyrano de Bergerac)

L'ombre des arbres dans la rivière embrumée
    Meurt comme de la fumée
Tandis qu'en l'air, parmi les ramures réelles,
    Se plaignent les tourterelles.

Combien, ô voyageur, ce paysage blême
    Te mira blême toi-même,
Et que tristes pleuraient dans les hautes feuillées
    Tes espérances noyées!

Mai, juin 72.

The poem consists of two quatrains with alternating lines of 12 and seven syllables. The alternation suggests a call–response structure, which to some extent characterizes the relation between the two stanzas also. The first quatrain presents a landscape. Like 'La Lune blanche', it establishes a play between elements located in the air ('les ramures réelles' and 'the tourterelles', for instance) and others positioned down on the surface of a body of water ('l'ombre des arbres'). This up–down interplay is introduced already in the epigraph. As a whole, the first stanza mediates between up and down; it mixes air and water, presenting the reader with ethereal elements such as the fog, smoke, and shadows that gently drift about, evaporating in the process.

The relation between the brevity of Verlaine's two stanzas and the long prose epigraph is remarkable. The epigraph contributes more than a third of the poem's word count. This unusual (im)balance, and the strong thematic overlap between poem and epigraph, creates a mirror effect that breaks down barriers between what is internal to the poem (Verlaine's stanzas) and what is liminal and pointing outwards (the epigraph). As a result, the poem overflows, drifts outside its lines ('comme de la fumée'). As we shall see at the end of this chapter, this is not the only *ariette* that blurs the distinctions between text and intertexts.

The second stanza begins with a move to the mental. The poem switches from present to past tense: the image ('ce paysage') encountered in the first stanza is considered in retrospect and through a comparison ('Combien...'). Two characters appear: a poetic voice addresses a 'voyageur' using the familiar 'tu' form (like in 'C'est l'extase...'). The key formulation, which blurs the landscape from the first stanza with a mental image, is found in the opening two lines of the second stanza: 'Combien, ô voyageur, ce paysage blême/ Te mira blême toi-même'. The ghostly landscape of smoke, fog, and shadows, drifting in the air and reflected in the water, is here cast as a match to the traveller's state of mind. The final lines of the poem drive this parallel home, bringing together the drowned hopes of the traveller and the lamenting doves in the tree-tops. The rhyme from the opening lines returns, giving the poem an aabb-ccaa structure that neatly encloses it within a hall of mirrors.

The important hinge-sentence at the beginning of the second stanza eloquently speaks of the complicated relations between landscape and mind, the environmental and the mental. Here the poem communicates – and demonstrates – how landscape and mind inform each other. This mainly happens through a play of repetition and difference. First, Verlaine uses the same word twice in close succession: 'blême'. Furthermore, the [ême] sound spills over into 'même', spinning out an impression of sameness. The alliteration of the 'm' sound with 'mira' (and internally with 'mê-me') adds to the homogeneity of the soundscape, and the double curves of the 'm' ensure that echoes, mirrors, and sameness can also be seen on the page – undermining any clear distinctions. There is unrest in these mirrorings, in this apparent proliferation of sameness. Counting syllables, for instance, we notice that the first 'blême' has one syllable, the second has two, and the following 'même' goes back to a single syllable. Such micro-movements keep the poem moving and rippling. In these many mirrorings, questions of agency, of original and reflection, become difficult to answer.

Indeed, who or what acts? The 'paysage' seems to act: it 'reflected you' ('te mira'). But 'to reflect' (in the sense of sending back an image) is a very passive act: a response to an initial impulse over which the reflecting surface has little control. But what does it mean, then, to 'mirer blême'? It would seem that the 'paysage' (which is 'blême') did *more than* simply reflect; it impressed its own paleness onto the mental slate of the traveller.[1] So in this sense the paysage *did* act. It sent back an image that was more than a simple reflection. This 'reflection' operated a transformation, a colouring (or more accurately, a decolouring) of the 'tu'. This brings us closer to a second meaning of the verb 'mirer'. 'Mirer' combines what we might call 'subject'-focused ideas about reflections and mirroring (making the reflective form 'se mirer' seem almost pleonastic) with more 'object'-focused ideas about objectification (as in 'ad-mirer' and finding oneself in the line of sight [and fire], ['ligne de mire']). The verb is therefore perfect to undermine any subject–object dualisms. We can then say that, in the interaction between landscape and traveller, a sharing of 'paleness' takes place. It is this complicated logic of sharing which the sounds and shapes of the 'm' so elegantly communicate. In this manner an environmentally constituted 'you, traveller' appears.

It is possible to sharpen this analysis by comparing Verlaine's poem to Baudelaire's prose poem 'Les Fenêtres'. At first, the two poems seem to bear no relation at all. Baudelaire's text is narrated by a character who is looking across the rooftops of Paris, seeing an old lady behind a window. The narrator tells us that he has composed a story about her, and he then boasts that his story is so beautiful and sad that it makes him cry. He does not know whether this story bears any resemblance to the life of the old lady, and he explicitly states that he could not care less about the story's veracity as long as it moves *him*. If the figure behind the closed window had been an old man – the narrator concludes – it would have been just as easy and just as satisfying to invent his story.

Baudelaire's poem can be situated in relation to mid-nineteenth-century debates about mimesis (and to his texts about realist literature and photography). As is frequently the case in Baudelaire, this narrator does not care for mimesis. 'Les Fenêtres' is not about art as a reflection of the world. In fact, the narrator explicitly prefers a closed window to an open window, presumably because it helps prevent him from

---

1   Everything seems to be bathing in the homogenizing moonlight, but in this poem there is no mention of the moon; also, the reader logically assumes that this is another poem about 'des saules pleureurs' (weeping willows), but the trees are never mentioned. The poem draws its reader in through such instances of underspecification.

becoming a slave to the real (but perhaps also because it affords him a chance to catch his own reflection in the window). Baudelaire's narrator is provocatively narcissistic, loudly solipsistic, interested only in how his imagination can give him pleasure. He cynically brags about his ability to take inspiration from anything, using the woman as a tool for the satisfaction of his desire. He takes the body of the old woman apart, breaks it into different elements, reassembles it, and is moved by the sadness of the story he composes: 'Avec son visage, avec son vêtement, avec son geste, avec presque rien, j'ai refait l'histoire de cette femme, ou plutôt sa légende, et quelquefois je me la raconte à moi-même en pleurant' (1975, 339) ['Out of her face, her dress and her gestures, out of practically nothing at all, I have made up this woman's story, or rather legend, and sometimes I tell it to myself and weep' (1970, 77)]. The poem rests on a very strong distinction between narrator and world.[2]

The comparison to Baudelaire helpfully brings out the pictorial character of Verlaine's first stanza: this stanza gives the *image* of a landscape.[3] It is an image we know from 'La Lune blanche', from many Japanese haikus (including the ones given in the first chapter), and from numerous romantic paintings: trees, birds, and a river bathing in the pale light. It is true that Verlaine destabilizes this landscape with the humorous epigraph, but the poem maintains its pictorial dimension. Whereas Baudelaire's narrator was in total control, and knew how he wanted to use his image, Verlaine's poem displays no such mastery. Two elements are important here. Firstly, Verlaine introduces two characters: a narratorial voice and a 'voyageur'. The text is about the relation between traveller and landscape, but the traveller is not telling his own story. Already, at this level, he is denied the control and mastery of Baudelaire's narrator. Secondly, the relation between traveller and landscape is unstable. A semi-mimetic, semi-performative logic is in play, in which the mental and the environmental interact.

Baudelaire's poem ends with a rhetorical question:

2   This brief reading stays with the perspective of Baudelaire's narratorial voice, but the poem is more complicated than suggested here. In so far as Baudelaire's narrator is *loudly* narcissistic and *demonstratively* solipsistic, his text turns outwards, provoking the reader through hyperbole. In this manner, the window is opened again, and Baudelaire's text can take on multiple other meanings (we shall briefly return to this poem in Chapter 4).

3   I am using the term 'image' here in the broader sense where it refers both to an actual landscape and the mental image – or recollection – of a landscape. The poem blurs this very distinction.

Peut-être me direz-vous: 'Es-tu sûr que cette légende soit la vraie?' Qu'importe ce que peut être la réalité placée hors de moi, si elle m'a aidé à vivre, à sentir que je suis et ce que je suis? (1975, 339)

[Perhaps you will say 'Are you sure that your story is the real one?' But what does it matter what reality is outside myself, so long as it has helped me to live, to feel that I am, and what I am? (1970, 77)]

In other words, the poem ends with a hyperbolic and narcissistic trumpeting of identity: the narrator claims to know who he is (saying 'je suis' twice in very close succession), having used literature to come to this knowledge. In Verlaine's poem, on the other hand, we have a traveller who precisely does not enter a dialectic relation to the world (but instead participates in a blurring); we have a mobile character, someone who continuously exposes himself to difference, someone traversing and traversed by the environment. In Verlaine's poem the image is neither projection nor representation: it is rather an action or an interface. This points to a different understanding of subjectivity, mimesis, and reflection – it points to the notion of individuation, to ecology and affect. It suggests that the image (like a haiku) is an active player in the process of individuation: a medium where a mutual specification of matter and sensitivity can take place.

At this point we can return to Barthes and Simondon. Previously we saw that Barthes considered the haiku to be an ecological practice that participates in a process of individuation. I also mentioned that Barthes's late seminar compared haiku-individuation to the kind of individuation he finds in photography. With this comparison, Barthes underlines the snapshot character of haikus: both photographs and haikus communicate what Barthes calls the 'ça a été', and as this singular moment registers it produces a tilt. In the light of how Barthes would develop his analysis of photography only a few months later, it is easy to see how 'the tilt' of the haiku anticipates *La Chambre claire*'s theorization of the photographic 'punctum'. In front of a (good) photographic image, the spectator is 'seized', connects with the real, and is revitalized. The final pages of *La Chambre claire* present this experience in a very dramatic and affectively charged manner. Writing about what he calls 'photographie folle' (2012, 183) ['mad photography' (1981, 119)], Barthes characterizes photography as an exposure to death, at once overpowering and revitalizing. When the seminars compare haikus with photography the tone is less dramatic, but even so, the photograph is always a way in which to 'surprise consciousness' (2003, 115). The 'tilt' that keeps open the process of individuation can thus be found in haikus and photographs alike. When Verlaine describes how the image of a landscape '[t]e mira blême toi-même', he ties image to individuation in a similar way. Landscape and poetic 'you' vibrate in the image and a particularly restless subject position is produced: only a 'traveller' could result from this environmental vibrancy.

Simondon's work also presents an 'ecological' take on this relation between images and individuation in so far as he sees images (whether mental or concrete) as mediating between the subject and the world, the concrete and the abstract, the past and the future. In *Imagination et invention (1965–66)*, images are described both as a process and a '"quasi-organisme"' (2014a, 9). Images help to organize the world, and in so doing they also organize the human being (who is aiming to organize the world). Simondon systematizes this mediation between human beings, images, and world in what he calls the 'cycle des images'. It lies beyond the scope of this chapter to detail this theory, but it is worth mentioning that, at the very beginning of his cycle, Simondon finds what he calls 'l'image intra-perceptive'. These first images may appear as we move about: either physically, such as when the infant moves its head and eyes, or mentally, through an anticipation of what may happen. Such movements generate schemata, a mental architecture in which perceptions later find place. These intra-perceptive images can therefore be thought of as a form of 'équilibre entre le vivant et son milieu' (19) ['equilibrium between the living organism and its environment'] – again, a kind of tuning.[4] Unlike the phenomenologists – with whom he

---

4 In slightly more detail: Simondon's cycle presents three stages that constitute another process of crystallization (or transduction). Avoiding anthropocentricity, he emphasizes the 'relative indépendance des images par rapport au sujet' (2014b, 9) ['images relative independence from the subject']. He also compares images to a mycelium, explaining that this network may momentarily produce an individual-mushroom. The first stage is then described as biological. At this level Simondon finds *a priori* images. The image is 'un faisceau de tendances motrices' (2014a, 3) ['a bundle of motor-tendencies']: a schema is established, a dynamic frame that is ready to host the meeting between object and subject. The second phase is that of hosting the information that comes from the environment. Simondon speaks of *a praesenti* images. To some extent such images escape our control; they contain more than we are able to perceive, but we channel (or concretize) some of their information. This is the stage of the experience. Images become functional, both organized and organizing forces. Finally, the third stage is where the systematization fully falls into place. Simondon writes of *a posteriori* images, and about how 'le monde des images-souvenirs réalise un véritable univers mental' (21) ['the world of memory-images

frequently shares so much – Simondon begins with movement, not with sense-perception or consciousness. In other words, consciousness and sense-perception result from movement (see also Chateau in Simondon, 2014a, xxix). This is worth emphasizing because it allows for a more thoroughly ecological understanding of the entanglements between human beings and the universe.

Verlaine's 'L'Ombre des arbres' similarly begins with movements and orientations that gradually coalesce into an image that then helps shape the traveller. In the process, the poem puts pressure on distinctions between inner and outer, subject and object, past and present. The same was obvious in 'La Lune blanche' and 'C'est l'extase…' – two other very pictorial poems. Indeed, this last poem was about gentle movements that only gradually (and hesitantly) coagulated as human presence. The poem suggested an always incomplete process of individuation (crystallization) that generated just enough subjectivity to allow the formulation of a question to the loved one (a question that remained unanswered). What the reference to Simondon allows us to see more clearly is how Verlainian haikus, through their image-like nature, explore vibratory environments and incomplete acts of formation. The reflective surfaces of gently moonlit water undermine subject–object dialectics, suggesting instead that (active) images generate individual-environments.[5] Critics have noted such logics before, but most of them have begun with subjects (and objects) rather than with processes of individuation, and therefore their

develops a real mental universe']. We now have an 'analogue du milieu extérieur' (19) ['analogue to the exterior environment']. When this third stage becomes too saturated, invention may throw open a new cycle. We begin a new process, but without neglecting the previous cycle, working from the ground of past experiences.

5   There are of course many pictorial poems in *Romances sans paroles*. A particularly striking image is the dystopian landscape found in Ariette VIII, 'Dans l'interminable ennui de la plaine'. Under a copper-coloured sky, Verlaine lays out a plain with famished wolves and a solitary crow: a dystopian landscape that anticipates twentieth- and twenty-first-century post-apocalyptic science-fiction films from Tarkovsky's *Stalker* (1979) to Villeneuve's *Blade Runner 2049* (2017). If this image sticks, it is also due to the multiple repetitions (two stanzas are given twice over just six stanzas). They suggest a landscape and an imagination that is dying, struggling to generate what might come next, but still trying. In this manner, Verlaine's spleen poem – very appropriately – *almost* terminates the genre. Unlike Baudelaire's 'Au lecteur', which is rich in imagery, energetic in its exploration of Dante'esque horrors (until the final incarnation of absolute indifference), Verlaine's poem lies leaden and exhausted, shimmering in the dying light.

readings have been less ecological than the one I am seeking to advance here. At this point, it is therefore time to consider how a Simondon-inflected reading of Verlaine compares with earlier well-known readings of Verlaine's poetry. I have chosen three readings that relate to the one I am offering here. What does the Verlainian subject look like for Arnaud Bernadet, Jean-Pierre Richard, and Clive Scott?

Three Verlaine Readers: Bernadet, Richard, and Scott

The most extensive recent engagement with Verlaine's work is found in the books and articles of Arnaud Bernadet. Drawing on the work of Gérard Dessons, Bernadet approaches Verlaine's work through the notion of the *manière* ['manner']. This notion was important in classical debates about aesthetics, and it was still alive at the time of Verlaine. But as Bernadet explains in *L'Exil et l'utopie, politiques de Verlaine*, it fell out of fashion and was replaced by partly overlapping notions such as 'style' and 'écriture' (2007, 12).

With the notion of *manière* Bernadet aims for the intersection of the personal, the political, and the act of writing. *Manière* refers to the ways in which writing becomes an individual engagement in the world. This characterization does indeed bring us close to Barthes's *écriture* as it is presented in his 1953 work *Le Degré zéro de l'écriture* (a presentation which I would like to keep distinct from Barthes's later notion of *écriture* from the 1970s). For early Barthes, *écriture* is a matter of literary form; it was his way of complementing Sartre's *Qu'est-ce que la littérature?* by arguing that form is a question of commitment too (see Barthes, 2002b, 1,026). It refers to the manner in which an individual author chooses to enter the stage of history by means of writing – it is 'un acte de solidarité historique' (1972, 14) ['an act of historical solidarity' (Barthes, 1967, 20)], and at the same time an act of authorial self-constitution.

Bernadet is in similar territory when he explains that 'la politique de la manière se révèle inséparable de l'acte d'individuation à travers lequel vers et proses se configurent' (2007, 17–18) ['The politics of manner turns out to be inseparable from the act of individuation through which verse and prose are configured']. In the later *Poétique de Verlaine* (2014), Bernadet presents the *manière* with reference to Jacques Rancière. He writes that Rancière's notion of a 'politique de la littérature'

> conserve ceci de fondamental qu'elle admet un rapport étroit entre la
> question du politique et l'invention de la valeur dans le langage. Ce

rapport, Verlaine lui a donné très précisément le nom de manière. En elle se conjuguent la subjectivité et l'historicité. (30)

[retains the fundamental feature of acknowledging a close relationship between the question of politics and the invention of value in language. This relationship is what Verlaine precisely gave the name 'manner'. In this word subjectivity and historicity combine.]

In this way Bernadet draws attention to the close links between the shaping of language, subjectivity, and the social, with 'manière' being the name for the knot where these efforts intersect.

It is not my intention to offer a detailed account of Bernadet's analysis of the Verlainian *manière* (which he develops over the 1,278 pages of *Poétique de Verlaine*, as well as in the earlier *L'Exil et l'utopie* and in many shorter texts). I am interested in the issue of Verlaine's subject position (or to use the term that Bernadet also employs: individuation). As we saw in Barthes's haiku analysis, individuation can tip towards a closed-off 'identity' or it can be associated with the more processual (and Simondonian) idea of a subject always in the making. On the whole, Bernadet goes further towards identity than I wish to do – tellingly using the key term 'manière' in the singular, with the possessive preposition 'de' ('la manière de Verlaine').[6] In this respect, he stays close to early Barthes and mid-century Sartre as he is thinking about the 'politiques de Verlaine'. However, in the present context, it is worth bringing out some of those passages in Bernadet's analysis where singularity and identity are opened up to more dynamic processes. Here Bernadet describes the poetic act as one less of subject constitution than of constant re-individuation – always moving the poet in new directions. For instance:

6   Seth Whidden leans in the same direction in *Leaving Parnassus*: 'Verlaine's poetry involves the poetic subject's search for identity through interaction with its object. Rather than being unique to *Poèmes saturniens*, I believe that this project extends throughout Verlaine's entire poetic work' (2007, 68). However, Whidden also specifies that in *Romances sans paroles* this search for identity finds itself under unusual pressure: 'In *Romances sans paroles*, where Verlaine's lyric subject is more destabilized than ever, he takes a bold step – perhaps as a result of the newfound freedom that Rimbaud inspired – and chooses to enter deeper into the inner chasm that torments his poetry. In these poems, Verlaine's poetic subject, while in a constant state of being confronted with a choice, bemoans his having to choose rather than actually choosing anything' (79). Whereas Whidden and Bernadet insists on the desire for subject constitution, I want to emphasize Verlaine's ability (in the haiku-poems) to open towards what Simondon calls the pre-individual environment.

Ainsi de même qu'elle [la démarche de Verlaine] lie un corps à un sujet, elle associe un corps et une voix. À son tour, cette voix ne se conçoit pas en dehors des lieux où elle s'incarne. Car elle ne peut s'énoncer qu'en se retirant aussitôt. Nomade, elle se déplace et se renouvelle dans l'inconnu et, à ce titre, fonde la quête de sujet qui est au cœur de l'entreprise littéraire de Verlaine. De déprises en reprises, l'instance poétique poursuit une même logique de continuation et d'excentrement, de changement et de perpétuation. Autrement dit, le sujet n'advient jamais dans ses textes que délocalisé. Toujours en avant, il ne coïncide pas avec lui-même; toujours autre, son identité est à venir, et se désigne par ce qu'elle cherche à être sans savoir ce qu'elle est. (2014, 1,147)

[In the same way that [Verlaine's approach] links a body to a subject, it associates a body with a voice. In turn, this voice cannot be conceived outside of the sites where it is embodied. Because it can only be pronounced by withdrawing immediately. Nomadic, it moves and rejuvenates in the unknown and, to this end, establishes the search for the subject that is at the heart of Verlaine's literary project. From deformation to reformation the poetic voice pursues the same logic of continuing and off-setting, of changing and perpetuating. In other words, the subject only occurs in his texts when it is delocalized. Always in front, it does not coincide with itself; always other, its identity is to come, and is indicated by what it seeks to be without knowing what it is.]

As this paragraph demonstrates, Bernadet finds in Verlaine's work a move between subject constitution ('la quête de sujet qui est au cœur de l'entreprise littéraire de Verlaine') and subject dynamization ('toujours autre, son identité est à venir'). This double insistence on formation and de-/re-formation ('de déprises en reprises') explains why Bernadet moves swiftly from more grounding formulations ('lie un corps à un sujet') to the ecological, haiku'esque aspect highlighted when he explains that the voice is as much an expression of the places in which it forms as it is an expression of a body and a subjectivity ('cette voix ne se conçoit pas en dehors des lieux où elle s'incarne'). Bernadet does not explain where he gets his notion of individuation from (of course, there may not be any single source), but I would like to push him towards the philosophies of Simondon, Deleuze, and Guattari, towards a thoroughly ecological process of individuation, towards the always ongoing co-emergence of subject and environment.

Other passages in Bernadet's analyses similarly take us toward this more processual ontology (or to use the Deleuzian term that Bernadet employed above: they take us toward the *nomadic*). For instance, Bernadet explains how Verlaine's literary criticism seeks to undo subject–object relations. Often criticism is an occasion for critics to manifest themselves (sometimes even at the expense of the object of criticism). However, for Verlaine, criticism is about giving someone or something else (author or text) a space in which to appear. Verlaine therefore abides by the principle that 'parler d'un poète, c'est surtout le citer' (1972, 949) ['to speak about a poet, one must first of all cite him']. Bernadet then explains that a special kind of criticism becomes possible when the critic withdraws from all subject–object dialectics. Giving up on commentary and exegesis, Verlaine responds to poetry with poetry, tenderly extending one poem with another. Presenting Verlaine's sonnet to Francis Poictevin in *Dédicaces*, Bernadet writes: 'à rompre ainsi et de façon définitive avec le dualisme logique du sujet et de l'objet qui gouverne toute analytique de la littérature, le sonnet absorbe finalement le geste critique dans son intégralité' (2014, 83) ['thereby breaking definitively with the logical dualism of subject and object that governs all literary analysis, the sonnet ultimately absorbs the critical gesture in its entirety']. Such a withdrawal from subject–object dialectics points to a radically new form of being-together which is found in Verlaine's poetry more generally. As Bernadet writes in his earlier study, Verlaine's intimacy becomes social, transsubjective:

> L'intime ne traduit jamais un repli autistique du moi mais tout au contraire une forme radicale d'*intersubjectivité* et même de *transsub-jectivité*. Il représente donc cet espace où, chez Verlaine, se construit virtuellement un modèle de socialité. (2007, 19)

> [The intimate never translates an autistic withdrawal of the Self but, on the contrary, a radical form of *intersubjectivity* and even of *transsubjec-tivity*. It therefore represents this space where, for Verlaine, a model of sociality is virtually constructed.]

Bernadet presents no further details about this move from radical intersubjectivity to transsubjectivity, but I would like to emphasize the prefix 'trans-' (as in transformation, transition, and Simondonian transduction). To go from 'inter-' to 'trans-' suggests that we are leaving the (Hegelian) dialectic, moving towards a dynamic, processual understanding of co-constitution in which intimacy can no longer be thought in terms of closure. This, admittedly, may be pushing Bernadet in a different direction from the one he imagines, but his vocabulary ('nomadic', 'transsubjectivity', and 'virtuality') opens this path.

Bernadet's analyses can therefore be said both to resonate with Barthes's early Sartre-inspired notion of *écriture* and with the same critic's later non-dialectic understanding of *écriture* (as presented in the writings on the haiku, for instance). If this is the case, it may of course have to do with an oscillation found in Verlaine's poetry. Bernadet makes precisely this point in the following passage, where he explains how the two tendencies operate within a single collection by Verlaine, *Poèmes saturniens*. Using Verlaine's vocabulary, Bernadet distinguishes between the 'chants bizarres' and the 'doux chants':[7]

> Alors que les 'chants bizarres' répondaient à une attitude stratégique, en conflit avec les réalités du moment, les 'doux chants' inventent une écriture qui entend transformer cette situation, et dépasser l'impasse d'une révolte contre le pouvoir.
>
> Si l'on préfère, ces chants d'un genre nouveau instituent leur caracté-ristique majeure, la douceur, en invariant du sujet. Ce qui signifie aussi que cette propriété entre immédiatement en corrélation avec sa configu-ration clivée et multiples dans 'Paysages tristes'. C'est elle qui crée les liens entre le je et les autres. Contre la violence de l'État et des conflits successifs, que sécrètent les formes contemporaines de régimes et de gouvernements, le poème verlainien inaugure une utopie de la douceur des rapports sociaux. (2007, 112)

[Whereas the 'strange songs' responded to a strategic attitude, in conflict with the reality of the moment, the 'soft songs' create a writing which aims at transforming this situation, and at overcoming the deadlock of a revolt against power.

In other words, these songs introduce, in a new way, their main characteristic of tenderness as a staple of the subject. This also means that this feature immediately correlates with the split and multiple configurations of 'Sad Landscapes'. It is this feature that creates the links between I and the Others. Against the violence of the state and successive conflicts secreted by contemporary forms of regimes and governments, the Verlainian poem inaugurates a utopia of tender social relations.]

On the one hand, Bernadet here presents the 'chants bizarres' as being 'en conflit avec les réalités du moment', 'une révolte contre le pouvoir'. We might call these the dialectical poems, in the sense that they belong to the world of the 'guerre des sens' (Barthes, 2002b, 517) ['war of meanings'] – the for and against, the subjects and the objects. On the other hand, there are the 'doux chants' that seek to escape this logic,

---

7 '[C]hants bizarres' is from the last poem ('Grotesques') in the second major section ('Eaux-Fortes') of *Poèmes saturniens*; 'doux chants' is from opening poem ('Soleils couchants') in the following section ('Paysages tristes').

insisting on a *douceur* that works to open the subject, reconfigure social space by avoiding the impasse of dialectics, and instead present – with a formulation that seems to come straight out of late-1970s Barthes – 'une utopie de la douceur des rapports sociaux' ['a utopia of tender, social relations'].[8] I strongly agree with Bernadet's emphasis on what Barthes might have called a non-Hegelian politics, but I also believe that Bernadet is a bit too quick to instrumentalize the *douceur* so that it becomes part of a new intersubjective logic ('immédiatement [c']est elle qui crée les liens entre le je et les autres') ['immediately [it] creates the links between I and the Others']. The consequence of this very rapid recovery of the *douceur* for the social sphere is that we do not sufficiently see how the *douceur* reworks traditional notions of subjectivity (and, therefore, more traditional notions of collectivity). Here Simondon's philosophy of individuation (and late Barthes's similar resistance to dialectics) seems more distinct from our dualist habits.

Bernadet's moves between subject constitution and continuous de- and reconstitution can also be found in Jean-Pierre Richard's famous text on the 'Fadeur de Verlaine' (in *Poésie et profondeur* [1955]). As in many of his writings from the 1950s and 1960s, here Richard recounts the *story* of a consciousness as it interacts with the world, but, unlike the optimistic story of *L'Univers imaginaire de Mallarmé*, the adventures of Verlaine's consciousness are tragic. What interests me in Richard's account is how Verlaine's work pushes him to theorize at the limits of the phenomenological framework that the critic used for most of his studies in the mid-1950s.

Richard's starting point is how Verlaine, 'spontanément' (165), makes himself available to the world. Richard writes about passivity and waiting, before he gives to the poet the slightly more active role of 'cultiver en lui les vertus de porosité qui lui permettront de mieux se laisser pénétrer' (165) ['cultivating in him the virtues of porosity that will allow him to be better penetrated']. The specificity of this phase, in which Verlaine makes himself 'porous' to the surroundings, has to do with the shapelessness of the world. Verlaine's world is full of sensations that have almost faded away. Richard uses an evocative and elaborate simile (inspired by Baudelaire's 'Spleen [LXXVI]' in *Les Fleurs du mal*): sensorial impressions reach Verlaine like odours from a perfume bottle

---

8 In Barthesian terms, Bernadet here promotes a politics of the neutral, of the non-vouloir-saisir. What matters for Bernadet and Barthes is to give to this 'douceur' a strong and active sense without falling into a war of meanings.

that has been left open for so long that the soft, lingering scents have liberated themselves from their point of origin. In other words, we are in a universe of

> sensations à demi mortes et qui ne contiennent plus en elles aucun renvoi précis à leur origine concrète [...]. Leur charme est justement de se délivrer de cette origine, d'en abolir en elles jusqu'à la notion, et de vivre une existence autonome. (166)

> [half-dead sensations that no longer contain in them any precise reference to their concrete origin [...]. Their charm is precisely in freeing themselves from this origin, abolishing even this notion within themselves, and leading an autonomous existence.]

The starting point for Richard's study is thus clearly on the side of de-constitution, giving space to the world that Whitehead conceptualizes as 'the vibratory continuum' (quoted in Hansen, 2015, 30). However, according to Richard the poet soon senses that he cannot linger with these fading sensations, because such a move would threaten his own being: 'À mesure que la sensation s'épuise, la conscience risque de s'engourdir et l'être de tomber en léthargie' (168) ['As sensation wears off, consciousness risks becoming numb, and being risks falling into lethargy']. To avoid being absorbed into a universe that is dying, Verlaine 'cultive donc la dissonance' (168) ['therefore cultivates dissonance']. As we saw in 'La Lune blanche', he attempts to create '"[u]n instant à la fois très vague et très aigu"' (168) ['"A moment that is, at once, very vague and very acute"'].⁹ In certain poems the vagueness dominates, in others the dissonance. This marriage of vagueness and precision is exactly what Richard attempts to capture with his titular word 'fadeur' ('blandness') – a noun that he rather idiosyncratically associates with a tactic of provocation: 'fadeur n'est pas insipidité: c'est une absence de goût devenue positive, réelle, permanente, agaçante comme une provocation' (170) ['blandness is not insipidity: it is the absence of taste that has become positive, real, permanent, irritating like a provocation']. This *fadeur* is on display in the most famous Verlaine poems, in particular in the key collection *Romances sans paroles*.

The *fadeur* can become overpowering, threatening 'la destruction de toutes les caractéristiques individuelles', bringing about 'un climat de neutralité indifférente' (175) ['the destruction of all the individual characteristics', bringing about 'a climate of indifferent neutrality']. But

---

9 Richard is citing Verlaine's 'Kaléidoscope' (from *Jadis et naguère*).

this is also, Richard emphasizes, where Verlaine's poetry is at its most original. Here Verlaine approaches his ideal of a 'lyrisme impersonnel' (176) ['impersonal lyricism']. This second stage presents a new risk for Verlaine's consciousness. Before, the danger was to slip into contourless regions, while now it is the bittersweetness that may overwhelm Verlaine.

Richard finds these two threats to subjectivity in the opening stanza of 'C'est l'extase...'. He comments:

> Extases, fatigues, délices qui semblent exister en eux-mêmes, et que la conscience paraît éprouver du dehors, par participation. Ou bien, et inversement, ce sont eux qui visitent la sensibilité, s'y glissent clandestinement comme des étrangers indésirables. [...] À ces moments à la fois douloureux et privilégiés la conscience a presque cessé de vivre sur le mode d'existence séparée. (176)

> [Ecstasies, weariness, delights that seem to exist in themselves, and that consciousness seems to experience from without, by participation. Or else, and vice versa, it is they who visit sensibility, who sneak into it like unwanted strangers. [...] At these moments that are simultaneously painful and privileged, consciousness has almost stopped living as a separate entity.]

In Richard's first sentence, the poet risks getting carried away by unanchored sensations; in the next, he faces the more invasive danger of being overwhelmed by the sharpness of the *fadeur*. Richard writes about a visit that almost escapes perception and consciousness, arriving 'clandestinement'. And he writes about the duplicity of the highlighted moments, at the same time painful and privileged. Finally, he emphasizes that in such moments 'la conscience a presque cessé de vivre sur le mode d'existence séparée' ['consciousness has almost stopped living as a separate entity'] – consciousness almost blurs into the general ecology.

But, as the adverb 'presque' suggests, this is not the end of the journey of Verlainian consciousness. Ultimately, Verlaine cannot 'épouser pleinement la neutralité' (180) ['fully embrace neutrality']: something in him resists. Instead he *reflects* on the experience of giving himself over, and this produces a split in his consciousness: 'Il sent sur le mode de l'anonyme, mais il se sent sentir sur le mode du particulier' (178) ['He senses in the anonymous mode, but he also senses himself sensing in the mode of the particular']. This precipitates the final – tragic – stage in Richard's account: Verlaine now gives up on the neutral, blames himself for 'charlatanisme', abandons the aspiration towards anonymity, and instead rethinks his poetic work as a form of spirituality anchored in Christ. This is the famous conversion to Catholicism in *Sagesse* where '[t]out s'explique et se réaccorde dans l'harmonie d'un ordre divin' (184) ['Everything is explained by and harmoniously re-tuned within a Divine order']. Verlaine becomes distrustful of sensation, and 'en arrive à chanter la patrie, les généraux et les gendarmes' (185) ['ends up singing the praises of the homeland, the generals and the *gendarmes*'].

Richard's reading – like that of Bernadet – thus detects in Verlaine a constant tension between writing as subject constitution and writing as subject de- or re-constitution through a move towards anonymity and neutrality. According to Richard (and here he differs from Bernadet), Verlaine's drama has to do with his inability to give himself over. In the end (an 'end' that is hardly an end, since *Sagesse* [1880] was published sixteen years before Verlaine's death, and multiple collections were still to come), Verlaine opts for the solid ground.

But hopefully it is also clear how Verlaine's poetry inspires Richard to theorize at the limits of the phenomenological. A traditional phenomenology emphasizes the role of sense perception for the constitution of a consciousness. It is through sense perception that we become aware of the world and ourselves. But in Verlaine's poetry sensations are close to having liberated themselves from their sources; they move about clandestinely, no longer giving form to the world, escaping from a consciousness which in turn almost ceases to be distinct from the universe. Lights have been dimmed, contours disappear, and it becomes difficult to map the relations between world and consciousness. Instead, we participate in incomplete and ecologically informed processes of individuation. We explore the affective – to the point at which subject–object dialectics no longer seem operative. Here, the always incomplete individuation results from a process of environmental unfolding, the participation in an 'humble antienne'.

It can be argued that Richard's text is as much a *symptom* of Verlaine's poetry as its analysis. Twice Richard considers moments of self-dissolution; twice he concludes that Verlaine cannot let go. An alternative reading would be that in his haiku-poetry Verlaine *does* let go, and that Richard struggles to follow him, unable to give the neutrality a more positive value. One cannot help but wonder what Richard's text might have looked like if he had begun *not* with the aim of describing the adventures of an individual consciousness, but rather (like Simondon) with the ambition of rendering an environment that sometimes crystallizes into an 'individual-environment'. We shall return to this issue shortly, but let us first consider Clive Scott's chapter about Verlaine in *The Riches of Rhyme* (1988).

In this chapter, Scott delivers a detailed analysis of rhyme in the *Fêtes galantes*, but first he offers a general presentation of Verlaine. This presentation resonates with Richard's: 'With Verlaine, feelings never develop beyond the primitive state of sentience, and a sentience peculiarly divorced from a sentient being' (1988, 237). This divorce of sentience from sentient being, this state of what Simondon calls affectivity, is precisely what Verlaine is able to render: 'It is Verlaine's ability to capture the unfocused, almost undifferentiated ripplings of consciousness at its lower levels, the kinetics of the psyche' (237–38). In this sentence, Scott pulls Verlaine's consciousness down to the level of 'undifferentiated ripplings', to what N. Katherine Hayles has recently called 'nonconscious cognition' (a concept we shall return to shortly). This second citation from Scott may seem more anthropocentric ('the kinetics of the psyche') than the first ('peculiarly divorced from a sentient being'), but soon Scott goes further, explicitly arguing that Verlaine brings us so far from individual consciousness that anthropocentricity is challenged:

> [Verlaine's] poems present, through the sensory encounter, the shifting polyvalence of moods which are inhabitable but not identifiable [...]. If Verlaine is an Impressionist, it is because he casts anthropocentricity in doubt with his impersonal constructions, because he relativizes experience, because he gives a peculiar substantiality to the half realities of shadow and reflection, because he depicts the mutual interpenetrations of objects or persons and their surrounding space. (238)

Scott's description is not incompatible with the analyses of Bernadet and Richard: in some passages Bernadet used the term 'individuation' to play up the processual and the environmental aspects of his interpretation; similarly, we saw that Verlaine prompted Richard to theorize at the limits of phenomenology, faced with a situation where the links between sensations, perceptions, and subsequent subject constitution seemed stretched to the point of breaking. Nevertheless, with his emphasis on the non-anthropocentric, Scott moves further into the realms of affect theory and ecocriticism (at a time when such terms hardly existed), realms that I have been exploring too.

Looking at these three sensitive readings, it is clear that in all cases Verlaine's poetry stimulates a kind of criticism that drifts away from classical analyses of subject–object relations. To read Verlaine's haiku-poetry through the conceptual framework of dialectics is to deny this poetry its specificity: Verlaine's haiku-poetry is not about intersub-jectivity. Instead, relations are difficult to map, giving way to a more generalized form of vibration. Smells and other sensorial stimuli have left their point of origin (did they ever have one?); impressions come from nowhere, are only partly captured, and consciousnesses therefore do not have the distinctiveness we would expect. To read this poetry we must begin with environments rather than individuals, and we will then realize (as Scott argued) that Verlaine casts anthropocentricity into doubt.

If we did this, we would no longer say that Verlaine's lyric subject flows into the world, or that his poetry is about mental states, sensations, and human moods as landscapes. As 'C'est l'extase...' suggested, we should go in the opposite direction instead. In the first ten lines, there are no human beings, only the discrete ecstasy of a landscape. These stanzas give us a universe in song.[10] Out of the universe of 'c'est cela', a poetic voice and a hesitant address to a lover ('c'est la nôtre, n'est-ce pas?') eventually emerge. Human beings are folded out of an environment, but the process of individuation clearly does not ossify into fixed identities or well-defined intersubjective relations. Rather, individuation has happened only just enough for there to be a question mark at the end. This poem – to borrow a term from the media theorist Mark Hansen – is about 'worldly sensibility' (see Chapter 6), about an 'humble antienne' that we might try to make 'ours'. We can then say that the narrator is trying to hook into – and to channel – the expressivity of the world; and with Simondon we may speak about how pre-individual affectivity enters and stimulates the individual-in-process. We thus find a minimal, vitalist materialism that plays out in pianissimo: environments express themselves through the lyric poet. This is, I believe, what Verlaine calls 'lyrisme impersonnel', and it is a subject position in tune with our times.

Verlaine Today

In the years since Simondon, Deleuze, and Barthes linked individuation, affect, and ecology, a number of different theoretical developments have taken place that resonate strongly with the readings presented above.

---

10   Conversely, 'Dans l'interminable ennui de la plaine' (mentioned in this chapter's footnote 5) gives us a universe in pain: the *ennui* belongs to the plain, the setting, before it belongs to any poetic voice (as we shall see in the next chapter, this also applies to Baudelaire's *Spleen de Paris*).

In the coming chapters I shall draw on writings by Brian Massumi and Mark Hansen, while here I would like to bring in N. Katherine Hayles's *Unthought: The Power of the Cognitive Nonconscious* (2017) to suggest how Verlaine's poetry relates to contemporary epistemologies.

Hayles's book presents what can be called an expanded theory of cognition. She distinguishes between three different levels, organized in the form of a pyramid. At the smallest, topmost level, we have 'modes of awareness'. This term refers to what are often called higher-order functions of consciousness, a level reserved for the human being: this is where *thinking* happens. In the middle of the pyramid we find 'nonconscious cognition', Hayles's key term. For Hayles, 'cognition' is a much broader term than 'thinking': '*Cognition is a process that interprets information within contexts that connect it with meaning*' (22). This broad definition allows her to argue that cognitive processes are found outside human consciousness too – in animals, plant-systems, and machines, for instance. Hayles draws on recent research in cognitive sciences and AI to present these forms of cognition, and she maintains a clear distinction between modes of awareness and nonconscious cognition. Finally, at the third, largest, and most basic level she speaks about 'material processes'. Not everything that changes can be said to cognicize.[11] The label 'material processes' thereby serves to demarcate nonconscious cognition at the lower level, whereas 'thinking' demarcated it at the higher level:

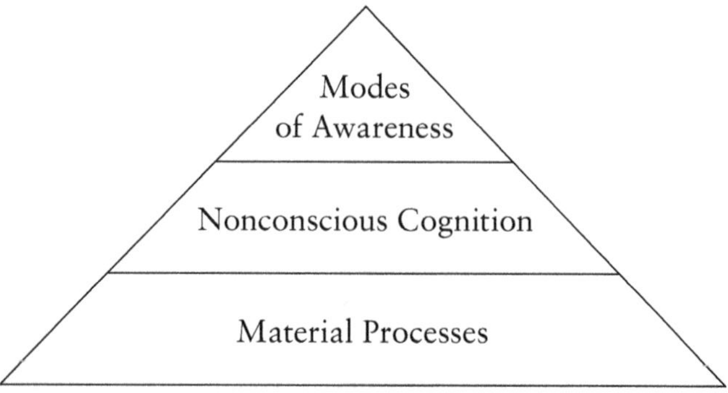

Figure from N. Katherine Hayles, *Unthought – The Power of the Cognitive Nonconscious*, p. 40 (University of Chicago Press, 2017). Permission to reproduce figure provided by N. Katherine Hayles.

11   At this point Hayles distances herself from new materialist thinkers, who, in her view, operate with an excessively broad understanding of cognition.

The figure is labelled 'The tripartite framework of (human) cognition as a pyramid' (40). The word 'human' underlines that we are present at all three levels: we think, we process information in a nonconscious manner, and we are assemblages of material processes. The parenthesis – '(human)' – underlines that this is not just about us: as we move down the pyramid we become increasingly embedded in the world more generally, and we are less and less alone. Focusing on the central level, it is therefore important to understand that nonconscious cognition is embedded, enacted, and environmental to a much larger extent than higher modes of awareness. This central level is, as Hayles writes, 'more in contact with reality than is consciousness' (28). Situating herself in relation to Simondon, she notes that for him too information and meaning arise in interpretation. This is why she can further define cognition by saying that '*Cognition is a process* [...] not an attribute [...] but rather a dynamic unfolding within an environment in which its activity makes a difference' (25). A key element in Hayles's argument, then, is a move from subject to environment – or more precisely, it is a move from the isolated individual towards what she describes as 'cognitive assemblages'. This term allows for the combination of human and other forms of cognition, it includes the affects.[12]

This theorization of cognition and sentience pushes at the framework of twentieth-century phenomenology. As mentioned, traditional phenomenology establishes strong links between sensorial perception, consciousness, and subject constitution. To a large extent this framework carries over into the analyses of Richard and Bernadet. However, as I have sought to demonstrate, both these readers are so sufficiently responsive to Verlaine's writings that they end up theorizing at the very limits of the phenomenological (and the anthropocentric): where sensations (or

---

12   I have not found space to also explore Verlaine's list-like poems in *La Bonne chanson* (such as 'Le foyer, la lueur étroite de la lampe' and 'Le bruit des cabarets') and *Romances sans paroles* ('Walcourt', for instance). These poems suggest what Verlaine had in mind in the letter cited above, when he told Lepelletier that he was planning 'un livre de poèmes [...] d'où l'*homme* sera complètement banni. Des paysages, des choses, malice des choses, bonté, etc., etc., des choses' (Verlaine, 2005, 313–14) ['a book of poems [...] from which *man* will be completely banned. Landscapes, things, malice of things [...], goodness of things, etc., etc. of things' (in Whidden, 2007, 78)]. The list poems may seem radically different from the ecological haiku-poems prioritized here, but Hayles's model suggests that these seemingly very different forms of poetry can both be seen as ways to participate in a more general assemblage and ecology, encouraging us to critically reconsider our anthropocentric habits.

affects) begin to evade our sensorial apparatus, and where the voice cannot therefore build consciousness from perceptions. Not only are many occurrences in Verlaine's poetry enigmatic (does this 'humble antienne' have anything to do with us?), even the material of sensation is evasive (is something happening?). This means that the subject loses its contours, vacillates, and seems unable to gather itself through its interactions with the universe; it cannot fully crystallize. Despite this seemingly negative vocabulary ('loose', 'unable', 'cannot'), we must not think of these experiences as being simply negative; sometimes they are, but as the previous chapter sought to demonstrate they may also be ecstatic, an 'heure exquise', a way of being alive.

Contemporary affect theory, media studies, and science and technology studies often begin here – with this 'individual-environment'. They begin at a historical moment in which we start to realize the extent to which we are influenced by things that escape our modes of awareness. Critics such as Hayles, Massumi, and Hansen attempt to theorize human action and interaction in this larger ecology. My contention is that Verlaine anticipated these developments, and that his haiku'esque poetry should be read as an effort to host that which escapes our perceptual apparatus, to mediate our relation to the affective (in this more precise sense).

The term 'Anthropocene' is just one sign of this growing understanding of how we are caught up in the world. Verlaine's poems can be understood as practical instruments for gaining such an understanding – exercises in non-anthropocentric ontology. Verlaine is thus offering an exploration of what we might call the Anthropocene system of language-, subject-, and world- imbrications – a world in which writing forth a landscape 'te mira blême toi-même'. This does not mean that human beings have no agency, or that the poet is entirely absent from the poetry (even if both Verlaine and Mallarmé explicitly advocate the absence of the poet as an ideal). As Simondon and Hayles make clear when insisting on assemblages, crystallizations, and distributed agency, human beings are part of – and operate in – the environments and networks. To explain how they 'operate', I have turned to the notion of practice, and in particular to the practice of haikus. Brian Massumi proposes another comparison, as he writes about the practice of 'improvisation' (see for instance 2014, 11–23; 2015b, 96–98). Improvisation is not simply a question of making something up on the spot; it is a skill (one which is essential for evolutionary purposes). When musicians improvise, they will generally have an idea about what to play, but they will not be following a predetermined route through a tune. Instead they respond to the other musicians, to the listeners, to changes in light, temperature, and to many more things, improvisation becoming a particularly heightened example of an art of the environment. In this context, words such as 'intention' and 'agency' have to be supplemented (and sometimes replaced) by ideas of 'channelling', 'co-creating', and (as we shall see in Chapter 4) 'mutually specifying'. Verlaine, too, is channelling environments: colouring, tuning, inflecting. My contention is that his poetry is particularly sophisticated when registering *and producing* the micro-movements that run through human beings and their environments. Verlaine clearly sensed the role that sound, rhythm, and other aspects of poetic form could play in this endeavour; nowhere is this more evident than in his most famous poem.

The Verlaine-Environment

Verlaine's third *ariette* is the logical choice to sum up what these first two chapters have argued about Verlaine's ecological, process-relational conception of subjectivity:

III

'Il pleut doucement sur la ville'

(Arthur Rimbaud)

Il pleure dans mon cœur
Comme il pleut sur la ville
Quelle est cette langueur
Qui pénètre mon cœur?

Ô bruit doux de la pluie
Par terre et sur les toits!
Pour un cœur qui s'ennuie
Ô le chant de la pluie!

Il pleure sans raison
Dans ce cœur qui s'écœure
Quoi! nulle trahison?…
Ce deuil est sans raison.

C'est bien la pire peine
De ne savoir pourquoi
Sans amour et sans haine
Mon cœur a tant de peine!

The poem begins with an impersonal 'il' found in an epigraph about the weather – the environment. The first lines of the poem then return to the impersonal 'il' through the use of a simile: 'Il pleure dans mon cœur/ Comme il pleut sur la ville'. The main characteristic of the poem is to continue this entanglement of 'cœur' and 'ville', human being and environment, giving the rain (or climate) a central role in this process.

Two elements are particularly important in the production and communication of this blurring between human and environment. First, the dense musical patterns. These are present in the opening lines where plosives [pl] and vowel patterns [eu] bring together the activities of the heart and the city ('pleure' and 'pleut'). In the fourth line another 'p' emphasizes the penetrability of the heart ('pénètre'), and in the eighth line the 'chant de la pluie' animates the rain, investing this natural phenomenon with expressiveness and lyricism. Towards the end of the poem the 'p's dominate ('pire peine/ De ne savoir pourquoi') to such an extent that Verlaine's text seems to mimic the percussive sound of the rain. This is what Ella Fitzgerald calls the 'pitter patter' in another famous song about rain and tears ('Don't be that way' by Benny Goodman, Mitchell Parish, and Edgar Sampson).

In addition to the 'p's, other aspects serve to homogenize the sounds of the poem – in particular the rhyme structure, AbaA, where the first and last rhyming words are identical.[13] Whereas famous sonic modulations such as Mallarmé's 'Aboli bibelot d'inanité sonore' (Mallarmé, 1998, 37) and Rimbaud's 'atroces fleurs qu'on appellerait cœurs et sœurs, damas damnant de langueur' (Rimbaud, 1972, 144) are so rich in internal plays that they force a slow reading, with semantics and sound competing for our attention, most of Verlaine's repetitions establish dense sound patterns without putting comprehension under too much strain ('Dans ce cœur qui s'écœure'). In this way, the poem dissolves more gently into sound, without confusing its reader. Even so, when drifting from semantics to sound the poem leaves the representational level behind and instead communicates at a sensuous level. There, language connects to a 'humble antienne' that testifies to the expressiveness of not only the poet but also the universe.

The second major aspect of this entanglement of human being and city has to do with a gentle cognitive collapse: the fact that the lyric 'I' (an 'I' manifest only through the possessive pronoun 'mon') has a limited (intellectual) understanding of what is happening. It can be said that we

---

13   In the fourth stanza, 'peine' carries two different meanings ('punishment' and 'pain').

move from Hayles's 'modes of awareness' to 'nonconscious cognition'. The voice is not able to rise above the situation and consider it analytically. Instead, it oscillates between 'not knowing why' and claiming 'there is no reason why'. More specifically, we have an unanswered question in the first stanza ('quelle est cette langueur/ Qui pénètre mon cœur?') followed by the more confident affirmation 'Il pleure sans raison' in the third, which the same stanza then immediately undermines with an exclamation, a question, and an ellipsis in quick succession: 'Quoi! Nulle trahison?...'. The voice then returns to the lack of explanation with 'Ce deuil est sans raison', before the last stanza drives home the idea of cognitive impotence ('ne savoir pourquoi'). In this manner, the poem communicates the impossibility of explaining – and thereby containing and distancing oneself from – the pain. However, even if there are no explanations, this does not mean that the voice gives up on trying to navigate the situation. For instance, the lyric voice is sufficiently self-aware to know that 'langueur' penetrates their heart and that their heart 's'ennuie'. The demonstrative pronouns 'ce' and 'cette' indicate an ability to map the environment, and the voice is capable of eliminating false explanations through the many negatives and privatives that dominate the short poem ('sans', 'nulle', 'ne').

These two ways of softening the distinction between human being and city obviously work together. There is no explanation to the pain and the voice cannot rise beyond it through explanation; however, there is a melodic modulation of this pain, an interweaving of impersonal lyric voice and environment, and a tuning that happens partly through the elimination of false explanations. This interpenetration of human being and environment is played out in a register neither outright masochistic nor therapeutic. It has shades of the masochistic (for instance with the question in the first stanza: 'Quelle est cette langueur/ Qui pénètre mon cœur?' and 'la pire peine' in the final stanza) and the therapeutic (through the cleansing powers of rain: 'Pour un cœur qui s'ennuie/ Ô le chant de la pluie!'), but overall this is another poem that avoids the extremes ('Sans amour et sans haine').[14] Instead, the poem emphasizes *douceur* right

14 I therefore read the poem differently from Seth Whidden. Whidden argues that Verlaine struggles with expression, and therefore with the subject constitution he hoped to achieve through his poetry. Whidden writes: 'In addition, the rhyme scheme ABAA adds a level of frustration (always waiting for the second B that never arrives), and the rhyme linking the first and last lines of each stanza is based on the repetition of words ("mon cœur," "de la pluie," "sans raison," "peine"). These repetitive structures, along with the repetition of the key words "cœur" and "sans,"

from the opening epigraph ('– il pleut doucement sur la ville'), which is then picked up in the second stanza ('Ô bruit doux de la pluie' and 'Ô le chant de la pluie') before overflowing the limits of the present poem and appearing in the epigraph to the next ariette ('de la douceur, de la douceur, de la douceur').[15] However, as already mentioned, Verlaine's avoidance of extreme emotions goes hand in hand with an enthusiasm for exclamation marks and interjections such such as 'Ô', 'Oh', and 'Hélas'. In this poem we find three exclamation marks and two interjections in just sixteen lines. This merits a short detour.

Texts such as 'Il pleure dans mon cœur', 'La Lune blanche', and many others are concerned with the ineffable, the vague, the ungraspable. The halftones and blurriness can be associated with a general poetics of 'évocation' or 'suggestion' that characterizes late-nineteenth-century French poetry, and which finds a canonical formulation in Mallarmé's response to Jules Huret's *Enquête sur l'évolution littéraire*: '*Nommer* un objet, c'est supprimer les trois quarts de la jouissance du poème qui est faite du bonheur de deviner peu à peu: le *suggérer*, voilà le rêve' (2003, 700) ['To name an object is to suppress three-quarters of the enjoyment of the poem, which is made of the pleasure of guessing little by little; to suggest it, there is the dream']. This does not mean that we can associate these poets with imprecision; as Verlaine writes in *L'Art poétique*, 'la chanson grise' is the place 'où l'indécis au précis se joint' (1962, 326) ['where the uncertain joins the precise']. A poem like 'Il pleure dans mon cœur' is both precise and indeterminate.

In our culture, the ideals of precision, completion, and perfection go so closely together that Verlaine's aesthetics almost seems paradoxical in its attempt to marry precision and indeterminacy. But, as we have seen,

all suggest a dearth of vocabulary (not a problem in the other "Ariettes oubliées"), which in turn underscores the lyric subject's difficulty with poetic expression. But how can one express that which one does not understand? Such, then, are the layers on which this poetic crisis operates; since the poetic subject cannot identify clearly the source of his sadness, it follows logically that he would lack the proper words to describe it' (Whidden, 2007, 87). I see less of a difference between 'Il pleure...' and the other *Ariettes oubliées*, and more generally I believe these poems excel at communicating what lies beyond the knowable, as precisely as possible, through a careful practice.

15 Verlaine is citing the opening verse of his own 'Lassitude' from *Poèmes saturniens* (1962, 63), and perhaps also responding to the haunting of another famous alexandrine: 'L'Azur, L'Azur, L'Azur, L'Azur' (from Mallarmé's 'L'Azur' [1998, 15]).

blurs and echoes may not be imprecise. A haiku is an echo: it makes itself available to the reader as vibration. This has nothing to do with imprecision. Closer to Verlaine's time and place, it would be misleading to characterize the late paintings of Claude Monet as imprecise. And, even more appropriately, someone like the contemporary master of blur, Gerhard Richter, dissolves any opposition between precision and blur: rarely have blurred images been so obviously precise.

What is at stake here goes further than a question about the meaning of aesthetic precision and imprecision. It relates to ideas about subjectivity and truth. As mentioned, the ideal of clear representational thinking dominates our culture, and with this comes an idea of how we can separate ourselves from the universe. 'Critical distance' is almost a pleonasm as we struggle to think critique as anything other than an exercise in distance. This is not helpful, however, when reading poetry like Verlaine's. Verlaine's is a poetry where distance between human being and universe is eroded, a poetry where a distinction between the vague and the precise has little analytic purchase, a poetry as precise and ineffable as a composition by Debussy. It is therefore also a poetry that combines *fadeur, brume,* ellipses, and halftones of all kinds with exclamation marks, repetitions, and multiple list-like enumerations that – at first – seem as far as possible from what we might think of as suggestion. In 'C'est l'extase…' the famous 'Ô le frêle et frais murmure!' brings together, perhaps better than any other line, exclamation marks and frailty, murmur and expletives. In such a way, Verlaine's poetry follows in the footsteps of Leibniz's famous critique of Descartes's notion of truth and subjectivity. For Leibniz, ideas could be both 'clear and confused' – indeed, this was precisely the kind of ideational thinking he associated with art. Art does not share the particular ideal of clarity that dominates so many thetic discourses, and as a consequence it is richer, more encompassing, less reductive and… more precise (as Hayles argues, thinking is in contact with a smaller fraction of reality than is nonconscious cognition).[16] If 'Il pleure…' occupies a unique position in the French literary imaginary (and in nineteenth-century French studies), it

---

16 Similarly, Norbert Wiener writes about the brain's advantages over the computer: 'Chief among these advantages would seem to be the ability of the brain to handle vague ideas, as yet imperfectly defined. In dealing with these, mechanical computers, or at least the mechanical computers of the present day, are very nearly incapable of programming themselves. Yet in poems, in novels, in paintings, the brain seems to find itself able to work very well with material that any computer

is because of the same seemingly effortless combination of precision and indeterminacy.[17]

And the poem *does* occupy a unique position in the French literary landscape. Few poems are as well known. From the first time you read it – or more accurately, hear it – it sounds familiar (hence the temptation to discard the poem as banal and quickly move on). What does it mean that this poem occupies such a prominent position in the collective imaginary? 'Il pleure dans mon cœur' communicates no knowledge, no view on anything. In one sense we may think of the poem as psychological (a lyric subject explores their soul); in another it is radically a-psychological (the soul-searching yields no result whatsoever). However, it does give readers an opportunity to settle in a soundscape, and in so doing, to mediate the relation between psyche and world. It is therefore the perfect poem to bring together the muted ecstasies of 'La Lune blanche' and 'C'est l'extase...' with the spleen tones of 'L'Ombre des arbres'. Like this latter poem, 'Il pleure...' is a spleen poem. But few spleen poems are as appealing and pleasant – few spleen poems have drawn in so many readers and satisfied their (perhaps unformulated) desire to experience their own porosity to a world in constant movement. In this manner, the poem becomes an almost zen-like practice that helps us into the universe, encouraging us to sense that we are and were always already part of the semiosis of the world.[18]

Coda: In the Grass...

This chapter has argued that Verlaine's haikus rest on an ecological conception of individuation that makes them contemporary with our Anthropocene condition. Other critics have sensed this, but because

would have to reject as formless' (Wiener, 1966, 72–73; we shall return to Wiener in Chapter 6).

17   Of course, there is nothing effortless about achieving this harmony between precision and indeterminacy. Steve Murphy recounts how the ariette was used for an advertisement for France Telecom – and how the advertising agents rightly alluded to the difficulty of being 'simple'. Underneath the poem, their slogan was: 'FRANCE TELECOM EQUIPEMENTS. RIEN N'EST JAMAIS SIMPLE PAR HASARD' (Murphy in Verlaine, 2012, 306) ['FRANCE TELECOM EQUIPMENTS. NOTHING IS EVER SIMPLE BY CHANCE'].

18   I speak of semiosis with reference to Hayles's definition of cognition as a process that connects information to meaning ('*Cognition is a process that interprets information within contexts that connect it with meaning*') (2017, 22).

they generally begin with the poetic subject, or a focus on the various character-relations in the texts, I do not think that they have sufficiently emphasized that Verlaine's haikus can be practised so that we come to understand ourselves as unfolding out of the 'humble antienne'. Someone who did understand this was Stéphane Mallarmé. Shortly after Verlaine's death in January 1896, he wrote a homage to his friend: a sonnet, entitled 'Tombeau', published on the first anniversary of Verlaine's death. Mallarmé had a habit of writing funerary homages; he published tributes to Gautier, Poe, and Baudelaire, and a more 'grumpy' ('boudeur' was Mallarmé's term [1998, 791]) homage to Wagner. The tribute to Verlaine is devoid of grumpiness. It aims to free Verlaine of his reputation as a drunken and scandalous man, remove all moral judgement, and bring attention to his poetry. This inspires one of the most charming alexandrines in Mallarmé's work (1998, 39):

Verlaine? Il est caché parmi l'herbe, Verlaine

As all of Mallarmé's *tombeaux* do, the sonnet takes the death of a great artist as an opportunity to celebrate the immortality of his art. These poems are also, to differing degrees, an opportunity for Mallarmé to write himself into the skin of a beloved colleague – a sort of ventriloquism beyond death, allowing Mallarmé to become a medium, adopting the *manière* of a fellow poet (and, in this particular case, responding to Verlaine's collection of *Dédicaces*).[19] This eleventh alexandrine in the sonnet shows Mallarmé brilliantly mimicking his friend. Verlaine is here *of* nature. Mallarmé uses Verlaine's name to suggest the green ('vert'), soft ('laine') grass in which Verlaine is hiding with his verse ('vers') like a worm ('ver') in the ground. Any distinctions between nature, creatures, and poetry are long gone – all three elements participate fully in the expressive assemblage. The phantom-word 'verbe' ('l'herbe Verlaine') suggests that in the case of Verlaine (and of Gautier, Poe, and Baudelaire also) 'à la fin était le Verbe': now poetry takes over. Another phantom word 'l'air' ('l'her-be') makes sure that nothing imposes itself. The fact that Mallarmé doubles up on the name of the poet references how Verlaine himself plays with repetitions, chiasms, and circularity to undo subject–object relations; Mallarmé has also found space – at the hemistich, of course – for Verlaine's favourite preposition 'parmi'. If this

---

19 In *Dédicaces* (1891), Verlaine responded to Mallarmé's poetry with a sonnet; now Mallarmé reponds, keeping alive what we (inspired by Bernadet) might call a transsubjective intimacy.

preposition so frequently figures in Verlaine's work (Murphy describes it as a 'véritable tic stylistique' [in Verlaine, 2012, 340], ['real stylistic tic']), it is because it constitutes the best one-word summary of his affective-ecological poetics and his view of individuation – the fact that we are always, as Massumi wrote about Simondonian ontology, 'in the middle', 'par le milieu'.

CHAPTER THREE

Affectivity and Ecology in Baudelaire's Twilight

The next two chapters focus on Baudelaire. Again, I do not claim that my readings are representative of all of Baudelaire's work; rather, they are concerned with texts and themes that speak to present debates. As we shall see, these chapters pursue the analysis of ecological and affective individuation that I began in my study of Verlaine, but they add to this a more explicit interest in collective individuation, in the social world.

This third chapter will focus on the prose version of 'Le Crépuscule du soir' in *Le Spleen de Paris* – and a limited number of recent texts associated with 'affect theory' and (less explicitly) 'new materialism'. It will closely analyze Baudelaire's poem, attempting to demonstrate what can be gained from reading Baudelaire's poetry non-anthropocentrically. The first part of the chapter brings Brian Massumi's writings on affectivity into dialogue with Baudelaire's poem. The second and third parts step back from the poetry and seek to clarify how this reading of Baudelaire differs from Georges Poulet's chapter on Baudelaire in *Les Métamorphoses du cercle* (1961); the relatively recent volume by Ross Chambers, *An Atmospherics of the City: Baudelaire and the Poetics of Noise* (2015); and Jacques Rancière's article 'Le goût infini de la République' (from *Le Fil perdu*, 2014a). By the end of the chapter, I will have given one possible answer to the question of how Baudelaire's poetry speaks to 'the present', arguing, in particular, that 'Le Crépuscule du soir' invites us to understand human beings as dynamic mediations of their environments, thereby disturbing our seemingly ingrained tendency to think agency in strictly individual and individualizing terms. Furthermore, I will have suggested that it is time for Baudelaire criticism to reconsider its commitment to the idea of Baudelaire as primarily a writer of urban modernity – a suggestion that will be developed in Chapter 4 on Baudelaire's writings about colour.

The Affective Ecology of 'Le Crépuscule du soir': Baudelaire and Massumi

'Le Crépuscule du soir' exists in a verse version published in 1852 and in a very different prose version: it is the latter that will be the subject of this chapter. It is the earliest of Baudelaire's prose poems and it is among those he revised most substantially. The first version is from 1855; the final text, discussed here, is from 1864:

XXII

LE CRÉPUSCULE DU SOIR

Le jour tombe. Un grand apaisement se fait dans les pauvres esprits fatigués du labeur de la journée; et leurs pensées prennent maintenant les couleurs tendres et indécises du crépuscule.

Cependant du haut de la montagne arrive à mon balcon, à travers les nues transparentes du soir, un grand hurlement, composé d'une foule de cris discordants, que l'espace transforme en une lugubre harmonie, comme celle de la marée qui monte ou d'une tempête qui s'éveille.

Quels sont les infortunés que le soir ne calme pas, et qui prennent, comme les hiboux, la venue de la nuit pour un signal de sabbat? Cette sinistre ululation nous arrive du noir hospice perché sur la montagne; et, le soir, en fumant et en contemplant le repos de l'immense vallée, hérissée de maisons dont chaque fenêtre dit: 'C'est ici la paix maintenant; c'est ici la joie de la famille!' je puis, quand le vent souffle de là-haut, bercer ma pensée étonnée à cette imitation des harmonies de l'enfer.

Le crépuscule excite les fous. – Je me souviens que j'ai eu deux amis que le crépuscule rendait tout malades. L'un méconnaissait alors tous les rapports d'amitié et de politesse, et maltraitait, comme un sauvage, le premier venu. Je l'ai vu jeter à la tête d'un maître d'hôtel un excellent poulet, dans lequel il croyait voir je ne sais quel insultant hiéroglyphe. Le soir, précurseur des voluptés profondes, lui gâtait les choses les plus succulentes.

L'autre, un ambitieux blessé, devenait, à mesure que le jour baissait, plus aigre, plus sombre, plus taquin. Indulgent et sociable encore pendant la journée, il était impitoyable le soir; et ce n'était pas seulement sur autrui, mais aussi sur lui-même, que s'exerçait rageusement sa manie crépusculeuse.

Le premier est mort fou, incapable de reconnaître sa femme et son enfant; le second porte en lui l'inquiétude d'un malaise perpétuel, et fût-il gratifié de tous les honneurs que peuvent conférer les républiques et les princes, je crois que le crépuscule allumerait encore en lui la brûlante envie de distinctions imaginaires. La nuit, qui mettait ses ténèbres dans leur esprit, fait la lumière dans le mien; et, bien qu'il ne soit pas rare de voir la même cause engendrer deux effets contraires, j'en suis toujours comme intrigué et alarmé.

Ô nuit! ô rafraîchissantes ténèbres! vous êtes pour moi le signal d'une fête intérieure, vous êtes la délivrance d'une angoisse! Dans la solitude des plaines, dans les labyrinthes pierreux d'une capitale, scintillement des étoiles, explosion des lanternes, vous êtes le feu d'artifice de la déesse Liberté!

Crépuscule, comme vous êtes doux et tendre! Les lueurs roses qui traînent encore à l'horizon comme l'agonie du jour sous l'oppression victorieuse de sa nuit, les feux des candélabres qui font des taches d'un rouge opaque sur les dernières gloires du couchant, les lourdes draperies qu'une main invisible attire des profondeurs de l'Orient, imitent tous les sentiments compliqués qui luttent dans le cœur de l'homme aux heures solennelles de la vie.

On dirait encore une de ces robes étranges de danseuses, où une gaze transparente et sombre laisse entrevoir les splendeurs amorties d'une jupe éclatante, comme sous le noir présent transperce le délicieux passé; et les étoiles vacillantes d'or et d'argent, dont elle est semée, représentent ces feux de la fantaisie qui ne s'allument bien que sous le deuil profond de la Nuit.

As its title suggests, 'Le Crépuscule du soir' expresses what happens when darkness falls. Responses to the fading of the light vary throughout the poem: it makes the poor happy, relieved that the day is over. It excites the mad people. The narrator writes about two mad friends who explode in apparently random acts of violence – much like the narrator in *Le Mauvais vitrier* (or the very contemporary characters analysed by the Tiqqun collective in their *Théorie du Bloom* [2004]). Eventually, one of these madmen died, whereas the other, still alive, is walking around harbouring a desire for recognition that no one seems able to satisfy. The darkness has a third effect on the city more generally: it is associated with happiness and family time. The narrator is standing on his balcony, overlooking the city, and the windows he contemplates reveal such instances of happiness. Finally, twilight takes yet another form in the poet himself – or rather, it takes several forms. First, he notes that it produces light in his spirit. This, however, makes him 'intrigué et alarmé' about the range of reactions that twilight can produce. The speaker then moves from this state of alarm straight back into a celebration of the night: we have a sequence of five sentences all ending with an exclamation mark, including a depiction that brings back the light by characterizing the twilight as 'le feu d'artifice de la déesse

Liberté!' ['fireworks celebrating the Goddess Liberty!' (Baudelaire, 1991, 63)]. Towards the end of the poem, a series of elaborate and subtly erotic metaphors describe the mix of light and darkness on the horizon. In the penultimate paragraph, the narrator evokes candelabras and dark draperies from the 'profondeurs de l'Orient' ['depths of the Orient' (63)] that imitate the emotions in the human heart. And in the final paragraph (one long sinuous sentence), he introduces the semi-transparent tutu of a dancer. It is tempting to link these last two chains of metaphors and see the contours of a dancer in a semi-transparent dress, behind heavily draped curtains… However, the poem does not offer a personification of darkness – there is no embodiment. Readers looking for a summative statement are therefore better served going back to the idea, found in the penultimate paragraph, that the spectacle of the sunset and the candelabres 'imitent tous les sentiments compliqués qui luttent dans le cœur de l'homme aux heures solennelles de la vie' ['reflect all the complex feelings that struggle in the heart of man at the solemn moments of life' (63)].

As mentioned, this is a poem that traces what happens when 'le jour tombe' ['evening falls' (62)]. It belongs to a category of poems by Baudelaire that lend themselves to a non-anthropocentric reading (other such prose poems include 'Le *Confiteor* de l'artiste', 'Les Bienfaits de la lune', 'Le Tir et le cimetière', and many verse poems). Obviously, there is a narratorial voice, and we encounter a number of characters. Nevertheless, I will suggest that the poem is less concerned with human characters and the ways in which they act and interact, than it is with an elusive, affective state that modulates the characters: the titular 'crépuscule'. From the beginning, the poem therefore presents a kind of hydraulic system: evening falls and sounds begin to rise from a mysterious 'noir hospice' ['black asylum' (62)] perched on the mountain; next, these sounds flood the city. Readers will feel inclined to tidy up and systematize the effects of this flooding by distinguishing between the emotions of the poor, the mad, the city more generally, and the narrator. This is exactly what I just did, for this is what the narratorial voice tries to do. But in the end, the poem's attempts at ordering the effects of darkness largely collapse, and as already mentioned we end up with 'everything': 'tous les sentiments compliqués qui luttent dans le cœur de l'homme' ['all the complex feelings that struggle in the heart of man'].

To analyse the poem, it is helpful to draw on Brian Massumi's Simondon-inspired writing on affects. We can then say that 'Le

Crépuscule du soir' is a poem about 'affects' rather than 'emotions'. For Massumi, affect is (to borrow from Steven Shaviro's concise summary)

> primary, nonconscious, asubjective or presubjective, asignifying, unqualified, and intensive; while emotion is derivative, conscious, qualified, and meaningful, a 'content' that can be attributed to an already-constituted subject. Emotion is affect captured by a subject [...]. Subjects are overwhelmed and traversed by affect, but they *have* or *possess* their own emotions. (Shaviro, 2010, 8)

Affects in-fluence human beings, but due to their fluidity they largely escape us; emotions or feelings, on the other hand, are affects recollected by a consciousness.

Massumi's early work received a lot of criticism for establishing a rigid separation of affects and emotions. The title of his key article (later incorporated in *Parables for the Virtual*) was 'The Autonomy of Affect', and indeed, his distinction between affects and emotions is stronger than the one we encountered in Simondon's work (see Chapter 1). However, even in this early presentation of affect, Massumi's formulations suggest that rather than a dichotomy between affect and emotion, we should think of a dynamic relation in which emotion can be seen as the always incomplete capture of affect. Massumi explains:

> affect is autonomous to the degree to which it escapes confinement in the particular body whose vitality, or potential for interaction, it is. Formed, qualified, situated perceptions and cognitions fulfilling functions of actual connection or blockage are the capture and closure of affect. Emotion is the intensest (most contracted) expression of that *capture* – and of the fact that something has always and again escaped. (2002, 35)

'Le Crépuscule du soir' – like many other late-nineteenth-century French poems – largely explores the realm of affectivity: it is a poem about elusive sensations, mysterious sounds, changes in the play between light and shadows. The poem and the narrator register the effects of darkness, but the effects are wildly dissimilar, and it is therefore impossible for readers to explain the poem by working their way back to a unifying cause. This is why readers are in the same position as the narrator: what both worries and excites us is that darkness can produce seemingly any response. As the narrator observes: 'bien qu'il ne soit pas rare de voir la même cause engendrer deux effets contraires, j'en suis toujours comme intrigué et alarmé' ['although it is not unusual for one cause to engender two contrasting results, I am always somewhat intrigued and alarmed when it happens' (63)].

But how far can one reasonably push such an affective reading of 'Le Crépuscule du soir'? To what extent does this poem move away from human figures that manifest themselves through choices and actions, and towards modes of happening, modes of doing that challenge both the narratorial voice and the characters we encounter in the poem? Most of Baudelaire's readers have tended to focus on the human subjects in the poem (and his work more generally), addressing complex issues relating to the voice of the narrator, the actions of his friends, intersubjectivity, and the problem of irony, for instance. I will leave such issues aside and concentrate on delivering an affective reading.

So let me propose a slight hyperbole: there is almost nothing about subjectivities and identities in this poem. At least, not in the humanist or existentialist sense of subjects becoming (and betraying) themselves through various kinds of individual action. In 'Le Crépuscule du soir', subjects are rather a momentary crystallization of a mood that seems to roll in from the mountains. This mood is filtered through the clouds before it eventually takes the immaterial form of an 'ululation' – a word that very appropriately seems to unravel syllable by syllable, delivering little more than a modulation of sound. Furthermore, darkness itself is constantly modulating. The poem moves swiftly from one metaphor to the next, thereby demonstrating the impossibility of capturing darkness. Already after the first two paragraphs, the twilight has been associated with (environmental elements such as) colours, sounds, a tide, and a tempest brewing in the distance. Using a contemporary vocabulary to characterize 'Le Crépuscule du soir', it can thus be said that the poem maps an affective ecology in which the various elements and characters struggle to find a stable form. It's true that it would be too much to suggest that there are no human characters in the text – that the poem is 'nonhuman' – but it is reasonable to say that human characters aren't privileged.

To understand this non-anthropocentric form of being, and its implications for how we think our relations to the world, we can refer back to Gilbert Simondon's idea of the 'individual-environment' (Chapter 1). With this notion, Simondon aimed to conceptualize the co-evolution of human beings and environments. Simondon bracketed off the more traditional questions of intersubjective, dialectic relations, and instead focused on what he called pre-individual processes of becoming that temporarily produce individuals as environments. The characters in 'Le Crépuscule du soir' seem to be precisely such *individus-milieux*, transitory figures modulated by the hydraulics of the dying light. They do not exhaust the affective environment presented in the poem; rather, the mood runs through them, and through the text. More precisely: this mood manifests itself *as* text. The poem registers how the mood (in-)forms the various poor and rich citizens – almost like a virus or an electronic pulse. And this virus (like most viruses) transmutes as it moves along: coming in from the mountains, affecting the characters it encounters, and (we must imagine) receding as the light reappears.

Brian Massumi writes that in our time 'affectivity and will are in a state of indistinction' (2015a, 47). Something similar can be said about the world of Baudelaire's poem. Agency cannot be located at any precise point – instead the poem offers a profound challenge to conventional ideas of choice, action, causality, and subjectivity.[1] Nowhere is this communicated more clearly than in the anecdote about the two mad friends. Their actions seem to happen independently of their will and independently of any form of conscious decision. Reusing Massumi's vocabulary, we can say that a deed is done through them, 'choice happens' and 'decision happens', as if a particular kind of intensity was seeking an outlet (2015a, 19–20). In Baudelaire's poem, this challenge to more classical ideas about subjectivity (and its relation to choice and agency) is not only established at the more macro-narrative level (as in the anecdote about the friends), but also results from complex and precise linguistic crafting, which largely amounts to a destabilization of linguistic conventions. A brief analysis of this linguistic work can demonstrate my point.

If we study the verbal and syntactical structures in the poem, it becomes clear how often these prevent us from determining 'whom', if anyone, is the cause of 'what'. This is communicated from the laconic beginning of the text: 'Le jour tombe' ['evening falls' (62)]. This three-word sentence presents an article, a noun, and a verb in the present tense; the grammatical subject is performing an act and the verb is active – it could hardly be more straightforward. But we might begin

---

1   Massumi presents the relation between freedom and distributed agency in different ways in his various writings. Here is one of his least provocative formulations, reminding us that we must rethink agency and freedom, not deny their existence: 'Our freedom doesn't consist in making a choice or decision that comes only out of our own subjectivity – in other words, out of nowhere. Our freedom is how we play our implication in the field, what events we succeed in catalysing in it that bring out the latent singularity of the situation, how we inflect for novel emergences. That is a relational question' (2015b, 158).

by asking to what extent 'falling' can accurately be described as an act. Grammatically, the verb is active, but semantically the idea of falling is more commonly associated with passivity; it is something that happens to you, typically against your will. Staying with the grammatical subject ('le jour'), it is remarkable not only that a nonhuman element 'acts' (our language is full of such expressions, but that does not make them any less noteworthy), but also that this subject could be replaced by its antonym ('la nuit') without causing the denotative meaning of the sentence to change ('le jour tombe' = 'la nuit tombe'), or by an intermediate solution 'le soir tombe' (hence Rosemary Lloyd's English translation 'evening falls'). The three-word opening thereby immediately constructs a zone of indistinction in which identities disappear ('jour' equals 'nuit' equals 'soir') and things happen without actions being clearly initiated. Although the poem cannot yet be called disturbing, these forms of indistinction begin to build a worrying universe, enhanced by the signification of 'tombe' as noun (a 'grave'), and the subversive take on the biblical links between order, light, and creation: *let there be darkness.*

The remainder of the opening paragraph continues to eat away at identities and individual agency. First, the text uses a passive voice ('Un grand apaisement *se fait* dans les pauvres esprits fatigués' ['A great sense of peace pervades poor spirits' (62)]) to undermine any clear idea of agency – who acts here? Then it repeats the trick from the opening sentence, introducing another grammatically active verb that confuses our attempts to determine who acts: 'et leur pensées prennent maintenant les couleurs tendres et indécises du crépuscule' ['and their thoughts now assume the tender and indeterminate colours of dusk' (62)]. Here the active verb 'prennent' might suggest that the subject ('leurs pensées') acts, but it actually seems to describe something like a reflection (as in the 'reflection of light': 'les pensées' reflect what is happening around them), thereby turning the grammatical subject into the object.[2] In this manner, the sentence brings together two different views of cognition. The more active reading of 'prendre' suggests a form of cognition that we might, schematically, call Cartesian, Hegelian, or Sartrean: thinking as a form-giving activity through which the subject gradually builds itself. On the other hand, the reactive meaning of 'prendre' points to an environmental conception of thinking: thinking

---

2   These ambiguities resemble those encountered with Verlaine's 'ce paysage blême/ Te mira blême toi-même' (see Chapter 2).

becomes a responsive-creative act in which we are affected by – and channel – impulses in the environment. In Baudelaire's grammatical construction, these two views of cognition – these two meanings of the word 'reflective' – are scrambled.[3]

At a more macro-narrative level, the poem creates a flat ontology, often doing away with distinctions between living and non-living entities. Not only '[l]e jour tombe', but windows speak and the poet addresses twilight apostrophically ('Crépuscule, comme vous êtes doux et tendre!' ['Dusk, how gentle and tender you are!' (63)]). At the crucial point towards the end of the text where readers might expect the narrative to come to an end and a moral (however ambiguous) to emerge, some very complex syntactical structures, introducing elaborate metaphors, guarantee that the ambiguity reaches a new climax. The metaphors in the final two paragraphs create a semantic overload which it is virtually impossible to bring back to a linear, narrative logic. The logic of the last paragraph can be summed up like this: the twilight resembles a dress decorated with stars that represent the sparks of a fantasy that only the night lights up. Again, it is difficult to pinpoint *whom* does *what*.

If we add to these observations the mysterious sounds that well forth from the mountains, it is clear that the poem pulls away from causal logics, away from subject–object dichotomies, and instead creates a climate of indistinction.[4] This climate points to a new conception of subjectivity – the 'individual-environment' – that resonates (and can be read) with contemporary affect theory. A partial and excessively succinct summary of the poem could sound like this: as night falls, Paris and its inhabitants become an environment in which modulations play out and a new ontology emerges. But how does such a reading compare to earlier

3 Massumi writes that 'a jellyfish is its brain' (2002, 36–37). By this he means that although the jellyfish does not think in the way that human beings do, it still adjusts and responds to the environments in which it finds itself. It is a reflective animal – engaged in what Hayles would call 'nonconscious cognition' (Chapter 2). The point here is not that Baudelaire's text (or Massumi's, for that matter) suggests that human beings are reflective *only* in this sense of the word; the point is that we are *also* (and to a much larger extent than generally admitted) reflective in this sense of the word.

4 See also Baudelaire's definition of pure art in 'L'art philosophique': 'C'est créer une magie suggestive contenant à la fois l'objet et le sujet, le monde extérieur à l'artiste, et l'artiste lui-même' (1976, 598) ['It is to create a suggestive magic containing at once subject and object, the world outside the artist and the artist himself'].

readings? As we shall see in the next section, this question will take us to Edgar Allan Poe, and to Baudelaire's writings about his American colleague.

Poulet and Poe: From Phenomenology to Spiritual Materialism

In some respects, the non-anthropocentric reading sounds familiar. Baudelaire himself writes about intensities, and as we shall see several of his readers have paid attention to the work that intensity and affectivity do in his poetry. More generally (and as previously mentioned), mid- to late-nineteenth-century French poetry has long been known as an art of suggestion, music, and everything that exceeds the representational. We might therefore ask why (or indeed 'if') it is helpful to bring in Gilbert Simondon, Brian Massumi, Steven Shaviro, and others who do not write about Baudelaire, when these topics have been approached by Baudelaire scholars. We might ask where the differences between a non-anthropo-centric reading and these previous readings lie. In particular, the points made in the section above may seem close to readings proposed by Geneva school critics such as Jean-Pierre Richard and Georges Poulet in the mid-1950s and early 1960s. In the previous chapter we studied Richard's reading of Verlaine; let us now turn to Poulet's reading of Baudelaire.

Poulet tends to focus on the sensuous aspect of Baudelaire's writings, the spatial and temporal characteristics of his poetic universe, and the various movements we find in the poetry. With this interest in space, sensation, and movement, Poulet largely brackets off individual psychology, sociology, and politics to concentrate instead on delivering sophisticated analyses of something that resembles the moods and affects described above. Consider, for example, the opening page of his chapter on Baudelaire in *Les Métamorphoses du cercle* (1961). Poulet begins with a short passage from Baudelaire's essay 'Edgar Allan Poe, Sa vie et ses œuvres' [1856]), then weaves this citation together with other brief excerpts from texts by Baudelaire and observations of his own. In this manner, a description of what I have called 'Baudelaire's affective ecology' emerges. But Poulet is not only describing – his particular style of writing *performs* the ecological ethos of Baudelaire's poetry. Destabilizing distinctions between critic and object of study, Poulet lets the poetry speak through a voice that no longer has a single point of origin (thereby, as we saw in the previous chapter, approaching

Verlaine's ideal for literary criticism: 'parler d'un poète, c'est surtout le citer' [Verlaine, 1972, 949] ['to speak about a poet, one must first of all cite him']):

> 'La nature… frisonne d'un frisson surnaturel et galvanique'. C'est par ce frisson que tout commence chez Baudelaire. A de certaines heures, 'admirables heures, véritables fêtes du cerveau', les objets se trouvent soudain parés de couleurs plus vives, doués d'un relief singulier, d'une résonance aiguë: 'Les sons tintent musicalement, les couleurs parlent.' Une extrême énergie fait frémir les choses. Elles chatoient, résonnent, trépident. Elles ne se contentent plus d'être, elles se mettent à vivre. A cette intensité qui éclate partout au-dehors correspond une même intensité au-dedans. C'est l'heure où 'les sens plus attentifs perçoivent des sensations plus retentissantes', où 'toute pensée sublime est accompagnée d'une secousse nerveuse'. Les choses vibrent, la pensée vibre. Vibration qui est en chaque contour, bruit ou teinte au-dehors, en chaque idée au-dedans. Ou plutôt il n'y a ni dedans, ni dehors, mais simplement l'apparition subite et multiple, quelque part, dans le champ perceptif, d'une même intensité vibrante. (Poulet, 1979, 407)

> ['Nature… quivers with a supernatural and galvanic quivering.' It is by this quivering that everything in Baudelaire begins. At certain hours, 'admirable hours, veritable festivals of the brain,' objects suddenly find themselves decked with more vivid colors, endowed with a strange setting off, with a keen resonance: 'sounds ring musically, colors speak.' An exceptional energy makes everything tremulous. They sparkle, resound, trepidate. To be is no longer enough with them, they come alive. To this intensity bursting everywhere outside, there corresponds a similar intensity within. It is the time when 'the more vigilant senses perceive more reverberating sensations,' in which 'all sublime thought is accompanied by a nervous shaking.' Things vibrate, thought vibrates. A vibration which is in every contour, noise, or color without, in every idea within. Or rather, there is neither within nor without, simply the sudden and multiple apparition, somewhere, in the perceptive field, of the same vibrating intensity. (1966, 266)]

According to Poulet, Baudelaire's imagination thus begins with *vibration,* with *intensity,* with 'une extrême énergie', or, as Baudelaire puts it in his texts on Guys and Wagner, with *electricity.* This is also, I argued above, what 'Le Crépuscule du soir' proposes: intense affective vibration. Poulet's opening paragraph can be said to give the optimistic counterpoint to the more ambiguous and at times outrightly disturbing nocturnal vibration (the 'ululation') that pulsates through – or *as* – 'Le Crépuscule du soir'. It suggests a flat, vitalistic ontology in which there are no strong distinctions between things and thought. Like contemporary new materialist philosophy, Poulet argues that in Baudelaire all is 'vibrant matter' (to borrow the title of Jane Bennett's influential study).[5] In his next paragraph, he goes on to specify that in this world 'il n'y a pas de relation' (408) ['there is no relation' (267)]: everything is so inextricably linked up that even the idea of relation is misguided. To put this in the Simondon-inspired terms used in the Verlaine chapters, we have moved from a logic captured by the prefix 'inter-' to one better captured by the prefix 'trans-'.

But Poulet's text does not stay this close to Massumi (or Jane Bennett) throughout. Instead, he moves back to the zone of relations, back towards a more dualist, phenomenological framework; eventually, he almost seems to forget his opening paragraphs. In most of the text, he describes the various stages that Baudelaire's consciousness goes through in its attempt to mediate its relation to the world. Poulet is now writing in a manner that reminds us of Jean-Pierre Richard's analysis of Verlaine. In a very narrative-driven, tripartite account we follow Baudelaire's search for a figure that is at once open and directed, mobile and concentrated, a figure capable of mediating between the eternal and the transitory. Poulet ends up claiming that the thyrsus is Baudelaire's answer to the problem of mediating between consciousness and world.

The difference between the Geneva school critics and the Simondon-inspired reading offered here can therefore be associated with the complex issue of how a phenomenological understanding of subjectivity compares with a Simondonian conception of individuation. As we have seen, Simondon's point is that, whereas most philosophers (including the phenomenologists) have begun their thinking of subjectivity by presupposing an individual which then has to negotiate its relations to the world (through perception, not least), we should begin instead with the pre-individual processes of individuation. For Simondon (and contemporary thinkers like Massumi), process, movement, vitality, and intensity precede (and help produce) individual consciousnesses. However, such distinctions between phenomenology and Simondon's thought are not

5   Readers familiar with new materialist philosophy will appreciate just how contemporary Poulet's description seems. It sounds as if it has been pulled from Jane Bennett's article on Lucretius's *De Rerum Natura* (2000), or from her later book on *Vibrant Matter* (2010). Reading Poulet's opening page anachronistically we may say that he is trying to convince us that Baudelaire's writings are a mix of new materialism and affect theory.

always easy to make. It can be argued that some of Maurice Merleau-Ponty's late writings – from the lectures on nature onwards (1956–60) – begin to bridge the gap between phenomenology and Simondon.[6] Poulet's opening paragraph on Baudelaire (written in the exact same period) is another example of this *almost* post-phenomenological writing. Lacing his text with the passages from Baudelaire, Poulet opens in Simondonian style, stressing that everything in Baudelaire begins with a 'frisson' ['quivering'] and an 'intensité'. But in the same paragraph, he also argues that this quivering takes place 'dans le champ perceptif' ['in the perceptive field']. This raises a number of questions: Who (if anyone) is perceiving? Does anyone 'own' the perceptive field? Are we meant to think that a perceiver precedes the quivering? Or is the perceiver perhaps produced by the quivering? When the following pages move back to a more classical (dualist) phenomenology, prioritizing an individual consciousness and its sense perceptions, the Simondonian moment seems to have passed. Even so, it is important to emphasize the significance of this Simondonian moment: just as Verlaine pushed Richard to theorize at the very limits of phenomenology, Baudelaire brings Poulet close to a Simondonian position.

Going back to Baudelaire, my point is that these complexities, these sometimes very delicate differences between a subtle phenomenological dualism and an affective, post-dualist ontology, are worth keeping in mind when approaching the poetic texts. We can imagine a reading of 'Le Crépuscule du soir' that is concerned with how a certain number

6   In a series of working notes for his third lecture course on 'The Notion of Nature' (1958), Merleau-Ponty explicitly engages with the work of Simondon (something he did not do with any other doctoral student). Here he notes that his own ambition is to 'sortir du cogito cartésien, de l'intersubjectivité sartrienne' (2005, 40) ['tak(e) us out of the Cartesian *cogito*, of Sartrean intersubjectivity' (42)], but this does not yet mean that he is ready to leave the phenomenological framework. In particular, Merleau-Ponty remains devoted to the centrality of the notion of perception. Responding to Simondon's work, Merleau-Ponty concedes that 'Nous ne percevons pas constamment, la perception n'est pas coextensive de notre vie' (40) ['We do not constantly perceive, perception is not coextensive with our life' (42)], but he then adds that perception nevertheless remains the manner in which we access (and are accessed by) 'l'être brut (ou perceptif)' (40) ['brute (or perceptive) being' (42)]. With famous later texts such as *L'Œil et l'Esprit* and the unfinished *Le Visible et l'invisible*, he arguably moves out of a dualist ontology. We shall return to this question in chapters 4 and 6 below. (On the relations between Merleau-Ponty and Simondon, see Merleau-Ponty, 2005.)

of characters behave in Paris at night. This reading might, for instance, be interested in modern psychology, that of the characters and that of the narrator; it could be interested in the question of irony, that of the narrator in particular. This reading would view Paris as the setting for a poem about human interactions. It is undeniable that many of Baudelaire's texts invite such a reading, and most readers have therefore approached his poetry in exactly that manner. For instance, there are good reasons to continue to read 'À une passante' as a poem about an encounter between a man and woman, a poem about inter-subjectivity. However, we can also read 'Le Crépuscule du soir' as a poem about how a specific affective ecology (in-)forms and modulates subjectivities. This reading – my reading – stresses that the challenge posed by Baudelaire's poem precisely lies with how it disturbs our desire to think agency in individual and individualizing terms. It highlights that Baudelaire's poem leaves little space for what might be called the fiction of the autonomous, liberal subject, that it instead suggests that the characters (who are obviously there) must be thought of as temporary 'individual-environments'. Such a reading might even inspire us to reconsider the focus on intersubjectivity in 'À une passante': clearly, the man and the woman are always already superseded by environmental factors such as the 'rue assourdissante' ['deafening street']; and we can speculate that the 'coup de foudre' only happens because the woman is a particular kind of *individu-milieu* – the host of a specific meteorological phenomenon ('son œil, ciel livide où germe l'ouragan' ['her eye, livid sky in which a storm brews']).

Another example: many readers will consider 'Spleen de Paris' to be the name of what is essentially a psychological condition shared by the different narrator(s) and characters that appear throughout Baudelaire's collection. On the other hand, I would argue that spleen is a mood that pervades Paris, that it is indistinguishable from Paris, and that the heterogeneous and complex gallery of people and narratorial voices which we encounter on our way through the collection are little more than different transient crystallizations of this elusive, affective state. In other words, Baudelaire's spleen is Parisian, and not simply the spleen of Parisians.[7] In my opinion, therefore, the widespread focus on characters (and at times, but not always, their psychology) does not fully capture

---

7   This is perhaps nowhere more obvious than in the personification of Paris found in Baudelaire's projects for an epilogue to the 1861 edition of *Les Fleurs du mal* (1975, 191–92).

what goes on in Baudelaire's poetry. As Poulet's opening page suggested, there is what we might call a vibrant or vitalist materialism that troubles those existential, psychological, and phenomenological frameworks; this is a poetry that invites us to think differently about the human subject.

It is here, at the level of subject position, that my main argument lies. Above, I separated the 'individual-environment' from what I called 'the fiction of the autonomous, liberal subject'. With these terms, I am reformulating Barthes's distinction between 'individuation' and 'individual' (see Chapter 1). For Barthes, the first notion referred to a processual, ecological, and open-ended subject, while the second referred to a fossilized version of the human subject. But Barthes's theorization of the 'individual' is not the only counter-figure to the 'individual-environment'. When I now refer to a 'fiction' of autonomy, I am borrowing from John Dewey's critique of the 'liberal individual' in *The Public and Its Problems* (1927):

> The idea of a natural individual in his isolation possessed of full-fledged wants, of energies to be expended according to his own volition, and of a ready-made faculty of foresight and prudent calculation is as much a fiction in psychology as the doctrine of the individual in possession of antecedent political rights is one in politics. The liberalist school made much of desires, but to them desire was a conscious matter deliberately directed upon a known goal of pleasures. Desire and pleasure were both open and above-board affairs. [...] Mind was 'consciousness,' and the latter was a clear, transparent, self-revealing medium in which wants, efforts and purposes exposed without distortion. (2012, 96–97)

Today, relatively few scholars in the humanities would feel targeted by Dewey's critique of the fiction of a natural individual with its transparent consciousness. We have read Freud, Marx, and many others, and we have developed some very fine-grained vocabularies for dealing with the intricate relations between individual and society. Nevertheless, I would argue that the fiction of the liberal subject continues to inform not only societal debates but also literary criticism and humanistic scholarship. Far from all aspects of Dewey's critique seem outdated. Shortly before the passage already cited, Dewey laments the fact that political and social sciences continue to operate with a notion of 'free men' that is out of sync with contemporary science:

> The familiar eulogies of the spectacle of 'free men' going to the polls to determine by their personal volitions the political forms under which they should live is a specimen of this tendency to take whatever is readily

seen as the full reality of a situation. In physical matters natural science has successfully challenged this attitude. In human matters it remains in almost full force. (96)

Dewey does not specify which 'physical matters' he has in mind, but there is little doubt he is referring to the ways in which quantum physics and Einsteinian relativity challenged the idea of objective, independent phenomena in the first decades of the twentieth century (see also Chapter 6). Dewey's text may be almost 100 years old, but it can be argued that much humanistic scholarship still struggles to catch up with this scientific revolution. On the other hand, when reading 'Le Crépuscule du soir' the fiction of 'free men' finds itself properly at sea in a more general vitalist ecology. To further explore this dimension in Baudelaire's work, let us now turn to the poet's fascination for Edgar Allan Poe.

Poulet's chapter began with a quotation from Baudelaire's 1856 text about Poe. Poulet erased (and paraphrased) a part of the passage he referred to. Here is Baudelaire's sentence uncut: '[l]a nature *dite inanimée participe de la nature des êtres vivants, et, comme eux*, frisonne d'un frisson surnaturel et galvanique' (1976, 318) ['So-called inanimate nature participates in the nature of living beings, and, like them, trembles with a supernatural and galvanic trembling' (1992b, 253)]. The restored part (which I have italicized) highlights what we now know from our reading of 'Le Crépuscule du soir': Baudelaire challenges distinctions between living and 'so-called' (i.e. 'wrongly called') non-living organisms. He is making the point that liveliness is more evenly distributed than we often care to think. And he is making a point about the inextricability of human beings and their environments, about 'des individus-milieux' and 'des milieux-individualisés' – about pervasive electricity, vibrant matter, and various forms of quivering ('frissonnement').

That Baudelaire should make this point in a text about Poe is far from accidental. His very first translation of Poe was of a short fictional dialogue called 'The Mesmeric Revelation' (1844). That text presents some of Poe's idiosyncratic speculations about ontological questions. A man is first hypnotized and then interviewed about life and death. At some point during the interview he dies, but the hypnosis allows the conversation to continue. As in Poe's more famous tales 'The Oval Portrait' (1842) and 'The Facts in the Case of Mr. Valdemar' (1845), we do not know exactly when the moment of death occurs, and we therefore do not know if the voice presenting its worldview is that of a subject (a living human being) or an object (a dead body). This is most appropriate because the voice, dead or alive, outlines a non-dualist ontology in which distinctions between mind, matter, and God disappear – an ontology of *participation* (as Baudelaire translated):

> The atmosphere, for example, impels the electric principle, while the electric principle permeates the atmosphere. These gradations of matter increase in rarity or fineness, until we arrive at a matter *unparticled* – without particles – indivisible – *one*; and here the law of impulsion and permeation is modified. The ultimate, or unparticled matter, not only permeates all things but impels all things – and thus *is* all things within itself. This matter is God. What men attempt to embody in the word 'thought,' is this matter in motion. (Poe, 1952, 552)

This passage contains its fair share of Spinoza-inspired, speculative metaphysics, but it clearly describes an ultimate level where matter can no longer be particled (thereby placing Poe's narrator alongside mid- to late-nineteenth-century anti-atomists such as the chemist Marcelin Berthelot).[8] This matter is first called God – and when it infuses (or impels) the particles, we call it 'thought'. Poe's hypnotized and possibly dead narrator thus presents a radical idea about God as unparticled matter (or perfected matter), God in motion as thought, and thought impelling all things, setting the world in motion.

On the one hand, what such passages point to is nothing new: a nineteenth-century version of 'materialism' that seems to disregard distinctions between what many twentieth-century thinkers would see as the fundamentally different fields of poetic and scientific discourses.[9] On the other hand, this 'nothing new' resonates strongly with recent critical

---

8 Poe seems particularly inspired by Spinoza's *Principles of Cartesian Philosophy* (2002, 148–49). (I thank Francesco Sticchi for pointing out this parallel.) This idea of a non-granular level of reality is no longer considered scientifically correct.

9 One aspect of this materialism was the interest in whether bodies produce electricity – what today is called bioelectromagnetics. The pioneer in this field was Luigi Galvani (1737–98) who famously experimented with frogs and electricity. When 'la nature frissonne... d'un frisson surnaturel et *galvanique*' ['Nature... quivers with a supernatural and *galvanic* quivering'], when bodies produce electricity as in 'A une passante', when Poe writes about mesmerized (and eventually dead) speaking bodies, and when Baudelaire (as we shall see in the next chapter) believes that colours must be linked to molecular energy consumption and production, we clearly have what Artaud calls 'une idée matérialiste de l'esprit' (2004, 701) ['a materialist idea of spirit'].

theory by new materialists such as Jane Bennett. Poe's and Baudelaire's texts invite us to think about happenings and events that challenge anthropocentric frameworks.[10] They promote an idea about human beings caught up in more general vital processes, a spiritual materialism, and they do this in a manner that is thought-provoking in our age of the Anthropocene. Obviously, this does not mean that we should rush to embrace what many twentieth-century critics considered to be a reactionary and mystical dimension in Baudelaire's work. Nevertheless, with our increased awareness of the inextricability of human beings and their environments, it may be possible to see Poe's and Baudelaire's *quiverings* in a different light. Before I explore this dimension of Baudelaire's thinking in the next chapter on colour, let me finish this chapter with two critics who attempt to think the political implications of Baudelaire's engagement with this question of atmospheres: Ross Chambers and Jacques Rancière. As we shall see, Rancière in particular is refreshingly undaunted when exploring the politics of Baudelaire's vitalism.

10 In May 1867, Stéphane Mallarmé and his friend Henri Lefébure were engaged in an intense exchange about idealism, materialism, and the ability of poetry to inherit the social role that religion used to play. Mallarmé's letter from 27 May is famous – it contains the oft-quoted sentence 'La Destruction fut ma Béatrice' (1998, 717) ['Destruction was my Beatrice'], and other equally famous passages about Beauty and *L'Œuvre* (that we will consider in the Conclusion). Lefébure's letter from the same day is not as well known, but it brings together Baudelaire, Poe, Lucretius, and Spinoza, attributing to the first a reflection on the other three: 'toutes les fois que l'homme a entrevu le vrai, c'est-à-dire la constitution logique de l'univers, il s'est rejeté avec horreur vers l'illusion infinie et, comme dit Baudelaire, n'a peut-être inventé le ciel et même l'enfer que pour échapper au Nevermore des Lucrèce et des Spinoza.' (Mondor, 1951, 247) ['[E]very time man has glimpsed the true, i.e. the logical constitution of the universe, he has pulled back in horror and turned towards infinite illusion; as Baudelaire says, perhaps man invented heaven and even hell simply to escape from the Nevermore of all Lucretiuses and Spinozas.'] Although these writers and thinkers can be understood in many ways, it is remarkable that Lefébure attributes to Baudelaire a statement in which the poet inscribes himself in a Lucretian–Spinozist lineage. It is tempting to borrow from a recent introduction to Spinoza and suggest that, just like Spinoza, Baudelaire 'naturalise l'esprit autant qu'il spiritualise la matière' (Lenoir, 2017, 167) ['is naturalizing spirit as much as he is spiritualizing matter'].

The Politics of Atmospheres: Chambers and Rancière

In some respects, my affective, ecological reading of Baudelaire resembles Ross Chambers's analysis in *An Atmospherics of the City: Baudelaire and the Poetics of Noise* (2015). However, this does not mean that Chambers references any of the critical theory this chapter has been drawing on, nor does it mean that he is keen to re-evaluate what I have called the spiritual materialism in Baudelaire's work. Let me begin with the issue of agency in Chambers's reading.

On the one hand, Chambers operates with a strong notion of Baudelairean agency. From the opening pages, he explains that Baudelaire sees 'the practice of modern art as an atmospherics of urban life [...] *making sensible* the dimension of strangeness inherent, most notably, in the "moving chaos"[11] of the familiar urban street' (2015, 3). This practice helps to 'awak[en] the poet's readers to the unconscious state of alienation in which they lived' (3). Chambers describes this *'making sensible'* as Baudelaire's poetic *act*, so it is clear that he sees Baudelaire as a poet with agency who is aiming to demystify and disalienate readers, making them sense and understand the modern world. Chambers (sensibly) does not suggest that Baudelaire's poetry proposes political solutions; rather, it promises 'disalienation – that is, the *recognition of human alienation*, something that is not the same as becoming in some miraculous way *un*alienated' (17). This account of Baudelaire's 'long struggle to invent an alternative poetics [capable] of drawing attention to [...] the dangerous reality of atmospheric noise' (147) is a key aspect of Chambers's analysis and entails a clear sense of the poet as an acting subject who is engaged in the project of helping readers understand the alienating logics of the modern world.

On the other hand, when analysing the poetry Chambers abandons the vocabulary of 'act[s]' and 'long struggle[s]', instead writing about what I have called in this chapter, processes of crystallization. Discussing 'Les Sept vieillards', he explains that the first *vieillard* materializes 'as a kind of condensation of the ambient atmosphere or an emanation from out of its damp fogginess' (95), and later he suggests that the poem as a whole can be seen as 'a phenomenon comparable with the way a storm evolves out of the build-up of atmospheric pressure that precedes and produces it, as if it were a precipitate of that heavy and foreboding atmosphere'

---

11   Chambers's quotation marks indicate that he is borrowing from Gérard de Nerval's *Sylvie*.

(101). In other sections, he insists that 'what is active both in Baudelaire's late verse and in his prose poems, therefore, is an atmosphere' (59). In such passages, Chambers draws near to the non-anthropocentric ontology I have explored here; agency is difficult to locate – or it is, as in this last citation, placed with the 'atmosphere'.

We may then wonder: what does it mean to disalienate a reader's relation to an atmosphere or an acoustic phenomenon? To answer this question, it is important to understand that Chambers has chosen to prioritize a different, purer set of city poems than 'Le Crépuscule du soir' (poems such as 'À une passante' and 'Perte d'auréole'). With Chambers's key examples we remain firmly within the well-known horizon of modern, Haussmannian Paris. If we seek to locate agency, it is therefore more straightforward than with 'Le Crépuscule du soir'. When Chambers notes that the atmosphere 'acts', this atmosphere – the noise, the horse manure on the streets, the gas lamps, etc. – can relatively easily be understood as the expression of human activity and enterprise. Haussmann (and many other human beings) changed Paris, and those changes (were) gathered in Baudelaire's noisy city poems. Chambers's text thereby remains anchored in a socio-political tradition in which the key term is 'modernity'; and in this tradition human beings are never far from the centre. As Chambers writes in a typical passage of his analysis of 'Les Sept vieillards',

> [the] *atmosphere* arises, therefore, as an effect of the city's noisy *inhabit-edness*, where inhabitedness implies also hauntedness; it is synonymous, in other words, with the urban crowd and the electricity it generates as it surges through the streets, its collective moods determining something like the variable weather – *le temps qu'il fait* in its relation to *le temps qui passe* – of community. (94)

Clearly, the atmosphere is here produced by the Parisians – and not by a more mysterious 'God'-'thought' that 'impels the electric principle' and moves the 'atmosphere' (as in Poe's 'Mesmeric Revelation'). Therefore, when Chambers presents *Le Spleen de Paris* as 'nearly anonymous writing' (156) in which a poet gives himself over to a particular atmosphere that readers must then relate to, we should remember that this atmosphere results from human efforts to modernize Paris.[12] Chambers's book

---

12   An alternative relation between cities and citizens is presented in Henri Laborit's *L'Homme et la ville* (1971). Using a framework from cybernetics and information theory, he establishes a feedback loop between human beings and cities: we form the city, but the city always already forms us as we begin to form the city (see Laborit, 2011, 27). Laborit's analysis leaves behind the fiction of the

can then be placed in relation to Benjamin's idea about Baudelaire's capacity to productively take on – and expose – the alienating (and very human) forces that dominate life in the modern, urban world. In the *Passagen Werk*, Benjamin writes: 'The unique significance of Baudelaire consists in being the first who in the most impeccable way apprehended self-alienated man and fixed him with a thing-like solidity [ding-fest gemacht], in the double meaning of this word: established his identity and armed him against the reified world' (in Markus, 2001, 36).

In this manner, the poet has the courage and sensitivity to allow his poetry to be a symptom of atmospheric changes; he can be understood (these are my terms and not Chambers's) as a seismograph for a particular quake in mid-nineteenth-century France, registering the entropic *Zeitgeist*. To understand the political aspect of this work, we must add that the seismographic poetry participates in the structures it expresses. Poetry is not a passive medium for the expression of a *Zeitgeist*; rather, it generates affectivity and subjectivity, and as such it is part of the social production and circulation of its time. Therefore, the idea of *giving form* goes hand in hand with an idea of Baudelaire's poetry as interference in the affective ecology of his time. Some readers may be keen to explain these interferences using the well-known grammar of subjects, objects, and actions, but Baudelaire's writings often encourage us to think critically about this grammar and our fidelity to it. With his emphasis on atmospheres and noise, Chambers goes a long way in this direction.

Even though I find much to admire in Chambers's reading and its attempts to think the social implications of a poetry that challenges subject–object dialectics, I do not think his analysis fully captures

liberal subject. On the one hand, it does so by looking at our biological make-up, in particular our brains and their constitution, and on the other, by considering social structures like the city, trying to understand how these express and interact with the biological level. In this interplay between the biological and the social, 'decision' and 'choice' become very local phenomena: 'la prétendue décision ne fera que se soumettre à des processus obligatoires qui, insuffisamment conscients et analysés, feront encore croire à un choix qui n'existe sans doute jamais' (56) ['the so-called decision is subject to a number of obligatory processes; if these remain only partly conscious and insufficiently analysed, we may still believe in a choice which no doubt never exists']. Laborit's aim is not to close off the possibility of human beings determining their lives, but on the contrary – as his set-off clause makes clear – to encourage further understanding and analysis of the intra- and extra-personal structures we live by.

the unruliness of a poem like 'Le Crépuscule du soir'. This is also a city poem, but it is a half-hearted one, less concerned with modernity than later prose poems. The narrator is not yet in the street but on his balcony; when darkness rolls in from the hills, his attention is directed towards a world beyond the perimeter of Haussmannian modernity (the mysterious asylum on the hill). Furthermore, 'Le Crépuscule du soir' is only half-noisy. It's true that there are several sounds in the poem, and some of them are brutal: the 'great howling' and 'discordant cries' modulate into the more discreet 'ululation'. But as we move into the darkness, all sounds disappear, and the uncanny atmosphere of the poem has as much to do with silence as it does with the noises of the modern city.[13] With 'Le Crépuscule du soir', a less anthropocentric world is foregrounded, and the twilight (in so far as it initiates the 'actions' in the poem) can hardly be called a modern phenomenon.

Because agency is more difficult to place in this poem than it is in the modern atmospheres prioritized by Chambers, 'Le Crépuscule du soir' is harder to reclaim for a traditional understanding of progressive politics.[14] This explains why Chambers's preference, like that of other Benjamin-inspired critics such as Marshall Berman (2010), leans towards the later city poems, and why it may be easy to conclude that 'Le Crépuscule du soir' is an example of a more romantic and mystical dimension in Baudelaire's work. But in the twenty-first century, as we become increasingly aware of the dangers of our inability to look beyond the human, we should no longer feel confident about marginalizing what disturbs our ideas of Baudelaire's modernity. Rather, I would suggest that the contemporaneity of a poem such as 'Le Crépuscule du soir' has to do with the fact that it offers a more profound destabilization of the anthropocentric perspective than the kind found in purer examples of city poetry: whereas 'Le Crépuscule du soir' disturbs our

---

13   As we saw in Chapter 1 (in relation to 'Les Chats'), Baudelaire is also a great poet of those mysterious moments where the universe holds its breath.

14   It is potentially misleading to present Chambers as someone who associates late Baudelaire with a progressive politics. Rather, Chambers explains how Baudelaire gives up on the ideology of progress in the wake of his disappointment with the events of 1848–51. But precisely because he gives up on progress, he manages to liberate himself from idealization and fetishization, instead assuming the role of a seismograph for the contemporary structures of feeling. This allows readers to respond to his writing, to judge the alienation, in a progressive way. In short, Chambers argues that Baudelaire's writings become progressive when he ceases to believe in progress.

inclination towards anthropocentrism, other city poems tend to feed this inclination through their very act of critiquing human behaviour. In other words: if we keep cementing the view of Baudelaire as the poet of urban modernity – essentially a sociological poet – we will only partly understand how radical a challenge to our anthropocentric habits and conventional understandings of subjectivity his poetry presents. Many readers will feel uncomfortable with this consideration – they will suspect a mystical dimension frequently associated with symbolism. But this unsettling ecology in which no reader feels at home has the positive effect of inviting us to imagine a life that doesn't begin and end with the human figure. To clarify what this can mean, to allay political concerns about Baudelaire's 'spiritual materialism', and to offer a very different take on the politics of atmospheres, let me conclude this chapter with an appraisal of Jacques Rancière's article 'Le goût infini de la République' in *Le Fil perdu* (2014a).

Rancière immediately distances himself from the dominant, Benjaminian reading of Baudelaire. He does this for instance by emphasizing that Baudelaire's preface to his Poe translations presents the 'sauvage' – and not the modern metropolitan – as the supreme incarnation of the *dandy* (2014a, 98; 2014b, 33); and by reading Baudelaire's texts on crowds through art criticism (as I shall also do in the coming chapter). Approaching poetry via art criticism means downplaying the human subject, for, as Baudelaire writes, 'En art, c'est une chose qui n'est pas assez remarquée, la part laissée à la volonté de l'homme est bien moins grande qu'on ne le croit' (2014a, 104) ['In art – and this is a thing which is not sufficiently observed – the portion that is left to the human will is much less great than is generally believed' (2014b, 28)].

To summarize Rancière's article we can say it delivers an argument about social space. In pre-romantic times, space was unified, and this allowed for actions to take place: 'L'action a besoin d'un monde fini, d'un savoir circonscrit, de formes de causalité calculables, et d'acteurs sélectionnés' (101) ['Action requires a finite world, a circumscribed body of knowledge, calculable forms of causality, and designated actors' (36)]. By the time that Baudelaire begins to write, this world no longer exists. Romantic and post-romantic texts are therefore often about what Rancière calls 'la faillite de l'action' (101) ['the failure of action' (35)]. We have meaningless actions such as Julien Sorel's famous gunshots in *Le Rouge et le noir*, we have the absence of actions as with Flaubert's indolent Frédéric Moreau in *L'Éducation sentimentale*, and we have those abstract, Baudelairean actions that are more akin to spasms than to actions proper (Rancière mentions the narrator in 'Le Mauvais vitrier', but he might just as well have mentioned the two friends in 'Le Crépuscule du soir'). Many (post-Benjaminian) readers have written about alienation in this modern, tragic world, analysed how commodity fetishism creates a social system in which objects and human beings are equally reified, and cited the famous Benjaminian idea about the 'loss of experience'. However,

> Ce geste interprétatif qui lit dans les mots et les respirations du poème la transcription héroïque d'une expérience sensorielle dévastée coupe peut-être un peu trop vite à travers le tissu esthétique au sein duquel prend sens la rêverie baudelairienne de la République infinie. Elle fait basculer du côté d'une 'déstruction de l'expérience' ce qui est bien plutôt une modification dans le système des rapports entre les éléments définissant une forme d'expérience: des manières d'être et de faire, de voir, de penser et de dire. (97–98)

> [This interpretative gesture, which takes the words and cadences of the poem as the heroic transcription of a devastated sensory experience, cuts perhaps too quickly through the aesthetic fabric within which the Baudelairean reverie of the infinite republic makes sense.
> It tips toward the side of a 'destruction of experience,' something that is much more a modification in the system of relations between the elements defining a form of experience: ways of being and doing, of seeing, of thinking, and of saying. (33)]

Rather than a shattering that alienates and crushes subjects, Rancière thus writes about what can be called a new relational web, a new ecology. He offers a much more positive characterization of this new ecology than the one suggested by critics who come to Baudelaire through the Benjaminian theorization of modernity.[15] Rancière writes about the 'infinitization' of both the social world and individual identity: 'Le monde social se perd en ramifications à l'infini. Et il en va de même pour le sujet qui était la cause de l'action. Son identité se perd dans l'infiniment petit des sensations' (103–104) ['The social world loses itself in infinite ramifications. And it is the same for the subject who was the cause of the action. His identity gets lost in the infinite smallness of sensations' (37)]. The important point here is that the pixelation of both

---

15   See for instance Chambers's very dystopian presentation of the late Baudelaire's conception of modernity: 'there is in fact no progress at all, just time that passes, as Baudelaire understands it, in the endless losing battle of human negentropy against the force of entropy' (2015, 156).

social situations and individual identities allows for a non-hierarchical, modern world of incessant movement. Borrowing from Baudelaire's art criticism, Rancière characterizes this new exploded reality as a 'floating world', and he explains:

> Le monde flottant est un monde où les lignes de partage entre identités sociales sont brouillées, de la même façon que, dans la peinture de Delacroix, la ligne [...] se trouve supprimée deux fois, selon la vérité des géomètres pour qui chacune en contient mille et celles des coloristes pour qui elle n'est jamais que 'la fusion intime de deux couleurs'. (107)

> [The floating world is a world where the dividing lines between social identities are blurred, just as, in the painting of Delacroix, the line – at once framework and emblem of the representational order – is twice suppressed, first, according to the truth of the geometer, for whom each one contains a thousand others, and then, for the colorist, for whom it is never more than 'the intimate fusion of two colors' ('Salon of 1846'). (40)]

The scrambling ('brouillage') which happens when colours explode a line is radically democratic. I shall return to this argument in my next chapter (where we shall also see that Mallarmé similarly builds from the explosive light effects in Édouard Manet's 'Le Linge' to bring out the democratic nature of an aesthetic that allows 'the multitude [...] to see with its own eyes' [Mallarmé, 2003, 467]).[16] Rancière calls this phenomenon the 'infinitisation républicaine de la sensation' (111) ['republican infinitization of sensation' (43)].

Benjamin therefore moves 'un peu trop vite' (as Rancière put it) when he worries about the 'loss of experience' in the modern world. True, the organic model in which experiences and actions unify human beings may no longer exist in the modern world, '[m]ais la réfutation du modèle organique, ce n'est pas le triomphe de l'inorganique. Ce qui s'oppose à l'organisme, ce n'est pas l'inorganique, c'est la vie comme puissance qui circule à travers les corps, excède leur limites et désorganise le rapport même de la pensée à son effet' (103) ['But the refutation of the organic model is not the triumph of the inorganic. What is opposed to the organism is not the inorganic, it is life as power that circulates through bodies, exceeds their limits, and disorganizes the very relation of thought

---

16   'The Impressionists and Édouard Manet' was written for *The Art Monthly Review* (30 September 1876). Mallarmé wrote the text in French, and then oversaw and authorized the English translation. The original text has been lost, so I am citing the English version (Mallarmé, 2003, 444–70).

to its effect' (37)]. We therefore encounter a new idea of subjectivity and a new idea about the world – both are dynamic, open, infinite. We have 'un sujet qui est réseau infini de sensations et un monde sensible qui excède toute clôture de terrain d'action stratégique' (104) ['a subject who is composed of an infinite network of sensations and a sensual world that exceeds any closure of the field of strategic action' (38)]. In this world, a new way of thinking and a new form of writing are required. Rancière calls this form of thinking the 'rêverie', and he believes that the prose poem is particularly 'rêveuse' (109) ['dreamlike' (42)]:

> [La rêverie] n'est pas le contraire de l'action mais un autre mode de la pensée, un autre mode de rationalité des choses. Elle n'est pas le refus de la réalité extérieure mais le mode de pensée qui remet en question la frontière même que le modèle organique imposait entre la réalité 'intérieure' où la pensée décidait et la réalité 'extérieure' où elle produisait ses effets. (105)

> [[Reverie] is not the opposite of action, but another mode of thought, another mode of the rationality of things. It is not the refusal of external reality but the mode of thought that puts into question the very boundary that the organic model imposed between 'interior' reality, where thought decided, and 'exterior' reality where it produced its effects. (38)]

The *rêverie* is thus a hospitable mode of thinking that is able to host the heterogeneous multiplicity of the floating world.[17] It does not require clear distinctions, hierarchies, or the cause-and-effect logics that dominated pre-romantic literature. In my vocabulary, it is a more ecological mode of thought, explicitly challenging the distinctions between inner and outer. Clearly this does not mean that Rancière is advocating anarchy; the rêverie is a form of *rationality* (as he writes) found in aesthetic objects that operate on specific individuals, changing specific situations

---

17 This floating world is presented already in the opening poem of *Le Spleen de Paris*. 'L'Étranger' can (anachronistically) be read as a subversive take on what would be known as the filmic convention of the establishing shot (a convention that comes straight out of realist writing à la Balzac). Rather than grounding the titular character (and the collection more generally) in a particular setting, 'L'Étranger' ungrounds. Rather than panning over a cityscape, zooming in on Paris, Baudelaire tilts his camera to the sky, weaving the title character into the movement of clouds in the sky: from the outset we are in a universe of pure kinesis, movements without direction; the poem communicates 'a kind of ambient, free-floating sensibility' (as Steven Shaviro writes about the contemporary structure of feeling [2010, 2]).

through 'infinitization' – 'une politique modeste mais fidèle' (111) ['a modest politics, but a faithful one' (43)].

If Chambers ultimately stuck to a more well-known conceptualization of the human being by prioritizing Baudelaire's urban poetry and holding on to an idea of his writing as a project of disalienation, Rancière goes via art historical writings to embrace the heterogeneity of social spaces and individual identities, arguing that these 'infinitizations' allow for local, swarm-like exchanges of a democratic, republican nature. It is therefore possible to present Rancière's analysis in such a manner that it resembles contemporary post-anthropocentric or new materialist philosophy. For instance, one may compare Rancière's anti-hierarchical and vitalist position ('la vie comme puissance qui circule à travers les corps, excède leur limites et désorganise le rapport même de la pensée à son effet' [103], ['life as power that circulates through bodies, exceeds their limits, and disorganizes the very relation of thought to its effect' (37)]) with Rosi Braidotti's argument that in our post-anthropocentric times, 'Life' must be 'posited as process, interactive, and open-ended [...] the transversal force that cuts across and reconnects previously segregated species, categories and domains' (2013, 60). In the next chapter we shall go further in this direction. However, there is a limit to how far in a new materialist direction Rancière himself intends to go. In *Vibrant Matter*, Jane Bennett recounts her experience of attending a talk by Rancière. When asked about the possibility of extending his theory about non-hierarchical human relationships to include relationships between human beings and their environments also, Rancière declined the invitation to flatten his ontology. Bennett continues: 'Despite this reply, I think that even against his will, so to speak, Rancière's mode contains inklings of and opportunities for a more (vital) materialist theory of democracy' (2010, 106). Indeed, when reading Rancière's analysis of Baudelaire's poetry, one may feel that it is difficult to contain the infinitization so that it does not also work towards a flattening of hierarchies between human beings and their surroundings. However, my point here is not that we must follow Bennett in her desire to speak of 'Thing-Power' (2), but rather that when we read Baudelaire we should be attentive to the force ('puissance') Rancière writes about. This 'puissance' is one that *we* (bodies and thoughts) pick up – or, more precisely, host. What this means will become clearer in the next chapter, which offers a more affirmative, vitalistic reading of Baudelaire than the one that can be argued through a reading of 'Le Crépuscule du soir'.

Conclusion

This chapter has taken on the complex question of how 'Le Crépuscule du soir' speaks to the present. I have argued that Baudelaire's poem invites us to consider subjectivities as ongoing mediations of a mid-nineteenth-century affective ecology, and that the poem thereby challenges our tendency to think agency in personalized terms. In Georges Poulet I found a reader that was sensitive to this non-anthropocentric dimension of Baudelaire's poetry, and in Poe (and in citations from Baudelaire's introduction to his work) we found a particularly vitalistic form of materialism. Here the liberal idea of 'the individual' was all at sea, with Poe and Baudelaire moving beyond subject–object distinctions in a manner that points back to earlier writers such as Lucretius and Spinoza and forward to contemporary new materialist philosophy. The final section of the chapter then engaged with two readers who explore the socio-political dimension of Baudelaire's challenge to subject–object dualisms. Chambers makes this point through an emphasis on atmospheres and noise, Rancière by looking at the 'infinitization' of subjects, social situations, and poetic forms. I demonstrated that Chambers's focus on the urban means that he ultimately keeps the human subject close, delivering (a sophisticated version of) the more recognisable, sociological reading of Baudelaire's modernity. And I argued that even if there is a limit to how flat Rancière intends his ontology to be, he still goes further in his challenge to individualism, insisting on the democratizing potential of the energetic pixelation that vibrates as Baudelaire's poetry. For Rancière, 'La beauté moderne n'est pas celle de ce "toujours semblable" qui obsède Benjamin depuis sa lecture de Blanqui et qu'il voit emblématisé dans la fantasmagorie des "Sept vieillards". Elle est à l'inverse celle du multiple anonyme, du corps qui a perdu les lignes qui l'enfermaient, de l'être dépouillé de son identité' (108) ['Modern beauty is not that of the "always the same" that obsesses Benjamin after his reading of Blanqui, and that he sees emblematized in the fantasmagoria of Baudelaire's "The Seven Old Men." It is, to the contrary, that of the anonymous multiple, of the body that has lost the lines that enclosed it, of a being stripped of its identity' (41)]. Despite their differences, both these readings demonstrate that the destabilization of the autonomous, humanist subject is not the end of politics. In the coming chapter, I will continue to explore Baudelaire's capacity to move beyond subject–object dualisms – reading some of his more 'mystical' texts – and I will insist that this move must also be thought of in its social dimension. To establish this argument, we shall begin by leaving the noisy city, seeking out (pictorial presentations of) pastoral landscapes before finally coming back to Paris.

CHAPTER FOUR

Baudelaire and the Power of Colour

This chapter studies Baudelaire's engagement with colour in selected art historical writings, first among these the 'Salon de 1846'. However, my interest lies less with the writings on colour in themselves than with the question of what these writings tell us about Baudelaire's view of the world and the place that human beings occupy therein. In other words, I will travel through colour to Baudelaire's understanding of ecology, ontology, and the human being. In moving between colour, worldview, and Baudelaire's understanding of subjectivity, I am following the example of numerous artists and thinkers for whom colour has been a privileged field for the study of relations between human beings and their worlds. I am thinking for instance of one keen reader of Baudelaire, Paul Cézanne, who famously and powerfully described colour as 'l'endroit où notre cerveau et l'univers se rejoignent' (in Gasquet, 2012, 153–54) ['the place where our brain and the universe meet' (1991, 153)]. And I am thinking of Maurice Merleau-Ponty who in *L'Œil et l'Esprit* (1964) first emphasizes that 'toute théorie de la peinture est une métaphysique' (1997, 42) ['Every theory of painting is a metaphysics' (1993, 132)], and then gives colour a key place in Cézanne's aesthetics, thereby effectively establishing the issue of colour as a metaphysical question. Both of these names will therefore reappear later in this chapter. We shall see that in Baudelaire's writings on colour the human subject is intricately caught up in the world. In this respect the chapter corroborates the reading presented in the previous chapter. Finally, the chapter also suggests that colour has a power that can be harnessed for the invention of a different social reality.

The Process-Relational World of Colour

Baudelaire frequently insists on the importance of colour, and nowhere more so than in the third chapter in the 1846 salon 'De la couleur'. Before we analyse this third chapter, let us consider its position in the salon. Baudelaire opens with the famous dedication *Aux Bourgeois*, before a first chapter presents his reflections on criticism ('À quoi bon la critique?'). The second chapter then turns to the key notion of 'romantisme', with Baudelaire arguing that 'le Romantisme est l'expression la plus récente, la plus actuelle du beau' (1976, 420) ['romanticism is the most recent, the most up-to-date expression of beauty' (1992b, 52)]: it is 'la morale du siècle' (421) ['analogous to the moral attitude of the age' (53)]. Therefore, Baudelaire continues, '[q]ui dit romantisme dit art moderne, – c'est-à-dire intimité, spiritualité, couleur, aspiration vers l'infini, exprimées par tous les moyens que contiennent les arts' (421) ['Romanticism and modern art are one and the same thing, in other words: intimacy, spirituality, colour, yearning for the infinite, expressed by all the means the arts possess' (53)]. He finishes the second chapter, 'Qu'est-ce que le romantisme?', with the announcement that he will turn to the greatest of all romantic painters. However, before doing this (in his fourth chapter, 'Delacroix'), he needs a chapter on colour. With this slightly syncopated presentation, Baudelaire puts emphasis on 'colour', suggesting that to get from the general ('le romantisme') to its incarnation in the individual (Delacroix) we must pass through colour. In other words, to understand romanticism, to understand modern art, to understand Delacroix as a modern, romantic painter, it is crucial to grasp how colour works. And, I would add, to understand Baudelaire's view of the subject and its relation to the world, it is important to examine what he writes about colour.

The first thing to notice is that Baudelaire describes colours as relational. Colours depend on neighbouring colours, and in that sense are ecological. This is an aspect which critics have frequently commented upon (e.g. Howells, 1996; Phillips, 2005; Smith, 2011), and it is in line with many nineteenth- and twentieth-century theories about colour, not least that of Michel-Eugène Chevreul. Chevreul was a chemist who worked at the Gobelins in the production of tapestries. When the Gobelins received complaints about faulty colours, Chevreul examined the issue. He found that colours were not simply a matter of chemistry, but also a matter of perception, and that we see colours differently depending on factors such as neighbouring colours, light, hue, and so on. On this basis he developed a theory of colour, integrating discoveries made by Goethe and previous colour theorists, putting an emphasis on perception and (to some extent unintentionally) distancing himself from the more physicalist theories of Isaac Newton, for example. As Bernard Howells (1996) points out, we do not know whether Baudelaire actually read Chevreul's *De la loi du contraste simultané des couleurs et de l'assortiment des objets colorés* (1839), but Chevreul was in the air.[1] Studying Baudelaire's remarks on colour, it is clear that he had knowledge of the scientific theorizations of his time.

It is important to add that the relational conception of colour does not just mean that two different, each in their own right homogeneous, colours interact. The law of contrasts reveals that 'individual' colours are heterogeneous, and that the encounters between colours bring out this heterogeneity. Chevreul's theory presents a system of internal differentiation, and it emphasizes that the interplay between colours works in such a way as to highlight contrast. In this manner, we might say that colours are not just relational, but also dynamic. To take the example that Baudelaire prioritizes: a juxtaposition of green and red will make each of these colours seem more intensely green and red. Or with Merleau-Ponty's slightly more complex and poetic example (from 'Le doute de Cézanne'): 'Une rose sur un papier gris colore en vert le fond' (1996, 19) ['A rose/pink upon grey colours the background green']. This is why Chevreul's treatise is called *De la loi du contraste simultané des couleurs*. It is not difficult to see why this theory of polarization might have appealed to the poet of shocks and electricity: this is a colour theory about heightened tensions – a non-essentialist, relativist, and dynamic theory of colour.

Baudelaire pushes the idea of dynamic, processual colours quite strongly, frequently arguing that colours *do* things. They alter the world, almost as if they had a will or an agenda of their own. This is evident in the description of Delacroix's *Chasse aux lions* (in 'Exposition Universelle, 1855, Beaux-Arts'). Here Baudelaire explains how the colours of the painting attack the spectator: 'La *Chasse aux lions* est une véritable explosion de couleur (que ce mot soit pris dans le bon sens). Jamais couleurs plus belles, plus intenses, ne pénétrèrent jusqu'à l'âme par le canal des yeux' (1976, 594) ['The *Chasse aux lions* is a veritable colour explosion (let the word be taken in the good sense). Never can

---

1 Ann Kennedy Smith (2011) highlights three possible influences on Baudelaire: Chevreul, and the painters Émile Deroy and Eugène Delacroix, with both of whom Baudelaire had personal contact.

colours more beautiful, more intense, have penetrated into the soul by way of the eyes' (1992b, 136)].[2] He then goes further in the attribution of agency to the painting, writing that 'cette peinture, comme les sorciers et les magnétiseurs, projette sa pensée à distance' (595) ['Delacroix's style of painting, like sorcerers and hypnotists, can project its thought at a distance' (136)], again emphasizing that this has to do with the work of colour in particular: 'Il semble que cette couleur, qu'on me pardonne ces subterfuges de langage pour exprimer des idées fort délicates, pense par elle-même, indépendamment des objets qu'elle habille' (595) ['It really seems as though the colour – I hope I may be forgiven these linguistic subterfuges to express what are highly subtle ideas – is itself capable of thought, independently of the objects it clothes' (137)]. Here the spiritu-alization – or animalization – of the painting clearly demonstrates that Baudelaire considers Delacroix's colours as an active force. Colours do not just result from an interplay with other colours; the explosion breaks the frame so the relational, active, polarising system implicates the spectators too. Colour flows over us, and brings us into the dynamism. This is why the topic of colour inspires some of the most vitalistic writing in Baudelaire's work.

Let us now turn to our key passage: the two first paragraphs in the third chapter of the 'Salon de 1846': 'De la couleur'. As several critics have argued, these paragraphs are so carefully worked through that they can be read as prose poems. Here the process-relational work of colour is clearly on display, as the colours give us the emergence of a world. This is the first paragraph:

> Supposons un bel espace de nature où tout verdoie, rougeoie, poudroie et chatoie en pleine liberté, où toutes choses, diversement colorées suivant leur constitution moléculaire, changées de seconde en seconde par le déplacement de l'ombre et de la lumière, et agitées par le travail intérieur du calorique, se trouvent en perpétuelle vibration, laquelle fait trembler les lignes et complète la loi du mouvement éternel et universel. – Une immensité, bleue quelquefois et verte souvent, s'étend jusqu'aux confins du ciel: c'est la mer. Les arbres sont verts, les gazons verts, les mousses vertes; le vert serpente dans les troncs, les tiges non mûres sont vertes; le

---

2   Between 1854 and 1861 Delacroix painted a series of five paintings entitled 'Chasse aux lions'. Baudelaire is writing about the largest painting in the series (175cm x 360cm) from 1855. Unfortunately – and ironically, given what I will soon argue about the incendiary nature of Delacroix's colours – this work was severely damaged in a fire at the Musée de Bordeaux in 1870.

vert est le fond de la nature, parce que le vert se marie facilement à tous les autres tons.[3] Ce qui me frappe d'abord, c'est que partout, – coquelicots dans les gazons, pavots, perroquets, etc., – le rouge chante la gloire du vert; le noir, – quand il y en a, – zéro solitaire et insignifiant, intercède le secours du bleu ou du rouge. Le bleu, c'est-à-dire le ciel, est coupé de légers flocons blancs ou de masses grises qui trempent heureusement sa morne crudité, – et, comme la vapeur de la saison, – hiver ou été, – baigne, adoucit, ou engloutit les contours, la nature ressemble à un toton qui, mû par une vitesse accélérée, nous apparaît gris, bien qu'il résume en lui toutes les couleurs. (Baudelaire, 1976, 422–23)

Baudelaire opens with an invitation to the reader's imagination: 'supposons' ['Let us imagine' (54)]. This is an invitation to participate in an exercise of world-making: a cosmopoesis that the rest of the paragraph unfolds for us, and with our help. The world that emerges before our inner eyes is presented as vibrant and mobile. Like Poe's world (in Chapter 3) it 'quivers', and this dynamism and vitality results from the work of colours. Significantly, the colours are no longer adjectives, attributes, but verbs, actions: 'tout verdoie, rougeoie'; consequently, they produce events, altering the environment: 'le vert serpente dans les troncs' ['green meanders in the tree trunks' (54)].[4] And Baudelaire knows that colours combine different aspects such as hue and tone, which he also describes as activities that make things 'poudro[yer] et chato[yer], en pleine liberté' ['shim(mer) in chaotic freedom' (54)], while the variations in light and shadow ('le déplacement de l'ombre et de la lumière' ['the interplay of light and shade' (54)]) further animate this universe in play.

It is clear that Baudelaire has been reading contemporary colour theory (or hearing about it from Delacroix). The passage contains scientific references to the 'constitution moléculaire' and 'le travail

3   Baudelaire adds the following footnote here: 'Excepté à ses générateurs, le jaune et le bleu; cependant je ne parle ici que des tons purs. Car cette règle n'est pas applicable aux coloristes transcendants qui connaissent à fond la science du contrepoint' (1976, 422).

4   In her analysis of 'La Beauté', Jennifer Yee perceptively argues that this sonnet should be read as a satire of the classicist ideals that many Winckelmann-inspired readers celebrated in the mid-nineteenth century. In the poem Beauty is allegorized as a statue, that advocates stillness: 'Je hais le mouvement qui déplace les lignes' (Baudelaire, 1975, 21). As Yee points out, this aesthetic of stillness 'present[s] a marked contrast to the impression of constant flux that Baudelaire so admired in Delacroix's painting. Indeed, Baudelaire's deprecation of sculpture is partly due to its lack of colour and movement (II: 434, 487–89)' (Yee, 2018, 10).

intérieur du calorique' ['molecular structure' and 'the inner workings of latent heat'] and it offers a contribution to contemporary art historical debates about the relations between colour and line, painting and drawing, with Baudelaire positioning himself alongside those who are keen to let the lines tremble.[5] But the paragraph also presents a more metaphysical ambition of using the imagined landscape to reach general conclusions about 'la loi du mouvement éternel et universel' ['the law of perpetual and universal movement' (54)], demonstrating Merleau-Ponty's remark that 'toute théorie de la peinture est une métaphysique' ['every theory of painting is a metaphysics' (1993, 132)]. Baudelaire's insistence on movement suggests a processual and vitalistic metaphysics that recalls Lucretius's cosmology.

From the second sentence, the passage takes on an almost incantatory dimension with the chanting of colour names bringing a pastoral landscape into being. First, the blue–green sea (and a reference to the sky) offers an overall frame. We may note how the naming of the sea is kept to the end of the syntagm, Baudelaire's syntax performing the very cosmopoesis he describes: the blue–green colours generate the sea. Then green takes over, appearing no fewer than seven times in the third sentence of the paragraph. These greens offer a bridge to other colours (Baudelaire combining poetry and scientific knowledge), as the natural universe rises from the page. He evokes different textures, he appeals to all our senses, he references different seasons (suggesting the rhythm of the year), and then he offers a complex comparison with a spinning top. This comparison is explained by the well-known visual phenomenon according to which colours, while hurling around as they do on a colourful spinning top, create the overall effect of a grey object. Even when nature appears grey, Baudelaire seems to suggest, it is in fact multicoloured (as we shall soon see, the grey rocks of Cézanne's Sainte-Victoire paintings demonstrate this).

This piece of cosmomorphic prose poetry raises the question of *where* colours are found. How do we come to more solid ground, if colours are produced relationally, if they are dynamic, and if they impact

---

5   The line versus colour debate plays an important role in French art history; originally associated with the names of Poussin (line) and Rubens (colour), the debate was revived in the 1830s with Ingres (line) and Delacroix (colour) in the starring roles. This (simplistic) dichotomy often opposes the line's classicism, rationality, and clarity to colour's emotion, affectivity, and romanticism. (For a short overview, see Le Rider, 1998.)

on – and flood – the spectators (the first of whom is the painter)? The short answer is: we do not find a solid ground, and we do not need it. In order to explain this, I would like to turn to Francisco Varela, Evan Thompson, and Eleanor Rosch's *The Embodied Mind: Cognitive Science and Human Experience* (1991, revised 2016). The eighth chapter in this classic book, which bridges cognitive science, phenomenology, and Buddhist thought, is devoted to the analysis of colour perception.

Writing on the basis of more recent research into colour and visual perception (in particular the so-called '*opponent-process theory*' [2016, 158] of Leo Hurvich and Dorothea Jameson), Varela, Thompson, and Rosch propose a view of colour that resonates with that of Chevreul, Delacroix, and Baudelaire. Once again, an analysis of colour is carried out to make a wider point about the relation between individual and world. From the beginning of the chapter, the authors stress that the complex issue of colour calls for an interdisciplinary approach. Cognitive science may be able to detail our neuronal responses to colour ('nothing short of a large and distributed neuronal network is involved in our perception of colour' [161]), and it can demonstrate that colours are intimately linked to other senses too.[6] But colour is also a perceptual category, and issues like the naming of colours matter for our perception. This leads to the observation that the perception of colour is a cultural phenomenon, some cultures naming and therefore seeing distinctions between (for instance) blue and green differently from other cultures. Through their various examples the writers are thus able to 'show that color categorization in its entirety depends upon a tangled hierarchy of perceptual and cognitive processes, some species specific and others culture specific' (171). This leads to their more general conclusion: 'We can now appreciate, then, how color provides a paradigm of a cognitive domain that is neither pregiven nor represented but rather experiential and enacted' (171).

This last conclusion is important in so far as it brings us to a broader philosophical point about human ways of being in the world (which will

---

6 Borrowing from an article by Oliver Sacks and Robert Wasserman, Varela, Thompson, and Rosch tell the true story of a man who, after an accident, lost his ability to see colours, and then had to live in a world of only black and white. This man soon lost interest in music, sex, and cooking, becoming increasingly dissatisfied with his life. Gradually, he turned his daily rhythm around and started living almost exclusively at night, discovering in the darkness a world that had hitherto escaped him (163–64).

soon bring us back to Baudelaire). Introducing their key terms 'embodied cognition', 'structural coupling', and 'enaction', Varela, Thompson, and Rosch now theorize a distinction between what they call 'chicken' and 'egg' understandings of reality:

> *Chicken position:* the world out there has pregiven properties. These exist prior to the image that is cast on the cognitive system, whose task is to recover them appropriately (whether through symbols or global subsymbolic states). (172)

On this position the authors comment: 'Notice how very reasonable this position sounds and how difficult it is to imagine that things could be otherwise. We tend to think that the only alternative is the *egg position*' (172). This egg position is then presented as follows:

> *Egg position:* The cognitive system projects its own world, and the apparent reality of this world is merely a reflection of internal laws of the system. (172)

Varela, Thompson, and Rosch's reason for going through a detailed analysis of colour is precisely to prepare the argument that *both* of these positions are wrong. Colour is neither 'out there' in the world as 'chicken' supporters claim, nor is it 'in here' in the individual psyche as 'egg' supporters argue; colour is neither an objective nor a subjective phenomenon:

> Contrary to the objectivist view, color categories are experiential; contrary to the subjectivist view, color categories belong to our shared biological and cultural world. Thus color as a study case enables us to appreciate the obvious point that chicken and egg, world and perceiver, specify each other. (172)

The authors therefore speak about 'mutual specification', emphasizing that their 'intention is to bypass entirely this logical geography of inner versus outer by studying cognition not as recovery or projection but as embodied action' (172). My point is that Baudelaire anticipates key aspects of this theory of mutual specification and embodied action. This becomes clearer when we read more widely in Baudelaire's art historical writings.

As is well known, there is a strong anti-representational dimension in Baudelaire's writings on aesthetics. In many texts he criticizes artists who think that faithfully representing nature (as many 'paysagistes' do) or human beings (as many 'portraitistes' do) is enough to be a good artist. This scepticism towards the 'chicken position' also goes some way towards explaining Baudelaire's often acerbic comments on the dangers of photography.[7] Baudelaire regrets that the public considers photography to be an art when it is in fact a kind of industrial – or at best, scientific – tool. For Baudelaire such confusion is problematic, because photographic representation poses a threat to the imagination. Anticipating twentieth-century critiques of spectacle (e.g. Debord) and simulacra (e.g. Baudrillard), Baudelaire argues that photographic representations prevent us from exercising our imagination, and thereby from experiencing our imbrication with the world; eventually our imagination will wither and our distance from the world will increase.

On the other hand, this does not mean that artists can form the world according to their own fancy, that they are entitled to impose their own world on the surroundings (the 'egg position'). It is true that Baudelaire's narratorial voice (a voice we shouldn't confuse with that of the author) plays with this idea in the highly ironic and cynical prose poem 'Les Fenêtres', as discussed in Chapter 2 on Verlaine (a poem I read as a warning against any naïve belief in art as empathy). But in Baudelaire's less ironic art historical writings, he often criticizes the 'egg position'. For instance, he points out that Ingres mistakenly 'croit que la nature doit être corrigée' (587) ['thinks that nature must be corrected']. Ingres therefore gets in the way of what nature holds, something that only a more responsive and imaginative engagement with nature would be able to bring out.

In this manner, Baudelaire carves out a position between (what he perceives to be) the direct representation of, for instance, photographic images, which so many artists strive for, and the moralising, intervening, and subjectivist position that Ingres represents. The position he advocates is associated with Delacroix, and it is neither objectivist nor subjectivist, but 'surnaturaliste' – this position largely relies on the work of colours.

Surnaturalism designates precisely this interactive and dynamic world–painter relation. For example, Baudelaire writes: 'Le dessin est une lutte entre la nature et l'artiste, où l'artiste triomphera d'autant plus

<hr>

7   As Marit Grøtta has convincingly argued, this critique of photography does not prevent Baudelaire from taking a keen interest in the technical innovations of his time, including the many innovations in the field of perception. In his book about Francis Bacon (which we will soon turn to), Gilles Deleuze similarly recounts that Bacon was sceptical of photography as art, because it makes us think that art is about representation, but very fond of scientific photography such as that of Eadweard Muybridge.

facilement qu'il comprendra mieux les intentions de la nature. Il ne s'agit pas pour lui de copier, mais d'interpréter dans une langue plus simple et plus lumineuse' (457) ['Drawing is a struggle between nature and the artist, and the better the artist understands nature's intentions, the easier will be his triumph over her. For him no question arises of copying; it is a matter of interpreting in a more simple and luminous language' (79)]. This interpretation – this act of 'tuning' wherein the artist first listens to the intentions of nature, and then helps it to express itself – is also a way for the artist to bring his temperament to the table.

It is true that Baudelaire sometimes seems to dance between chickens and eggs. For instance, he emphasizes the temperament of the artist to such an extent that certain passages come close to subjectivism:

> Si tel assemblage d'arbres, de montagnes, d'eaux et de maisons, que nous appelons un paysage, est beau, ce n'est pas par lui-même, mais par moi, par ma grâce propre, par l'idée ou le sentiment que j'y attache. C'est dire suffisamment, je pense, que tout paysagiste qui ne sait pas traduire un sentiment par un assemblage de matière végétale ou minérale n'est pas un artiste. (660)

> [If the assemblage of trees, mountains, waters and houses that we call a landscape is beautiful, it is not so in and of itself, but thanks to me, through the idea or feeling which I attach to it. For this reason, I believe a landscape painter unable to convey his feelings through a vegetal or mineral assemblage cannot be called an artist.]

However, when we read on, we understand that the assemblages that Baudelaire writes about give a role to *all* the gathered elements: trees, mountains, waters, houses, and the artists themselves. And again, Baudelaire also warns us against the 'egg position', noting how many paysagistes make the mistake that he previously associated with Ingres, and now with Jean-François Millet: 'Au lieu d'extraire simplement la poésie naturelle de son sujet, M. Millet veut à tout prix ajouter quelque chose' (661) ['Instead of simply extracting the natural poetry from his chosen subject, M. Millet always seeks to add to it']. When Baudelaire borrows from Delacroix the metaphor that 'la nature n'est qu'un dictionnaire' (624) ['nature is but a dictionary' (303)], the sentence must therefore not be read in a subjectivist manner; rather the artist understands nature as something to compose with, and this act of composing draws on the body of the artists, who must bring out the force of the landscape using their own imagination and temperament. Painting is an act of mutual specification.

Varela, Thompson, and Rosch are of course not the only thinkers that have sought to navigate outside the subject–object dialectic. As we saw in previous chapters, Gilbert Simondon is another such thinker; but the primary reference for Varela, Thompson, and Rosch is one of Simondon's teachers and interlocutors: Maurice Merleau-Ponty. Before we briefly consider Merleau-Ponty's way out of subject–object dialectics, I will read – in some detail – a key source for his *L'Œil et l'Esprit*: Joachim Gasquet's conversations with Paul Cézanne.[8] It is my contention that this text offers a remarkable point of resonance for Baudelaire's chapter 'De la couleur', and it does so partly because it adds a more speculative dimension to the understanding of colour that we find in *The Embodied Mind*. Let us begin by asking: what does it mean to be an artist for Cézanne, and what role does colour play?

The Colour of the Sun: Baudelaire with Cézanne

In his conversations with Joachim Gasquet, Cézanne characterizes the artist as 'un réceptacle de sensations, un cerveau, un appareil enregistreur' (Gasquet, 2012, 149) ['a receptacle of sensations, a brain, a recording machine' (1991, 150)]. The genitive ('de') is ambiguous, but as we shall soon see, the sensations are both those of the painter and those *received* by the painter: sensation is worldly too (see also the discussion of Verlaine's 'humble antienne' in chapters 1 and 2). To be the host and channel for these sensations, an artist must, as the phenomenologists would soon say, perform something akin to an *epoché*: 'Toute sa volonté doit être de silence. Il doit faire taire en lui toutes les voix des préjugés, oublier, oublier, faire silence, être un écho parfait. Alors sur sa plaque sensible, tout le paysage s'inscrira' (150) ['His whole aim must be silence. He must silence all the voices of prejudice within him, he must forget, forget, be silent, become a perfect echo. And then the entire landscape will engrave itself on the sensitive plate of his being' (150)]. Cézanne

---

8 Joachim Gasquet's *Cézanne* was first published in 1921. It consists of a biographical study of Cézanne, and three conversations with Cézanne. The conversations took place in the late 1890s, but Gasquet only composed the book in 1912–13. There has therefore been some debate about the accuracy of these conversations (to what extent is Gasquet reporting? to what extent is he reinventing?), but the text nevertheless remains a key source for the understanding of Cézanne's aesthetics (and for our understanding of Merleau-Ponty's approach to Cézanne).

here introduces the metaphor that will run through his presentation of the work of an artist: the artist as 'plaque sensible'. Going back to Baudelaire, we now see that Millet and Ingres failed to be this 'plaque sensible': they did not silence their own voices, and therefore they got in the way of both nature and their own paintings.

Cézanne held Baudelaire's art criticism (and his poetry) in high esteem, singling out the writings on Delacroix and Guys as rare successes in the genre. It is therefore unsurprising that some of Cézanne's most acerbic comments are about Ingres, a painter that he too plays off against Delacroix, largely for the same reasons as those given by Baudelaire. On Ingres's side Cézanne puts drawings, academism, tedious moralism, and lifelessness; on Delacroix's side colours, originality, intensity, courage, and life. The problem with Ingres's famous *La Source* is that 'ça ne tourne pas dans l'air' ['it doesn't turn in space'], says Cézanne with an expression that brings to mind Baudelaire's spinning top.[9] Cézanne then hastens to add that the bracketing off of an artist's will is only a first step, and that once the artists have been im-printed, they must use their craft to exteriorize the im-pression ('le métier interviendra ensuite' [150], ['after that he will have to use his craft' (150)]). The role of that first essential epoché-like move is to take us to the heart of sensation.[10]

When Cézanne addresses the stage at which artists make themselves available to sensation, he immediately drifts towards a multisensory realm. Looking critically at one of his Sainte-Victoire paintings, he regrets that he has not sufficiently rendered this multisensorial experience. The regret leads him to a comparison with Baudelaire and Zola, who were able to use words to render the sensations he should have communicated with his

9   See Cézanne's dismissal of *La Source*: 'J'ai le plaisir de la ligne, quand je veux. Mais il y a là un écueil. Holbein, Clouet ou Ingres n'ont que la ligne. Eh bien!, ça ne suffit pas. C'est très beau, mais ça ne suffit pas. Regardez cette *Source*... C'est pur, c'est tendre, c'est suave, mais c'est platonique. C'est une image, ça ne tourne pas dans l'air' (183). ['I can take pleasure in line if I want to. But there are snags, Holbein, Clouet or Ingres have nothing but line. Well, it's not enough. It's very beautiful, but it's not enough. Look at this *Source*... It's pure, it's delicate, it's smooth, but it's platonic. It's an image, it doesn't turn in space' (178).]

10   It can be argued that Cézanne's explanations leave space for confusion. In this passage he seems to operate with a distinction between (1) an experience of nature and (2) the communication of this experience (where 'le métier interviendra'). In most passages, however, this distinction falls away, as the practice of painting intensifies the experience of nature.

colours. This inspires a bold idea about the proximity between sensation and Being, achieved, once again, in a movement of intense gyration:

> Quand la sensation est dans sa plénitude, elle s'harmonise avec tout l'être. Le tourbillonnement du monde, au fond d'un cerveau, se résout dans le même mouvement que perçoivent, chacun avec leur lyrisme propre, les yeux, les oreilles, la bouche, le nez… (151–52)

> [Whenever sensation is at its fullest, it harmonizes with the whole of creation. Nature's stirrings are resolved, deep down in one's brain, into a movement sensed equally by our eyes, our ears, our mouth and our nose… (151)][11]

In this manner, Cézanne's description opens up a more speculative register. We understand that to explode into sensation is not just a question of multisensorial sensitivity, it is a question of approaching Being. A remark by Gasquet prompts Cézanne to insist: '[c]e que j'essaie de vous traduire est plus mystérieux, s'enchevêtre aux racines mêmes de l'être, à la source impalpable des sensations' (153) ['What I'm trying to convey to you is something more mysterious, more entangled in the very roots of being, in the impalpable source of all sensation' (152)]. This prepares the most mythical and speculative part of Cézanne's reflections:

> Et puis, le milieu où nous nous mouvons habituellement… ce soleil, écoutez un peu… Le hasard des rayons, la marche, l'infiltration, l'incarnation du soleil à travers le monde, qui peindra jamais cela, qui le racontera? Ce serait l'histoire physique, la psychologie de la terre. Tous plus ou moins, êtres et choses, nous ne sommes qu'un peu de chaleur solaire emmagasinée, organisée, un souvenir de soleil, un peu de phosphore qui brûle dans les méninges du monde […]. Moi, je voudrais dégager cette essence. La morale éparse du monde c'est l'effort qu'il fait peut-être pour redevenir soleil. (153)

> [And then this element in which we habitually move… this sunshine, here's another thing… The chance fashion in which its rays fall, the way it moves, infiltrates things, becomes part of the earth's fabric – who will ever paint that? Who will ever tell that story? The physical history of the earth, its psychology. All of us, to a greater or lesser degree, all things

---

11   'Nature's stirrings' does not fully capture the whirling or swirling movements of Cézanne's original '[l]e tourbillonnement du monde'. The reader should have in mind a vibrant world like that of Lucretius's *De Rerum Natura*. Indeed, as we shall soon see, Cézanne makes this reference explicit.

animate and inanimate, are a bit of solar heat that has been stored up and organized, a reminder of the sun, a little phosphorus burning in the membranes of the earth's brain. [...] Personally, I'd like to extract this essence. Perhaps the earth's diffused morality represents the effort it's making to return to its solar origin. (152)]

Here we see that Cézanne understands 'êtres et choses' ['all things animate and inanimate'] as stored heat. Everything comes from the sun, and everything yearns for a return to the sun; the painter is the one who communicates – and seeks to satisfy – this yearning. In this, colour plays a key role:

La délicatesse de notre atmosphère tient à la délicatesse de notre esprit. Elles sont l'une en l'autre. La couleur est le lieu où notre cerveau et l'univers se rencontrent. C'est pourquoi elle apparaît toute dramatique, aux vrais peintres. Regardez cette Sainte-Victoire. Quel élan, quelle soif impérieuse du soleil, et quelle mélancholie, le soir, quand toute cette pesanteur retombe... Ces blocs étaient du feu. Il y a du feu encore en eux. (153–54)

[The delicacy of our atmosphere is linked to the delicacy of our qualities of mind. They exist one within the other. Colour is the place where our brain and the universe meet. That's why colour appears so entirely dramatic, to true painters. Look at Sainte-Victoire there. How it soars, how imperiously it thirsts for the sun! and how melancholy it is in the evening, when its weight sinks back... Those blocks were made of fire and there is still fire in them. (153)]

These formulations present colour as an event in which fire or heat manifests itself, and an encounter between human being and universe – atmosphere and spirit – takes place. It is this dramatic event Cézanne aims to create in painting.

For both Baudelaire and Cézanne the question of colour therefore inspires an ontology. Colours bring us into a multisensory, rotating universe. Colours are verbs, producing events that impact on us. In Cézanne's account, they remind us that everything comes from the sun and is yearning to return to the heat of the sun. Similarly, in Baudelaire's opening paragraph the world was put in motion and heated up by a 'travail intérieur du calorique' ['inner workings of latent heat'] which takes place in the colours of the world. In these vibratory, thermic, germinating universes, we encounter the release of intense movements that no longer distinguish between 'êtres et choses' (153) ['all things animate and inanimate' (152)].

It is worth mentioning that Merleau-Ponty follows Cézanne (and Baudelaire) along these speculative lines, proposing a number of formulations that allow us to see more clearly what Cézanne describes. For instance, *L'Œil et l'Esprit* criticizes Descartes for developing a theory of vision (*La Dioptrique*, 1637) that does not pay attention to colours. Had he thought about colours, 'il se serait trouvé devant le problème d'une universalité et d'une ouverture aux choses sans concept, obligé de chercher comment le murmure indécis des couleurs peut nous présenter des choses, des forêts, des tempêtes, enfin le monde' (1997, 43) ['he would have found himself faced with the problem of a conceptless universality and opening onto things. He would have been obliged to find out how the uncertain murmur of colors can present us with things, forests, storms – in short the world' (1993, 133)]. So, for Merleau-Ponty too, *colours open Being*; they allow the expression of the world. This description, of course, points to the 'vibration ou rayonnement' (77) that Georges Poulet found in Baudelaire (Chapter 3), and to that which 'gazouille et murmure' in Verlaine's 'humble antienne' (chapters 1 and 2).

What is the status of the painter – and the human being – in this event? For Merleau-Ponty painting is not about mimesis (chickens), nor is it about the projection of an inner world onto an outside (eggs). As with many of the grammatical structures we encountered in 'Le Crépuscule du soir' (and in the poetry of Verlaine), Merleau-Ponty instead challenges conventional ideas about agency with the beautiful suggestion that the painter is born of visibility: 'le peintre [...] naît dans les choses comme par concentration à soi du visible' (69) ['it is the painter to whom the things of the world give birth by a sort of concentration or coming-to-itself of the visible' (141)]. In this manner he too invites us to move out of subject–object dialectics, to a more intimate co-emergence of universe and human being (what Varela, Thompson, and Rosch termed 'mutual specification'). This is why the birth of the painter cannot be reduced to a subjective event. Merleau-Ponty instead presents the painter as a human being on fire, in a sentence that closes with a quotation by Paul Klee:

> Au fond immémorial du visible quelque chose a bougé, s'est allumé, qui envahit son [le peintre] corps, et tout ce qu'il peint est une réponse à cette suscitation, sa main 'rien que l'instrument d'une lointaine volonté'. (86)

> [In the immemorial depths of the visible, something has moved, caught fire, which engulfs his body; everything he paints is in answer to this incitement, and his hand is 'nothing but the instrument of a distant will'. (147)]

Going back to Cézanne, we can now bring in a self-reflexive passage from his text. Here the painter explains that he struggled to paint the Sainte-Victoire when he still thought its shadow was concave. Only when he realized that it was convex, that the mountain participates in its environment, was he able to paint it. The Sainte-Victoire 'fuit de son centre' (154) ['it disperses outside from the centre' (153)], and this puncture takes everything else with it in the process. Cézanne now presents a general cosmopoesis – including a reference to the atom-showers (the *clinamen*) of Lucretius's *De Rerum Natura*:

> Voilà le bain de science, si j'ose dire, où il faut tremper sa plaque sensible. Pour bien peindre un paysage, je dois découvrir d'abord les assises géologiques. Songez que l'histoire du monde date du jour où deux atomes se sont rencontrés, où deux tourbillons, deux danses chimiques se sont combinées. Ces grands arcs-en-ciel, ces prismes cosmiques, cette aube de nous-mêmes au-dessus du néant, je les vois monter, je m'en sature en lisant Lucrèce. Sous cette fine pluie je respire la virginité du monde. Un sens aigu des nuances me travaille. Je me sens coloré par toutes les nuances de l'infini. À ce moment-là, je ne fais plus qu'un avec mon tableau. Nous sommes un chaos irisé. Je viens devant mon motif, je m'y perds. Je songe, vague. Le soleil me pénètre sourdement, comme un ami lointain, qui réchauffe ma paresse, la feconde. Nous germinons. [...] Il faut la nuit pour que je puisse détacher mes yeux de la terre, de ce coin de terre où je me suis fondu. (154–55)

> [That's the bath of experience, so to speak, in which the sensitized plate has to be soaked. In order to paint a landscape well, I first need to discover its geological structure. Think of the earth's history as dating from the day when two atoms met, when two whirlwinds, two chemical dances, joined together. When I read Lucretius, I drench myself with those first huge rainbows, those cosmic prisms, that dawn of mankind rising over the void. In their fine mist, I breathe in the new-born world. I become sharply, overwhelmingly, aware of colour gradations. I feel as if I'm saturated by all the shades of the infinite. At that moment, I and my painting are one. Together, we form a blue of iridescent hues. I come face to face with my motif; I lose myself in it. My thoughts wander hazily. The sun penetrates my skin dully, like a distant friend, warming, fertilizing my laziness, and together we germinate. [...] Only with nightfall can I withdraw my eyes from the earth, from this corner of the earth with which I've merged. (153)]

What interests me here is not only the Lucretian ontology, which we may cautiously relate to the infinitization that Rancière wrote about (see Chapter 3), but also how Cézanne superimposes two temporal rhythms in his presentation of the 'germination'.[12] On the one hand, we go back to the moment when life on earth began with the encounter between two atoms; the passage is as cosmopoetic as the opening to Baudelaire's 'De la couleur'. On the other hand, this cosmic dimension is played out over the rhythm of the day: as the sun rises, Cézanne reads *De Rerum Natura*, paints, fuses with his work, and gets caught up in the world; it is only when night falls that he is again able to detach himself from the painting and the earth. At this point of detachment, he continues, he is able to return to the experience that played out in the intensity of daylight. And he then understands what it means 'to see':

> Une tendre émotion me prend. Des racines de cette émotion monte la sève, les couleurs, une sorte de délivrance. Le rayonnement de l'âme, le regard, le mystère extériorisé, l'échange entre la terre et le soleil, l'idéal et la réalite, les couleurs! Une logique aérienne, colorée, remplace brusquement la sombre, la têtue géométrie. Tout s'organise, les arbres, les champs, les maisons. Je vois. (155)

> [A tender feeling comes over me and from the roots of this feeling rises the sap – colour. A sort of deliverance. Colour that expresses the radiance of the heart, that gives an outward form to the mystery of vision, that links earth and sun, the ideal and the real! An airy, coloured logic suddenly ousting sombre, stubborn geometry. Everything becomes organized: trees, fields, houses. I am seeing. (154)]

What Cézanne seeks in his paintings is thus a recovery of the fire of Being. Fire is what we all were, what nature is; it is lodged in the rocks of the Sainte-Victoire as the mountain seeks a return to the sun – fire is what colours express when paintings become events and lift humans too.[13] As the passage explains, this exchange between earth

---

12   In Chapter 2, I mentioned Simondon's processual theory of 'le cycle des images'. It is striking that when Simondon presents this cycle (anticipation, experience, retrospection… and new anticipations), he notes how it plays out over the course of a day, a year, and the history of civilizations (Simondon, 2014a, 24–28).

13   This elemental dimension – fire as force and environment – is the one Merleau-Ponty translates into his idea of 'la chair du monde'. As Galen Johnson writes, this doesn't mean that flesh or fire is some all-pervasive cosmic substance, but rather that things can become fleshy and fiery (in Merleau-Ponty, 1993, 50). Building from Spinoza, Galen Johnson explains that 'Being itself, for Merleau-Ponty, as the incarnate principle of Flesh, is imbued with a kind of energy, longing, desire

and sun culminates as geometry is replaced by a new 'aerial logic' through which 'everything falls into place' ('tout s'organise'). This is how Cézanne 'is born of visibility' (as Merleau-Ponty put it), and can triumphantly announce: 'Je vois'.

Before we return to Baudelaire, I would like to mention the largely comparable – but more radical, more oppositional – analysis of colour that can be found in Gilles Deleuze's *Francis Bacon: Logique de la sensation*. Deleuze's analysis brings us closer to our time, and closer to thinkers that appear elsewhere in this volume (Simondon, Braidotti, Massumi, Rancière, and others). For Deleuze, 'Bacon est cézanien, beaucoup plus que s'il était disciple de Cézanne' (1994, 28) ['Bacon is Cézannean, even more so than if he were a disciple of Cézanne' (2006, 26)], and it is therefore not surprising that references to Cézanne abound in his study of Bacon's work. First of all, Deleuze argues that the two painters give the same key role to colour. For Deleuze,

> C'est très simple. La peinture se propose directement de dégager les présences sous la représentation, par-delà la représentation. Le système des couleurs lui-même est un système d'action directe sur le système nerveux. [...] Libérant les lignes et les couleurs de la représentation, elle [la peinture] libère en même temps l'œil de son appartenance à l'organisme. (1994, 37)

> [It is very simple. Painting directly attempts to release the presences beneath representation, beyond representation. The color system itself is a system of direct action on the nervous system... [Painting] liberates the eye through color and line. But *it does not treat the eye as a fixed organ*. (2006, 37)]

Rather than 'to represent', the task of painting is thus to 'peindre les forces' (the title of Deleuze's eighth chapter) so that these forces can work directly on the viewers. This is why no art is simply figurative:

> En art, et en peinture comme en musique, il ne s'agit pas de reproduire ou d'inventer des formes, mais de capter des forces. C'est même par là qu'aucun art n'est figuratif. [...] Et n'est-ce pas le génie de Cézanne, avoir subordonnée tous les moyens de la peinture à cette tâche: rendre

or *conatus*' (49). And further: 'The desire or *conatus* of the Flesh is the demand for expression, the demand that the world be brought forth over and over again into visibility' (51). Mauro Carbone adds to this that the notion of '"chair" est un autre nom de l'"élément" qu'il [Merleau-Ponty] appelle aussi "Visibilité"' (2011, 7) ['"flesh" is another name for the "element" he also calls "Visibility"' (2015, 1)].

visibles la force de plissement des montagnes, la force de germination de la pomme, la force thermique d'un paysage... etc? (39)

[In art, and in painting as in music, it is not a matter of reproducing or inventing forms, but of capturing forces. For this reason no art is figurative. [...] And was it not Cézanne's genius to have subordinated all the techniques of painting to this task: rendering visible the folding force of mountains, the germinative force of a seed, the thermic force of a landscape, and so on? (41)]

How may painters express these forces? How can they 'liberate the eye'? According to Deleuze, the key operation, for both Cézanne and for Bacon, lies with the 'modulation *de* la couleur' (77). Here the genitive case 'de' works in all of its multi-directionality. It refers to the manner in which the painters modulate colours, but also to the ways in which colours modulate both the represented and the painters. Precisely by keeping these movements together, the painters produce sensation. As Deleuze puts it: 'Il n'y a pas plus de dedans que de dehors, mais seulement une spatialisation continuée, l'énergie spatialisante de la couleur' (86) ['There is neither an inside nor an outside, but only a continuous creation of space, the spatializing energy of colour' (93)].[14] At this point he introduces a footnote to explain that he is building from Simondon's distinction between moulding and modulating. As Simondon writes (in the passage cited by Deleuze): 'mouler est moduler de manière définitive, moduler est mouler de manière continue et perpétuellement variable' (86) ['to mould is to modulate in a definitive manner: to modulate is to mould in a continuous and perpetually variable manner' (140)]. What Deleuze highlights here is the continuous process of colour modulation through which Bacon (and Cézanne) undo the work of figuration and representation, creating an opening onto the world of forces that representations hide. As was the case for Merleau-Ponty, Deleuze suggests that colours open Being. And again, the idea of heat and energy reappears: we saw

14   Rancière may be critical of Deleuzian aesthetics (see Rancière in Alliez, 1998, 525–36), but Deleuze's analysis of colour resonates strongly with Rancière's description of 'la vie comme puissance qui circule à travers les corps, excède leur limites' (2014a, 103) ['life as power that circulates through bodies, exceeds their limits, and disorganizes the very relation of thought to its effect' (2014b, 37)], and with his definition of 'la beauté moderne' as 'celle du multiple anonyme, du corps qui a perdu les lignes qui l'enfermaient, de l'être dépouillé de son identité' (108) ['that of the anonymous multiple, of the body that has lost the lines that enclosed it, of a being stripped of its identity' (41)].

that Baudelaire associated colour with 'le travail intérieur du calorique' ['the workings of latent heat'], that Cézanne spoke about everything – beings and things – being 'un peu de chaleur solaire emmagasinée' ['a bit of solar heat that has been stored up'], that Merleau-Ponty talked about the visible catching fire and invading the body of the painter, and now we see Deleuze highlighting Cézanne's ability to make us see 'la force thermique d'un paysage' ['the thermic force of a landscape']. What Deleuze's account makes clearer is how painting as a heat-colour-quake is a force so powerful that it carries us beyond a phenomenological framework, 'libérant [...] l'œil de son appartenance à l'organisme' (as he wrote above). This is what happens when an image 'tourne dans l'air' (as Cézanne said), when a painting spins the universe. In this gyratory state, bodies no longer anchor movements; instead, *seeing* is, as Cézanne put it, '[l]e rayonnement de l'âme, le regard, le mystère extériorisé, l'échange entre la terre et le soleil, l'idéal et la réalite, les couleurs!' ['Colour that expresses the radiance of the heart, that gives an outward form to the mystery of vision, that links earth and sun, the ideal and the real!' (154)]

With these reflections on colour, fire, intensity, and a spinning cosmos – by Cézanne and some of his philosopher-commentators – it is time to return to Baudelaire, and consider the second paragraph in 'De la couleur'. Here Baudelaire continues the cosmopoesis that opened the chapter, and like Cézanne, he now maps the unfolding of the universe onto the rhythm of the day (having thereby placed his text on three different temporal scales: evolutionary history, the rhythm of the year and its seasons, and the rhythm of the day). In other words – and again like Cézanne – he gives a key role to the sun (and its heat) as it colours throughout the day:

> La sève monte et, mélange de principes, elle s'épanouit en *tons mélangés*; les arbres, les rochers, les granits se mirent dans les eaux et y déposent leurs *reflets*; tous les objets transparents accrochent au passage lumières et couleurs voisines et lointaines. À mesure que l'astre du jour se dérange, les tons changent de valeur, mais, respectant toujours leurs sympathies et leurs haines naturelles, continuent à vivre en harmonie par des concessions réciproques. Les ombres se déplacent lentement, et font fuir devant elles ou éteignent les tons à mesure que la lumière, déplacée elle-même, en veut faire résonner de nouveau. Ceux-ci se renvoient leurs reflets, et, modifiant leurs qualités en les *glaçant* de qualités transparentes et empruntées, multiplient à l'infini leurs mariages mélodieux et les rendent plus faciles. Quand le grand foyer descend dans les eaux, de rouges fanfares s'élancent de tous côtés; une sanglante harmonie éclate à l'horizon, et le vert

s'empourpre richement. Mais bientôt de vastes ombres bleues chassent en cadence devant elles la foule des tons orangés et rose tendre qui sont comme l'écho lointain et affaibli de la lumière. Cette grande symphonie du jour, qui est l'éternelle variation de la symphonie d'hier, cette succession de mélodies, où la variété sort toujours de l'infini, cet hymne compliqué s'appelle la couleur. (Baudelaire, 1976, 423)

Clearly, Baudelaire finds pleasure in following the movement of the sun. He begins with 'la sève monte' ['the sap rises' (55)], an energising movement (and an expression we also found in Cézanne's conversations). The sap is the effect of the rising sun (and the return of spring) – trees, rock, and granite are reflected in the water, the universe becomes animated: this is exactly what Cézanne called 'la germination' (and Poulet 'the quivering'). Soon the sun more explicitly enters the stage ('l'astre du jour'), contributing to the vibration, altering relations, making the ecological, process-relational ontology felt. This opens the door to a multisensory universe where musical metaphors abound: Baudelaire emphasizes the harmonious nature of the interplay between colours, as well as the natural alliances that some of them form (according to both nineteenth-century and more recent theorizations of colour). Finally, the sun sets, disappearing into the waters and thereby bringing about another marvellous interplay between colour tones, a dramatic 'sanglante harmonie éclate à l'horizon' ['blood-red harmony spreads over the horizon' (55)], playing the final melodies in the complicated hymn that we call 'la couleur' (as he did in his opening paragraph, Baudelaire brings his prose-poetic paragraph to rest on the keyword *colour*).

This paragraph is not simply describing the unfolding of a universe from dawn to dusk. Baudelaire is undermining any distinction between describing and creating, and precisely because he moves to a more performative register, he is inventing a relation to the world, for himself and for his readers. In the passage quoted above, the musical metaphors bring this out. They signal (if not the futility, then at least) the fragility of all distinctions between representation and performance, between the objective and the subjective, a nature 'out there' and a man-made culture. In this paragraph, colours produce a forceful symphony that captures and explodes the reader. We enter a mobile yet harmonic system; as Cézanne might say, this is what it means 'to see'.

We can therefore propose the following understanding of Baudelaire's colour-ontology. *The Embodied Mind* argues that colour is a phenomenon that allows us to move beyond the debates between subjectivist and objectivist positions, chickens and eggs, to the idea of mutual specification. This mutual specification is dynamic, processual, and ecological. Merleau-Ponty, Cézanne, and Deleuze give a dramatic and existential dimension to the process of mutual specification. If colour is a privileged place for the encounter between the mental and the environmental (the meeting of mind and universe), it is because this is where a force (or fire) shared by humankind and universe animates the process of mutual specification. The artist's role is to help bring out this force, this 'chair du monde', and in that process both tune and animate the relation between humans and world.

When considering Baudelaire's paragraphs, we see how this vitalistic dimension is found in his texts on colour. The first paragraph suggests that individual colours are animated by an inner heat which functions like an engine keeping the processes of germination and vibration alive. Colour is an event in which expression (that of nature, that of man) takes place. In the second paragraph, the sun and its movements take centre stage, as both cause (ensuring that 'la sève monte') and endpoint ('le grand foyer' ['the great ball of fire' (55)], an expression that again seems to chime with Cézanne's idea of the sun as the original element that we are longing to return to).

Throughout these two paragraphs, it may seem as if Baudelaire is more interested in vibration and movement than he is in constitution; it may seem that this is all about formlessness and vitalism. However, that would be a superficial reading. These paragraphs end with an insistence on colour as composition, as 'hymn'. Though on a larger scale than Verlaine's 'humble antienne', for Baudelaire too the universe is a 'melody' that we join in ('La mélodie laisse dans l'esprit un souvenir profond' [425], ['a melody leaves an unforgettable memory in the mind' (57)]). And Baudelaire's careful poetic writing in the opening paragraphs of 'De la couleur' clearly does its best to make readers participate in the hymn.

If the opening paragraphs of 'De la couleur' are concerned with cosmopoesis, the remaining paragraphs of the chapter increasingly turn to human beings, in order to detail how we too are environments, and how we are caught up in other environments through the work of colours. Previously, Baudelaire played with timescales; now he switches spatial scales, considering what he calls – with a thoroughly post-anthropocentric formulation – 'le détail dans le détail [...] par example, la main d'une femme' (423) ['the detail within a detail [...] a woman's hand, for example' (55)]. This is a move reminiscent of the

American designers Charles and Ray Eames's famous film *The Power of Ten* (1974). In this film, we first observe a couple having a picnic in a park. The camera zooms out, increasing the frame to the power of ten, and a voice-over helps us adjust our eyes, explaining what we see. This simple move is repeated over and over again until we are far beyond our own galaxy, lost in abstract patterns. Then we return to the couple, and the camera begins to zoom in to the power of ten. This takes us into the body, the skin, the microbes... eventually producing other very abstract landscapes, reminiscent of the ones we encountered beyond our galaxy. Similarly, Baudelaire's 'De la couleur' opened with landscapes and cosmopoesis, and now he brings out a magnifying glass, and moves close to the palm of a woman's hand. He goes into the joints, studies the veins, and finds a multicoloured (and multi-tonal) landscape of greys, browns, greens, blues, oranges, and whites which points back to the landscapes we encountered at the beginning of the chapter.[15] Baudelaire thereby emphasizes the interactive play between human beings, universe, and colours. And he specifies that it wouldn't be enough to simply reproduce colours as we see them. The expert 'coloriste' is someone who is able to fully participate in the hymn of colours (which we can find in a landscape and on the palm of a hand) whilst transforming this experience in such a way as to make it available to others too. This is what it means when an image 'turns', when a universe 'sings', and the human being participates in the movements of the cosmos.

Baudelaire Was Never Modern: Art as Ecological Practice

At the end of Chapter 3, I addressed the oft-debated question of Baudelaire's modernity in relation to the half-hearted city poem 'Le Crépuscule du soir'. At the end of this chapter on the pastoral idylls of 'De la couleur' and Baudelaire's art criticism more widely, I would like to

---

15   This blurring of body and landscape is also found in other Baudelaire texts; for instance, in the famous exercise in seduction entitled 'L'Invitation au voyage'. In both the verse and prose versions of this poem, the narrator conjures up the image of a marvellous universe ('un pays de Cocagne' [1975, 301], ['a country of Cockaigne']), likens the landscape to his lover, and promises to travel up its/ her 'canaux' ('channels') – a word that brings together the anatomical and the maritime (just as the neighbouring word 'vaisseaux' does) – 'pour assouvir/ ton moindre désir' (1975, 54) ['to satisfy/ your every desire'].

return to this issue via two well-known texts on 'l'homme des foules': the third chapter from Baudelaire's study of Constantin Guys *Le Peintre de la vie moderne* and (to a lesser extent) the prose poem 'Les Foules' from *Le Spleen de Paris*.[16] My aim is to compare the experience that plays out when brain and world mingle in the event called 'colour' with the experience offered by urban crowds. In order to make this comparison, we will need to understand the experience of crowd-swimming, and we should therefore also explore why Baudelaire compares the crowd-swimmer with a child. To complete the comparison, the last component in my small textual network will be the 1853 text 'Morale du joujou', which will deal with crowds, toys, and colours. As we shall see, the fiery vitalism found in Baudelaire's writings on colour seeps into these writings also.

The third chapter of *Le Peintre de la vie moderne* begins with a short, idiosyncratic summary of Poe's 'Man of the Crowd' (1840). Poe introduces a narrator who is recovering from a recent illness. He is sitting in a café, looking out on the streets of London as darkness falls. When the narrator spots an interesting-looking passer-by, he plunges into the crowds in pursuit of the man. Most of Poe's text then follows the narrator as he chases the man of the crowd. Baudelaire's summary ignores the many pages devoted to the pursuit; he gives up on the cat-and-mouse game and instead concentrates on the narrator. As a result, the summary wrongly gives the impression that the titular 'Man of the Crowd' is Poe's narrator, not the man pursued.

Omitting the cat-and-mouse game is only one aspect of Baudelaire's deliberate move away from questions of intersubjectivity and towards a relative depersonalization. If Baudelaire introduces Poe's text into his study of Constantin Guys it is precisely to emphasize that the latter is an anonymous artist. He does not sign his drawings and watercolours, he does not want to be written about, and he does not even want to be seen as an artist. Instead (explains Baudelaire), Guys can be seen as an 'homme du monde' and an 'homme de la foule'. It is Guys's anonymity that inspires the parallel with Poe's text.

16   Although Baudelaire's writings on colour centre on the vibrancy of beautiful landscapes, less idyllic and less pastoral elements can be spinning tops also. 'Une Charogne' is as vibrant and vitalistic as any other landscape, and it is therefore not surprising that this was Cézanne's favourite poem, one he knew by heart. (It is of course also the most Francis Bacon'esque of Baudelaire's poems – a poem that explicitly compares the process of decomposition to the emergence of a painting.)

Having introduced his man of the crowd, Baudelaire insists on the curiosity of this character. The man of the crowd is excited, ready to rediscover the world, insatiable with curiosity. This description provides the springboard for a comparison between the man of the crowd, the child, and the genius. A child, too, is curious and explorative: '[l']enfant voit tout en *nouveauté; il est toujours ivre*' (1976, 690) ['the child sees everything as a novelty; the child is always "drunk"' (1992b, 398)]. Constantin Guys is such a character: man of the crowd, child, and genius. There is, however, an important difference between these last two figures: the child is in the grip of its experiences, whereas the genius is in control. The genius has stronger nerves (as Baudelaire puts it), and can therefore master the process of immersion into – and discovery of – the world. Famously, Baudelaire sums up this difference:

> le génie n'est que l'*enfance retrouvée* à volonté, l'enfance douée maintenant, pour s'exprimer, d'organes virils et de l'esprit analytique qui lui permet d'ordonner la somme des matériaux involontairement amassée. (690)

> [genius is no more than childhood recaptured at will, childhood equipped now with man's physical means to express itself, and with the analytical mind that enables it to bring order into the sum of experience, involuntarily amassed. (398)]

Clearly the distinction is between absorption into the experience of the world (child), and a certain practice that allows the genius to not only *see* the world (Baudelaire italicizes) but also to order and express it. The poet emphasizes the controlled nature of this vitalistic experience of *ivresse* ('à volonté'). Cézanne's artist was a 'plaque sensible' ['sensitized plate'], ready for nature's inscriptions and in possession of a 'métier'; similarly, Baudelaire's artists are capable both of sensing and of communicating their experiences and sensations.

It is worth mentioning that, throughout his text, Baudelaire keeps alive the theme of colour. First he emphasizes how our earliest childhood impressions are 'vivement colorées' (690) ['vividly coloured' (398)], then he explains that the child's drunken experience of worldly sensation has to do with 'la joie avec laquelle l'enfant absorbe la forme et la couleur' (690) ['the joy the child feels in drinking in shape and colour' (398)]; finally this theme culminates in a longer anecdote about a friend who, as a child, was absorbed by the spectacle of his father's morning routine ('la toilette de son père' [690]). The friend's fascination was largely the result of studying,

> les dégradations de couleurs de la peau nuancée de rose et de jaune, et le réseau bleuâtre des veines. Le tableau de la vie extérieure le ['un de mes amis'] pénétrait déjà de respect et s'emparait de son cerveau. [...] Ai-je besoin de dire que cet enfant est aujourd'hui un peintre célèbre? (691)

> [the colour tones of the skin tinged with rose and yellow, and the bluish network of the veins. The picture of the external world was already beginning to fill him ['one of my friends'] with respect, and to take possession of his brain. [...] Need I say that, today, the child is a famous painter. (398–99)]

Like the female hand in 'De la couleur', the father is a landscape, and future painters are folded out of the spectacle of such multicoloured landscapes. Baudelaire thus offers an artistic primal scene: an illustration of how 'la couleur est le lieu où notre cerveau et l'univers se rencontrent' (Cézanne in Gasquet, 2012, 153–53) ['Colour is the place where our brain and the universe meet' (1991, 153)], and how 'le peintre naît dans les choses comme par concentration à soi du visible' (Merleau-Ponty, 1997, 69) ['it is the painter to whom the things of the world give birth by a sort of concentration or coming-to-itself of the visible' (1993, 141)].

Despite Baudelaire's initial remarks, we must not overestimate the extent to which the genius is in control. Coming back to the man of the crowd, Baudelaire describes how difficult it is to render his experience in clear language:

> Être hors de chez soi, et pourtant se sentir partout chez soi; voir le monde, être au centre du monde et rester caché au monde, tels sont quelques-uns des moindres plaisirs de ces esprits indépendants, passionnés, impartiaux, que la langue ne peut que maladroitement définir. (692)

> [To be away from home and yet to feel at home anywhere; to see the world, to be at the very centre of the world, and yet to be unseen of the world, such are some of the minor pleasures of those independent, intense and impartial spirits, who do not lend themselves easily to linguistic definitions. (399–400)]

Attempting to wrestle his way out of the logic of chickens and eggs, these paradoxical 'and'–'and' constructions (e.g. 'hors de chez soi' *and* 'partout chez soi') lead Baudelaire to the conclusion that language struggles to render the experience he is trying to communicate. Why does language struggle? Because it orders, assigns places, distinguishes between inner and outer, and distributes agency between subject and object positions. As Barthes (1978) (in)famously argued in *Leçon* – language is 'fascist'

(14) because it forces you to order the world and ties you to a position. However, as he also went on to specify, there is one exception: literature is 'cette tricherie salutaire' (16) ['salutary trickery'] that allows us to escape the violence of dialectics. This was demonstrated in 'Le Crépuscule du soir' as the text carefully wriggled its way out of subject–object relations, avoiding simplistic ideas about agency. What the prose poem performatively conveyed via linguistic artistry, *Le Peintre de la vie moderne* expresses in a more direct way: Baudelaire continues to explore a zone where subject–object distinctions no longer hold sway.

But Baudelaire's text also gives more direct grounds for questioning the extent to which the *génie* remains in control. In another famous passage, he writes:

> Ainsi l'amoureux de la vie universelle entre dans la foule comme dans un immense réservoir d'électricité. On peut aussi le comparer, lui, à un miroir aussi immense que cette foule; à un kaléidoscope doué de conscience, qui, à chacun de ses mouvements, représente la vie multiple et la grâce mouvante de tous les éléments de la vie. C'est un *moi* insatiable du *non-moi*, qui, à chaque instant, le rend et l'exprime en images plus vivantes que la vie elle-même, toujours instable et fugitive. (692)

> [Thus the lover of universal life moves into the crowd as though into an enormous reservoir of electricity. He, the lover of life, may also be compared to a mirror as vast as this crowd; to a kaleidoscope endowed with consciousness, which with every one of its movements presents a pattern of life, in all its multiplicity, and the flowing grace of all the elements that go to compose life. It is an ego athirst for the non-ego, and reflecting it at every moment in energies more vivid than life itself, always inconstant and fleeting. (400)]

Here we witness the tension between control and loss of control, between throwing yourself into the electric current and bringing impressions (more or less) together in an exploded kaleidoscopic conscience. With this comes a tension between the idea of representation (implicit in the mirror metaphor, explicit with the kaleidoscope 'representing' life through broken pieces of coloured glass) and an expression of 'images plus vivantes que la vie elle-même'[17] – precisely the kind of intensities that Delacroix, Cézanne, and Bacon sought to communicate (as did Nietzsche

---

17   The English translation has 'energies' for 'images'; this may be an error, but it may also be a deliberate attempt at communicating the high-voltage image-consciousness of the man of the crowd.

and Barthes when they wrote about the kaleidoscope-consciousness, as discussed in Chapter 1).

It is possible to take this question of 'representation' versus 'mutual specification' further. As is well known, Baudelaire used these pages as a starting point for the prose poem 'Les Foules' (in *Spleen de Paris*). The poem returns to a number of the elements we found in the text on Guys, but the central role is now occupied by 'le poète'. Baudelaire seemingly turns up the element of control and mastery, defining the poet as the one who masters the art of crowd-swimming. The description of this art has changed very little. It is still a vitalizing experience; it is still associated with an ability to flow freely between self and others, to give oneself up, and perhaps to recompose oneself after an ecstatic experience in the crowds of the city. What interests me in this prose poem is the fundamental idea that 'jouir de la foule est un art' (1975, 291) ['to take pleasure in the crowd is an art']. The formulation ties to the much larger question of what art is for Baudelaire.

On the basis of the texts about crowd-swimming, it is clear that art is first of all a practice, a verb. This practice is ecological and revitalizing. It allows the discovery (and experience) of a world beyond the representational. It is therefore possible to draw on Isabelle Stengers's idea of the 'ecology of practices'. Referencing A.N. Whitehead, she describes practice as a matter of 'giving to the situation the power to make us think' (and *feel*, we might add without betraying Stengers's intentions [Stengers, 2005, 185]). In Baudelaire's text, art appears as a practice of immersion, discovery, and transformation that has less to do with the production of artworks than it does with certain practices of life. In this manner, his writings on crowd-swimming anticipate twentieth-century avant-garde practices with their insistence on art as process, practice, and intensification, rather than object and masterpiece.

This understanding of art is also found in 'Morale du joujou' – a key text about children and art in Baudelaire's work. Here the interaction between children and toys is described as a practice. The child manipulates the toy, and the toy forms the child:

Je crois que généralement les enfants agissent sur leurs joujoux, en d'autres termes, que leur choix est dirigé par des dispositions et des désirs, vagues, il est vrai, non pas formulés, mais très réels. Cependant je n'affirmerais pas que le contraire n'ait pas lieu, c'est-à-dire que les joujoux n'agissent pas sur l'enfant, surtout dans le cas de la prédestination littéraire ou artistique. (1975, 585)

[I believe that children in general act upon their toys; in other words, that their choice is governed by their disposition and desires, vague, if you wish, and by no means formulated, but very real. However, I would not deny that the contrary can occur – above all in cases of literary or artistic predestination. (2012, 17)]

The passage presents a process of 'mutual specification'. And as the last lines suggest – and the overall argument of the text makes clearer – this practice is part of an aesthetic education.[18] Art is a practice in which distinctions between producers (such as Guys), users (such as the reader of Poe), and the 'object' in question (whether this is a walk in the crowd, the drawing of a crowd, or a short story about a man walking in the crowd) become fuzzy.

And art is not the only practice that play prepares for. Play also anticipates the kind of experiments we find in the sciences. Indeed, many toys – not least optical toys such as the kaleidoscopes and panoramas mentioned in *Le Peintre de la vie moderne*, and the stethoscopes and phenakistiscopes mentioned in 'Morale du joujou' – are closely related to scientific instruments. Baudelaire distinguishes between the aesthetic education that certain toys facilitate and the scientific training that other toys stimulate, between aesthetic pleasure and desire for knowledge. But he does not give one priority over the other, recommending instead that a child engage in both. Baudelaire's text therefore links manipulation (in the etymological sense of appropriating with one's hands), beauty, and knowledge, delivering an argument for enactive practices, for the abandonment of any mind–body dualisms, for the capacity of practices to transcend subject–object dialectics. This is a wonderfully non-discriminatory approach that clearly illustrates that Baudelaire saw no reason for a logic of two cultures. As Bernard Howells observes: 'When [Baudelaire] wrote that imagination was "la plus *scientifique* des facultés" (Corr. I, 336) he intended to shock, but also to break down a divide – to claim a truth for imagination and to reclaim imagination for science' (1996, 86).

Following this brief exposition of the parallels between art, play, and crowd-swimming as practices that give both knowledge and aesthetic pleasure, we can attempt a more direct comparison between the experience of colour and that of urban crowds. First, it is impossible

---

18   As Marit Grøtta also writes in *Baudelaire's Media Aesthetics*: 'The intricate relationship between our senses and technology is also what makes uncertain the boundaries of the human' (2015, 144).

to maintain a strong distinction between the texts on colour and those on crowd-swimming and related activities such as play. We have seen that colours and aesthetics make their way into the texts about crowds, toys, and cities, and we have seen that all these practices are capable of challenging conventional dualisms. For example, the aesthetic power of life ('la forme et la couleur') easily overpowered the child: 'Le tableau de la vie extérieure le pénétrait déjà de respect et s'emparait de son cerveau' (691) ['The picture of the external world was already beginning to fill him with respect, and to take possession of his brain' (398–99)]. Such formulations are typical of Baudelaire (and especially of his art criticism); they distribute agency evenly between what we would usually call subjects and objects, thereby inviting us to find alternative ways to speak about how things happen. It's true that the artist and the crowd-swimmer must retain an element of control, but this 'control' precisely has to do with the ability to continue navigating at times when strong subject–object distinctions no longer apply. As such, art can be described as an exercise in navigating non-anthropocentric environments. I therefore propose to push the famous crowd- and toy-focused texts further away from ideas of intersubjectivity, of cat-and-mouse logics, than most of Baudelaire's readers have done. I would like to emphasize that children, artists, and reconvalescents emerge as crystallizations of the active environments in which they are swimming. For this reading, there is no particular reason to prioritize between texts frequently considered modern and those that appear more pastoral. Indeed, the urban electricity and the 'travail intérieur du calorique' do the same work on the individuating subject (and colours are of course also present in Baudelaire's urban poetry).

But since this distinction between a pastoral and a modern Baudelaire has been important in Baudelaire criticism, let me add a second point.[19] As suggested in the third chapter, some readers will likely place 'De la

19   The idea of a pastoral Baudelaire is developed in Marshall Berman's classic *All That Is Solid Melts into Air*. There, 'pastoral' does not refer to Baudelaire's (relatively few) writings on landscapes or nature but to an attitude towards modernity that leaves no space for the heightened tensions of the urban environment. The pastoral is idyllic and idealizing; it is a gaze that erases frictions. It is therefore debatable whether the idyllic but also fiery and vitalist landscapes in 'De la couleur' are 'pastoral' in Berman's sense of this term. However, it is still revealing that Berman uses the term 'pastoral' to designate an attitude that represses all tensions. In Berman's constellation of the modern, the contradictory, and the urban there is no space for the kind of forces we find in the landscapes of 'De la couleur'.

couleur' and 'Le Crépuscule du soir' among Baudelaire's more romantic and less adventurous texts in so far as the poet–narrator either dreams up a timeless pastoral idyll ('Supposons...') or remains on his balcony instead of throwing himself into the crowd, the city, and the dusk. By contrast, if 'Perte d'auréole' has become such a key text for (Benjamin-inspired) critics, it is precisely because the poet and his halo get down in the dirt (and into a dive bar). By embracing the contradictions of the modern, urban environment, this poem (and other often-studied texts such as 'Les Yeux des pauvres' and 'Le Mauvais vitrier') have long seemed more contemporary, more political, and more challenging than poems and paragraphs about non-urban settings. Certainly, my point is not that we should no longer pay attention to the ways in which Baudelaire can help us understand power-relations in early (and contemporary) capitalist culture. Rather, my point is that a dive into colour and landscape can be as productively self-alienating (Chambers) and as radically democratic (Rancière) as any urban experience. Moreover, many readings of Baudelaire's modernity unintentionally reveal a desire to keep human beings at the heart – and in control – of their environments. More problematically, they testify to a tendency to think agency in individualizing (often individualist) ways, which are precisely those challenged by Baudelaire's texts. I therefore contend that, in a research context strongly dominated by the urban Baudelaire, the paragraphs about the interplay between granite rocks, shimmering waters, and a fiery sun are even more explosive for the idea of the liberal individual than his writings about the (man-made) city and crowd dives.

Over these last two chapters I have proposed that Baudelaire's texts *tournent dans l'air* (as Cézanne put it) because of their ability to host a fiery force or vitality. This force can be experienced in the interaction with toys, art, colours, and crowds. When you climb the spinning top called 'La Chasse au lion', when the lion jumps at you, the result is a destabilization of individual identities and social structures. I do not think it would be wise to try to move beyond Rancière's insistence on the anti-hierarchical work that takes place in such aesthetic experiences – Baudelaire's explosions do not produce well-known ideological patterns. In fact, as the current chapter brought Baudelaire, Cézanne, and Deleuze together, it ventured far from conventional political thought, far from human perspective and scale, exploring a heat-fire-force which 'libère en même temps l'œil de son appartenance à l'organisme' [*does not treat the eye as a fixed organ*] (as Deleuze put it). When Baudelaire's writings bring together human and geological timescales, fiery rocks, the veins on a hand, electricity, nature, and urban crowds, rapidly zooming in and out, he is pushing us to think differently about the multiple ways in which we are caught up in – and exploded by – the aesthetic and the natural world; he is challenging our anthropocentric habits, and renewing our understanding of ourselves.

Coda: From Baudelaire to Mallarmé

For the final section of this chapter, I borrowed a title from Bruno Latour to suggest that Baudelaire was never modern. Baudelaire's writings do not respect the principles of Latour's 'modern constitution': he is not observing strict distinctions between the social sphere (including its arts) and the sciences, he does not separate the urban from the pastoral, the transitory from the eternal, the subjective from the objective.[20] In this little coda, I would like to sum up this argument by drawing, once more, on the visual artists and philosophers mentioned throughout the chapter; however, I will add in a few more names to point towards the last two chapters of this book. I will leave aside the well-known idea about Baudelaire as a poet of the urban and the modern, and instead present two versions of the not-quite-so-modern Baudelaire.

Let me begin with a story about Baudelaire's *lack* of modernity. We can find this story at the beginning of the (wonderful) book that Georges Bataille wrote about Manet towards the end of his life (*Manet*, 1955). Here, Baudelaire is presented as a persuasive advocate for the art of Delacroix, and a half-hearted supporter of Manet. Although Baudelaire defended the young Manet when his work was met with an avalanche of criticism and mockery, Baudelaire never fully appreciated the painterly revolution that bears the name 'Édouard Manet'. Baudelaire's aesthetic and generational sympathies went to Delacroix; when he wrote about Manet, he mainly celebrated his work from around 1860, whose Spanish style points to Velazquez (and, arguably, to Delacroix). According to Bataille, the modern Manet escaped Baudelaire. That is to say, he did

---

20   Readers unfamiliar with *Nous n'avons jamais été modernes* (1991) should know that Bruno Latour criticizes the 'modern constitution'. He distances himself from the modernists, who believe that science is distinct from politics, or distinct from the kind of creativity we find in the arts. Modernists have – unsuccessfully, Latour argues – attempted to purify a world that has always been messier and more complex than they wanted to acknowledge. Nature and society are coproduced.

not understand how Manet's work destroyed the subject of painting, nullified the motif, pulled it into silence, thereby liberating art from all bourgeois conventions, paving the way for a new abstract art: the sovereign interplay of colours and forms.[21]

To corroborate this reading, Bataille cites some of the conservative passages in Baudelaire's art criticism (and briefly engages with Baudelaire's 'La Corde').[22] In particular, he draws on Chapter 17 in the 'Salon de 1846', where the poet regrets the disappearance of 'les écoles' and their apprentice-system (young painters being formed in the ateliers of older masters). Baudelaire argues that this development has led to a relaxation of conventions and a loss of the 'grande tradition'; now there is nothing but 'le chaos d'une liberté épuisante et stérile' (1976, 492) ['the chaos of an exhausting and sterile freedom' (1992b, 103)]. He worries that in this new anarchic situation only the most singular geniuses – Delacroix, and to a lesser extent Ingres – can stay afloat and thus only they can impose a new order. But these painters, objects Bataille, are only the lingering of a noble but outdated form of art. Baudelaire has not understood that Manet was putting into practice one of the key principles of modern art: 'Prends l'éloquence et tords-lui son cou!' ['Take eloquence and twist its neck!'] (as Verlaine later put it in his 'Art poétique'). Baudelaire therefore teases Manet, semi-seriously writing 'vous n'êtes que le premier dans la décrépitude de votre art' (33) ['you are but the first in the decrepitude of your art'].

The current chapter has presented a different story about Baudelaire, Delacroix, and modern painting. In my chapter, the destruction of the subject – and more generally, the (Hegelian) theme of production through negation – was less important than it is for Bataille. Instead, we saw Baudelaire focus on colour, and we saw colour breaking lines, spinning the world, pixelating (but not negating) motifs and spectators.

21 As Bataille puts it, 'Manet supprima la signification du sujet. Supprimer le sujet, le détruire, est bien le fait de la peinture moderne' (1994, 38) ['Manet wrung the last drop of meaning out of the subject. To suppress and destroy the subject is exactly what modern painting does' (1955, 52)]. From Manet onwards, painting therefore became 'l'art d'arracher des objets, des images d'objets, à ce monde qui, dans son ensemble, se subordonna à la lourdeur bourgeoise' (43) ['the art of wresting objects, and the images of objects, from a world that has surrendered to a bourgeois torpor' (58)].

22 Baudelaire's prose poem 'La Corde', dedicated to Manet, takes inspiration from the tragic event of a young boy who modelled for Manet, and committed suicide in his workshop.

In this manner, Delacroix and Baudelaire liberated intensities and forces that lie beyond the representational, and this was one reason they continued to inspire twentieth-century thinkers and artists. We saw how the explosive colour-vitalism was picked up in the work of Paul Cézanne and Francis Bacon, and (in different ways) worked through in the writings of Merleau-Ponty and Gilles Deleuze. As Rancière suggested in his analysis, this electrifying power of colour is also politically liberating. Colour does democratic work, it forms a basis for Baudelaire's 'politique modeste mais fidèle' (Rancière, 2014a, 111) ['a modest politics, but a faithful one' (2014b, 43)].[23]

This second lineage – emphasizing the explosive intensities of colour – is not preoccupied by the question of modernity. When Cézanne goes to the Louvre, he finds as much intensity in Paolo Veronese's 'Wedding at Cana' (1562–63) as he does in Gustave Courbet's 'Un enterrement à Ornans' (1849–50) – and he loves both works. It has been my contention that Baudelaire's interest in the modern (which is undeniable) was similarly an interest in the intensity of life. Baudelaire was modern,

23   More names could be added to this list of colour-vitalists. Radical filmmakers Danièle Huillet and Jean-Marie Straub similarly went back to Cézanne and colour in their *Cézanne* (1990) and *Une visite au Louvre* (2004). *Une visite au Louvre* is a particularly powerful film. It consists almost exclusively of fixed-framed shots of the artworks on which Cézanne comments when he visits the Louvre in the company of Gasquet. A female voice-over uses a highly unusual diction to render the energy and force of Cézanne's way of seeing, speaking, and painting; everything we hear is taken from the conversations with Gasquet. In addition to the static shots of artworks, the directors introduce two panning shots to open and close the film (plus a static shot of the Seine, approximately halfway through the film). The final shot is remarkable. This is the directors' signature shot, the so-called 'plan straubien': a slow circular shot, showing a lush green forest clearing – a bit of the natural world about which Cézanne has been speaking. The shot has been lifted from Straub and Huillet's earlier film *Ouvriers, Paysans* (2001), which was based on texts by the Italian, communist author Elio Vittorini. Even if we should be careful about translating aesthetics into politics, Straub and Huillet clearly connect the colour-forces that Cézanne mentions with the utopian communities dreamt of by Vittorini's workers and peasants. The film seems to ask: Can colours help to open a new world? Can colours do political work? Baudelaire – and the painter friend who as a boy admired his father's morning ritual (in 'Morale du joujou') – would be able to answer: 'they did for us'. (Unsurprisingly, Straub and Huillet's films play an important role in Deleuze's books on cinema (in particular in *L'image-temps* [2002]) and Rancière's writings on the politics of film (in particular in *Les Écarts du cinéma* [2011]).

okay, but he was not just modern: his desire for intensity, electricity, and vitality could be satisfied in nature as well as on the boulevard.

In conclusion, let me complicate matters further and add that this intensity-argument about the democratic nature of nineteenth-century painting can also be made with Manet. Even if Delacroix and Manet are very different artists, even if they proceeded in very different ways (Delacroix's operation being that of the spinning top, Manet relying on negation), we can reduce the distance between them if we emphasize their ability to generate electrifying powers. This ability explains why Mallarmé's reading of Manet in 1876 comes remarkably close to Rancière's analysis of the relation between Baudelaire and Delacroix in 2014. When Mallarmé writes about Manet's 'Le Linge' (1875), he makes the same two points that Rancière made about Baudelaire – but less cautiously. First, Mallarmé argues that Manet's work is an example of what I called an aesthetics of pixelation. In the case of Manet, this has more to do with light than with the work of colour. Manet floods his motif with light, this light works at the contours (and colours), liberating the energy of the painting, which then flows over the spectators. Again, the result is a revitalization. Secondly, this revitalization is presented in political terms. Rancière argued that Baudelaire's analysis revealed the democratizing nature of Delacroix's colours; Mallarmé compares Manet's use of light with the revolution of 1789. Manet makes art for a new democratic era, for men who want to see with their own eyes. We are given the chance to recompose the pixelated painting, to reinvent ourselves (and our relations to others and the world more widely) in the encounter with the light of Manet. Exactly how this happens – how Mallarmé's media-theory operates, and to what extent it informs his own writings – will be the topic of the next two chapters.

CHAPTER FIVE

Mallarmé – Becoming *Individu-Livre*

In the humanities, the word 'instrument', and related terms such as 'instrumentality' and 'instrumentalization', generally come with a host of negative associations, quickly leading towards ideas about reification and alienation. In literary studies, having an instrumental approach to literature and language is associated with treating writing as transitive, overlooking – at your own peril, as deconstructive and psychoanalytic readers have repeatedly shown us – that language contains an excess; that it speaks us, as much as we speak it. Instrumentality is linked to dogmatic politics and conceptual naïveté; occasionally Jean-Paul Sartre's *Qu'est-ce que la littérature?* and its famous assertion that 'la fonction d'un écrivain est d'appeler un chat un chat' (Sartre, 2003, 281) ['the function of a writer is to call a spade a spade'] are given the dubious honour of illustrating this. On the other hand, it is commonly accepted that Mallarmé represents the antithesis of this simplistic view of language and literature. Mallarmé, we are told, was a poet who forged his entire poetics on the basis of a distinction between an instrumental approach to language, which he called 'l'universel *reportage*' (2003, 212), and a poetic vision which he hoped would come together in the form of a 'Livre [...] explication orphique de la Terre' (1998, 788) ['Book [...] Orphic explanation of the Earth'].

Yet, we also know that one of Mallarmé's most famous *Divagations* was entitled 'Le Livre, instrument spirituel' (1895), and that Sartre considered Mallarmé to be 'notre plus grand poète' ['our greatest poet'], not least because '[s]on engagement me paraît aussi total que possible: social autant que poétique' (1972, 14) ['his commitment seems to me to be as total as is possible – socially as well as poetically']. This idea of the book as a spiritual instrument indicates that instrumentality was less irredeemable for Mallarmé than it has been for many of his modern and postmodern readers. Obviously, the term 'instrument' evokes music as well as technics, and some readers may argue that Mallarmé has in mind this musical sense of the word. That is correct – for instance, 'Le Livre, instrument spirituel' describes reading as '[u]n solitaire tacite concert' (2003, 226) ['a solitary tacit concert' (2007, 228)]. However, as this chapter aims to demonstrate, firstly Mallarmé does not operate with a strong distinction between the musical and the technical understanding of the word 'instrument'; and secondly, Mallarmé's view of literature can indeed be called 'instrumental'.[1]

My chapter thereby communicates with (at least) two earlier studies. In 2010, Anna Arnar presented a comparable argument in her excellent *The Book as Instrument*. From the outset Arnar affirms that Mallarmé's work was simultaneously 'wildly idealist and fundamentally pragmatic' (2010, 1), and at the end of her volume she returns to this idea, stating that 'Les Notes en vue du "Livre"' were 'pragmatic and speculative' (274). I agree with Arnar's insistence on these seemingly opposing adjectives, and on the importance of highlighting the pragmatic, practical dimension of Mallarmé's approach to literature. In order to understand this practical dimension, the idea of the instrument is key. In this chapter, I shall take a complementary route to Arnar's in an attempt to explain how Mallarmé marries pragmatism and wild idealism. Arnar situates Mallarmé's work in French fin-de-siècle cultural history, analysing his aesthetic in the context of the birth of the artist's book and late-nineteenth-century ideas about reading and pedagogy. In her last chapter, she then examines the influence of Mallarmé's work on selected twentieth-century avant-garde artists and briefly mentions the idea of networked and wired books. I will approach the idea of instrumentality with a view to thinking the role that Mallarmé's work can have today, two decades into the twenty-first century, and I shall therefore spend more time than Arnar with the idea of the networked book (although I will not use this term). As in previous chapters, my argument will therefore be concerned less with nineteenth-century culture than with showing how Mallarmé's idea of the book as a spiritual instrument relies on an ecological conception of subjectivity that anticipates contemporary theorizations of the relations between human beings, technical processes, and the environment. In this reading, Mallarmé emerges as a thoroughly ecological writer, defiantly dreaming about how fiction can help to align humans and their environments.

---

1   Another (rare) positive engagement with arts and instrumentality can be found in John Dewey's *Art as Experience* (2009 [1934], 144–45).

The second study with which my chapter resonates is Bernard Stiegler and Ars Industrialis's *Réenchanter le monde* (2006). Although this text has little to do with literary criticism, and devotes only relatively few pages to Mallarmé, the idea of the spiritual instrument plays a key role. I shall therefore return to Stiegler and Ars Industrialis at the end of the current chapter.

The Book-Event: Politics and Beauty

One of Mallarmé's most famous statements can be found in the interview he gave for Jules Huret's *Enquête sur l'évolution littéraire* (1891): 'le monde est fait pour aboutir à un beau livre' (Mallarmé, 2003, 702) ['the world is made to end up as a beautiful book']. Four years later, 'Le Livre, instrument spirituel' begins with a reference to this remark, thereby inviting us to consider the article in relation to other aspects of Mallarmé's work. In what follows, I will accept this invitation and offer an intertextual reading of the first two paragraphs of 'Le Livre, instrument spirituel', setting aside the relation between 'le Livre' and newspapers that emerges as a key concern in later paragraphs. My aim is to give a brief but general presentation of Mallarmé's poetics by drawing out three connected strands in his theorizations of the book (which will form the foundation of the argument developed in the later parts of this chapter and in the next chapter). I will examine the social role of the book, the beauty of the book, and introduce the complex issue of agency, asking who creates the book and whether a book can 'act'.

'Le Livre, instrument spirituel' begins: 'Une proposition qui émane de moi — si, diversement, citée à mon éloge ou par blâme — je la revendique avec celles qui se presseront ici — sommaire veut, que tout, au monde, existe pour aboutir à un livre' (2003, 224) ['A proposition said to emanate from me, cited in my praise or dispraise — but I claim it here, along with others that will gather around — says, briefly, that everything in the world exists to end up as a book' (2007, 226)]. This statement can be linked to alchemistic traditions, to Victor Hugo, to Jules Michelet, and to Friedrich Nietzsche's idea about the aesthetic justification of existence (Nietzsche, 2003). Contrary to what readers have often suggested, the 'world as book' is a social and ontological idea as much as an aesthetic one.[2]

---

2 See Arnold Hauser's damning (and factually incorrect) description of Mallarmé: 'He lived in the vacuum of his intellectualism, completely cut off from

More accurately, in Mallarmé's texts such distinctions fall away as art, social life, and ontology become intimately linked.

Many passages in Mallarmé's work consider the socio-political function of the book. One of the best known is found in 'Sauvegarde' (1895), where Mallarmé reminds his readers of the political importance of 'maintaining' the book:

> À savoir que le rapport social et sa mesure momentanée qu'on la serre ou l'allonge, en vue de gouverner, étant une fiction, laquelle relève des belles-lettres — à cause de leur principe mystérieux ou poétique — le devoir de maintenir le livre s'impose dans l'intégrité. (2003, 272)

> [Meaning that, since the social relation at any particular time, condensed or expanded to allow for government, is a fiction, it belongs in the domain of Letters — because of their mysterious or poetic principle — and thence flows the duty of maintaining the book in general in its integrity. (2007, 290)]

Here Mallarmé posits that the social bond is a matter of fiction. This obviously does not mean that the social bond is unimportant, that it is 'just a fiction'. On the contrary, fiction, or 'le Livre', is presented as a model for social relations, a key component in the construction of the socio-political sphere. There are several complex reasons for this.

First, it is important to understand that the book, or fiction, on which social relations must be modelled has no ground other than itself. There is no transcendental power, no God to underwrite its value. As Mallarmé puts it in 'Le Livre, instrument spirituel': 'Le livre, expansion totale de la lettre, doit d'elle tirer, directement, une mobilité et spacieux, par correspondances, instituer un jeu, on ne sait, qui confirme la fiction' (2003, 226) ['The book, total expansion of the letter, should derive from it directly a spacious mobility, and by correspondences institute a play of elements that confirms the fiction' (2007, 228)]. In *La Musique et les lettres* (1894), Mallarmé similarly explains that fiction is only fiction if it is sufficiently self-aware to realize that it is not grounded. This absence

ordinary practical life, and having almost no relationships at all with the world outside literature [...]. No one ever followed Flaubert's example more faithfully. "Tout, au monde, existe pour aboutir à un livre" – the master himself could not have put it more Flaubertishly. "À un livre", Mallarmé says; but what results is, in fact, hardly a book. He spends his whole life writing, rewriting and correcting a dozen sonnets, two dozen shorter and about six larger poems, a dramatic scene and some theoretical fragments' (Hauser, 1989, 186).

of ground is a good thing, because it allows readers to participate in the 'game' of constructing the fiction, making it as compelling as possible, and at times even creating fictions that surpass our own ability to explain them ('un jeu, on ne sait', as Mallarmé put it).[3]

To clarify these ideas, we can introduce a counterexample to Mallarmé's ungrounded, self-aware, and politically progressive fictions: those pretentious fictions that forget their own 'ungroundedness' and instead masquerade as the incarnation of eternal truths. Mallarmé's most famous example here is Richard Wagner, an impressive artist who is no longer content to produce fictions, but instead sees himself, and expects others to see him, as the communicator of immutable truths. In 1885, Mallarmé writes about '[l]e dieu Richard Wagner' (1998, 40), much as Nietzsche, two years later, would mock Wagner as 'the ventriloquist of God' (Nietzsche, 1998, 72).

If we return to Mallarmé's opening statement about the world becoming book and read it intertextually, we can thus propose that it speaks about the production of a book which will be ungrounded, open to future rewritings, and therefore a model for how to establish social relations.

The second paragraph of 'Le Livre, instrument spirituel' considers the aesthetics of the book, introducing the idea of beauty and raising the question of agency (who does what, and how?):

> Les qualités, requises en cet ouvrage, à coup sûr le génie, m'épouvantent un parmi les dénués: ne s'y arrêter et, admis le volume ne comporter aucun signataire, quel est-il: l'hymne, harmonie et joie, comme pur ensemble groupé dans quelque circonstance fulgurante, des relations entre tout. L'homme chargé de voir divinement, en raison que le lien, à volonté, limpide, n'a d'expression qu'au parallélisme, devant son regard, de feuillets. (2003, 224)

> [The qualities required for such a work, assuredly genius — which scares me, since I'm one of the ones who lack it — don't stop there, given that the volume entails no signatory, so what is it like? Hymn, harmony, and joy, a pure cluster grouped together in some shining circumstance, tying together the relations among everything. The man charged with divine sight, because of the willing limpidity of the links, has only, before his gaze, the parallelism of pages as model. (2007, 226)]

3 This reading largely refers to *La Musique et les lettres*. I am proceeding rapidly here, but the reading has been presented in greater detail by several other critics. See for instance Bourdieu, 1992, 380–83, and Marchal, 1988, 486–89.

Beginning with the question of aesthetics, the passage makes clear that the book-hymn must be harmonious and joyous – and that it should express, in an instant, the relations among everything ('des relations entre tout'). This points back to the interview with Jules Huret, where Mallarmé presented his idea about the world as book while highlighting beauty: 'le monde est fait pour aboutir à un *beau* livre' (2003, 702, emphasis added) ['the world is made to end up as a *beautiful* book']. In modern Mallarmé criticism, the idea of beauty has often been marginalized, with critics preferring to cite the formulation that opens 'Le Livre, instrument spirituel' ('tout, au monde, existe pour aboutir à un livre' [2003, 224] ['everything in the world exists to end up as a book' (2007, 226)]). This is understandable, given that the interview was penned by Huret, whereas 'Le Livre, instrument spirituel' was entirely from the hands of Mallarmé. However, as this second paragraph shows, the idea of beauty (hymn, harmony, and joy) appears in both texts, and therefore must not be overlooked. What role does beauty play?

The point of highlighting beauty is not to pull Mallarmé back to romanticism, but to emphasize that the ungrounded 'Livre' must live up to certain standards in order for it to be of general interest. Beauty becomes a marker for this general interest; it links back to the social role of the book. Beauty, which also lingers in Mallarmé's formulation about the book being grounded in the '*belles*-lettres' (emphasis added), guarantees that the fiction is more than simply a private fancy. We can therefore say that Mallarmé anticipates Antonio Negri's view of beauty when the philosopher writes: 'The beautiful is an invention of singularity which circulates and reveals itself as common in the multiplicity of subjects who participate in the construction of the world' (2011, xii). Mallarmé and Negri share the idea that beauty 'proves' (to use a Mallarméan term) that an artwork has general interest, it brings the collective together. Negri stresses this activist dimension of beauty when he suggests that 'the beautiful is [...] an imagination that has become action. Art, in this sense, is multitude' (2011, xii). Mallarmé's activism – that of 'L'Action restreinte' – plays out differently, but Negri's formulations should be allowed to resonate in our reading of Mallarmé, because they bring out the social dimension in his idea of the beautiful book.

If we look to Mallarmé's production more widely, we can trace how beauty acquires this activist role (and we can note that just like Negri, Mallarmé links beauty and the multitude). In July 1863, the young, pre-Parnassian Mallarmé advocates a conservative ideal of eternal, transcendent beauty. At the time of a Polish uprising against Russia, he asks his friend Henri Cazalis, 'Henri, est-ce que l'homme qui a fait la *Vénus de Milo* n'est pas plus grand que celui qui sauve un peuple, et ne vaudrait-il pas mieux que la Pologne succombât que de voir cet éternel hymne de marbre à la Beauté brisé?' (1998, 650) ['Henri, don't you think that the man who made the Venus de Milo is greater than the one who saves a race, and wouldn't it be preferable that Poland should fall rather than see that eternal marble hymn to Beauty lying in pieces?' (1988, 24)]. But by 1876, this dichotomy between 'the people' and 'eternal beauty' has disappeared, and Mallarmé credits Édouard Manet with inventing 'a strange new beauty' (2003, 464) that is in touch with a modern age in which 'the multitude demands to see with its own eyes' (467). As we saw at the end of the previous chapter, Mallarmé thereby offers a perfect anticipation of Georges Bataille, who in 1955 also wrote about Manet as a crucial moment in the history of art: the inventor of a modern and democratic kind of beauty.

Having seen that the social role of the book goes hand in hand with its beauty, let us turn to the complex question of agency. The second sentence in the paragraph from 'Le Livre, instrument spirituel' quoted above introduces the figure of 'l'homme chargé de voir divinement' (2003, 224) ['man charged with divine sight' (2007, 226)]. Mallarmé furthermore suggests that 'voir divinement' is to observe the correlation between pages and universe, bringing the two together in such a way that the book and the universe allow each other to make sense, so that we can understand the 'relations entre tout'. This is what Bertrand Marchal calls reading as 'divination' (1988, 500). But who is able to perform this task? Who (or what) does the hiring that is suggested by 'chargé'? Where does the initiative lie in this assemblage of writer, reader, book, and world?

Mallarmé begins by downplaying his own role. He suggests that the work needs a genius, and that he himself is simply 'un parmi les dénués' ['one of the ones who lack [genius]']. He then proposes that the book can be without a single author. It is therefore tempting to conclude that 'l'homme chargé de voir divinement' refers to the reader: that we are all invited to play the role of the genius, when we weave these relations between page and universe. That is not untrue, and some passages in Mallarmé's work very explicitly present this view. We have already seen that 'the multitude demands to see with its own eyes', and the sentence that Dr. Bonniot (Mallarmé's son-in-law) placed as an epigraph to *Igitur* also comes to mind: 'ce conte s'adresse à l'Intélligence du lecteur qui met les choses en scène, elle-même' (1998, 475) ['this story is addressed to the Intelligence of the reader which stages things itself']. Roland Barthes gave one canonical expression of this idea when he proposed that 'toute la poétique de Mallarmé consiste à supprimer l'auteur au profit de l'écriture (ce qui est, on le verra, rendre sa place au lecteur)' (1984, 64–65) ['Mallarmés entire poetics consists in suppressing the author in the interests of writing (which is, as will be seen, to restore the place of the reader)' (1977b, 143)]. This allowed him to present Mallarmé as paving the way for the famous conclusion that 'la naissance du lecteur doit se payer de la mort de l'Auteur' (69) ['the birth of the reader must be at the cost of the death of the Author' (148)].

But as I suggested in my Introduction, Barthes's insistence on the birth of the reader *coming at the expense of the author* (to use the economic vocabulary that Barthes deploys in both passages cited above) does not fully capture the complexity of Mallarmé's thoughts on this issue. First of all, Barthes seems too keen to transfer agency from writer to reader. In 1967, he reads Mallarmé's poetics in accordance with the dialectic between master and slave: the slave/reader achieving self-consciousness by opposing the master/author. But Mallarmé does not always rush towards a dialectic reversal. In the passage under consideration, it is hard to detect any such urgency; in fact, with his 'ne s'y arrêter' ['don't stop there'], Mallarmé sidelines the question of who does what. Secondly, and as a consequence of this, Barthes's reading appears too anthropocentric. In his autobiographical letter to Verlaine, Mallarmé notes that the 'le rythme' should be 'impersonnel et vivant' (1998, 788) ['impersonal and alive'], and in 'L'Action restreinte' he goes on to write: 'Impersonnifié, le volume, autant qu'on s'en sépare comme auteur, ne réclame approche de lecteur' (2003, 217) ['Impersonified, the volume, to the extent that one separates from it as author, does not demand a reader, either' (2007, 219)]. As Jacques Rancière remarks, this obviously does not mean that the book should not be read (1996, 66). It rather means that even *before it is taken up* by a reader (as it eventually should be), the book is a site for 'des relations entre tout'. Mallarmé's work is full of such speculative statements that critics have either left untouched or used to build the image of an idealist Mallarmé (which could then be dismissed).

Another example of this more speculative tendency can be found if we reconsider the 1876 text on Manet. This text is also more complicated than a simple switch of powers from the artist to the spectator would entail: nature complicates things. Mallarmé writes that nature recruits artists to work for her, so that she can express herself to – and through – the new democratic citizens:

> At that critical hour for the human race when natures [*sic*] desires to work for herself, she requires certain lovers of hers — new impersonal men placed directly in communion with the sentiment of their time — to loose the restraint of education, to let hand and eye do what they will, and thus through them, reveal herself. (2003, 468)[4]

Whereas Barthes's famous formulations suggest an opposition between author and reader (and its dialectic resolution), Mallarmé – just like Baudelaire and Cézanne did in our previous chapter – troubles this anthropocentric framework. He does this both by giving nature a role, and by presenting the book itself as place and event. Mallarmé is concerned with what I will call 'the book-event', with how 'entre les accessoires humains, il [le livre] a lieu, tout seul: fait, étant' (217) ['among human accessories, it takes place all by itself: finished, it exists' (219)]. The 'avoir lieu' is to be understood in a very active sense, as in the English translation '*take* place'. Mallarmé is interested in how the world can express itself through the book, and (remembering that the 'relations entre tout' include humans too) in how this book can also stimulate and influence writers and readers. Of course, this does not mean that Mallarmé entirely eliminates the author. The topological and active nature of the book still relates to what Mallarmé called the task ('le devoir') of the writer in 'Sauvegarde'. As we saw, Mallarmé insisted on '[l]e devoir de maintenir le livre' (272) ['the duty of maintaining the book' (290)], because this allows fiction to inform the ever-ongoing creation of the social bond.

Again, a counterexample might help to clarify. We know from Mallarmé's writings that places do not always take place. For instance, Mallarmé was not sure that Paris 1895 was taking place. He wrote about his time and place being (in) a tunnel, and he explained that in this (non-)situation, it was impossible to be contemporary to oneself: 'Il n'est pas de Présent, non — un présent n'existe pas.. Faute que se déclare la Foule, faute — de tout. Mal informé celui qui se crierait son propre contemporain' (217) ['there is no such thing as a Present, no — a present doesn't exist... For lack of the Crowd's declaring itself, for lack of — everything. Uninformed is he who would proclaim

---

4   As mentioned in Chapter 4, the original French manuscript has been lost, so I am citing the English translation which Mallarmé oversaw and authorized.

himself his own contemporary' (218)]. By contrast, the book *can* take place, and if it does, it can allow its readers to take place too. The poet's task is to make sure that this happens: 'la poésie [...] doue ainsi d'authenticité notre séjour' (782) ['poetry [...] thereby endows our stay with authenticity'].

With this short intertextual reading of the first two paragraphs in 'Le Livre, instrument spirituel', I have attempted to map the relations between three strands in Mallarmé's thinking about the book. First, we have seen that the book comes with a socio-political dimension, offering itself as a model for the social bond, the writing of which must be open-ended and collective. Second, that beauty plays a key role in the attainment of this social status. Beauty 'proves' that the book is working for the collective. It ensures that the artwork takes place, reaching beyond the private realm to a common sphere. Finally, I have considered the question of agency, in what is still an inconclusive way. Clearly, Mallarmé minimizes his claim to authorship, leaving the initiative to readers and presenting the book as a collectively produced phenomenon. But we have also seen that the book is given a form of agency which exceeds the human perspective: it takes place by itself. In order to further explore this question of agency, it is necessary to examine the issue of instrumentality: how do we interact with the book? What is the practice of the book?

The Book as Practice

As the term 'instrument' suggests, there is a hands-on aspect to Mallarmé's proposition about the book taking place, the world becoming book. This I will call 'the book as practice', and 'practice' will be understood in the sense that Isabelle Stengers gave it (see Chapter 4) when she wrote about 'giving to the situation the power to make us think' (2005, 185). We can already now see that this definition resonates with Mallarmé's writings on the book insofar as it distributes agency evenly between the practitioner and the situation, inviting us to abandon the anthropo-centric perspective.

The word 'pratique' appears in several key passages, not least when Mallarmé is considering the reading process. In 'Le Mystère dans les lettres' (1896), defending himself against Proust's critique in 'Contre l'obscurité' (1896), Mallarmé writes:

Lire —

Cette pratique —

Appuyer, selon la page, au blanc, qui l'inaugure son ingénuité, à soi, oublieuse même du, titre qui parlerait trop haut: et, quand s'aligna, dans une brisure, la moindre, disséminée, le hasard vaincu mot par mot, indéfectiblement le blanc revient, tout à l'heure gratuit, certain maintenant, pour conclure que rien au-delà et authentiquer le silence — (2003, 234)

[To read —

That practice —

To lean, according to the page, on the blank, whose innocence inaugurates it, forgetting even the title that would speak too loud: and when, in a hinge, the most minor and disseminated, chance is conquered word by word, unfailingly the blank returns, gratuitous earlier but certain now, concluding that there is nothing beyond it and authenticating the silence — (2007, 236)]

Here, the practice of reading is characterized as a movement from white to white, from silence to silence. Throughout this journey, the initial 'blanc' or silence – the white paper that precedes the title, or the silence that precedes a reading – undergoes a transformation and is replaced by a meaningful white (or silence). The 'mystère' of the title has found expression, and we are able to see more clearly the relations between various aspects of the universe. In this particular passage, Mallarmé no longer writes about mapping the 'relations entre tout' (224) ['relations among everything' (226)], but his well-known idea about overcoming chance expresses the same thought. In the next paragraph, this idea culminates in the harmonious image of the 'preuves nuptiales de l'Idée' (234) ['nuptial proofs of the Idea' (236)], Mallarmé thereby reinstating the idea of a proof also found in his writings on beauty.

We should also note how the mechanics of reading are conveyed. Mallarmé recommends a step-by-step (or word-by-word) procedure for the overcoming of chance. Through this process, the task of reassembling – and finding a place in – the universe is accomplished. In order to make this reading-practice palpable, Mallarmé is simultaneously literal and abstract: 'appuyer' might refer to the finger pressing on the page, following the sentence as it unfolds; he writes about paper, titles, words, and spaces, and in the next sentence introduces the more technical terms 'fleuron' (finial) and 'cul-de-lampe'. Going back to Anna Arnar's formulations we clearly see that this is at the same time 'wildly idealist and fundamentally pragmatic' (2010, 1).

As mentioned, Mallarmé minimizes the difference between the activity of the writer and that of the reader. It is therefore not surprising that another famous text about the practice of writing from 1896, 'L'Action restreinte', resonates strongly with the passage just considered:

> Écrire —
>
> L'encrier, cristal comme une conscience, avec sa goutte, au fond, de ténèbres relative à ce que quelque chose soit: puis, écarte la lampe.
>
> Tu remarquas, on n'écrit pas, lumineusement, sur champ obscur, l'alphabet des astres, seul, ainsi s'indique, ébauché ou interrompu; l'homme poursuit noir sur blanc. (2003, 215)
>
> [To write —
>
> The inkwell, crystalline like consciousness, with its drop, at bottom, of shadows relative to letting something be: then, take the lamp away.
>
> As you noted, one doesn't write, luminously, on a dark field; the alphabet of stars alone does that, sketched or interrupted; man writes black upon white. (2007, 216)]

Here, we find the same layout on the page (isolating the key verb, performatively surrounding it with 'blancs'), the same interplay between black and white, the same striving for light, and the same combination of the concrete ('l'encrier de cristal', 'la goutte d'encre', 'la lampe') and the metaphysical. The passage from 'Le Mystère dans les lettres' considered above linked reading to the possibility of overcoming chance; this second passage similarly suggests a cosmic architectonics relying on the communication between the white page and the black sky, the black letters and the white stars.[5] The passage thereby points to numerous other famous pages in Mallarmé's works, not least the penultimate key sentence in *Un coup de dés* – 'RIEN [...] N'AURA

---

5   On Mallarmé's play with black and white, see Harrow (2021).

EU LIEU [...] QUE LE LIEU [...] EXCEPTÉ [...] PEUT-ÊTRE [...] UNE CONSTELLATION' (1998, 384–87) ['NOTHING [...] WILL HAVE TAKEN PLACE [...] BUT THE PLACE [...] EXCEPT [...] PERHAPS [...] A CONSTELLATION' (2001, 46–49)] – where the mirroring of place, page, and sky becomes so intricate that 'constellation' demands to be taken both in its astronomical sense and as a reference to the layout of the text. In both practices (reading and writing), the physical and the metaphysical become indistinguishable: it is via the practice of reading, writing, going step by step, while paying attention to the black and the white on the page and in the sky, that Mallarmé and his reader close the gap between book and world.

Finally, *La Musique et les lettres* presents a third – and perhaps the most famous – expression of this idea of a creative, step-by-step mapping and harmonization of the structures of the world. Now, the practice is no longer theorized as reading (as in our first example) or writing (as in our second example); it is simply creative:

> La Nature a lieu, on n'y ajoutera pas; que des cités, les voies ferrées et plusieurs inventions formant notre matériel.
>
> Tout l'acte disponible, à jamais et seulement, reste de saisir les rapports, entre temps, rares ou multipliés; d'après quelque état intérieur et que l'on veuille à son gré étendre, simplifier le monde.
>
> À l'égal de créer: la notion d'un objet, échappant, qui fait défaut.
>
> Semblable occupation suffit, comparer les aspects et leur nombre tel qu'il frôle notre négligence: y éveillant, pour décor, l'ambiguïté de quelques figures belles, aux intersections. La totale arabesque, qui les relie, a de vertigineuses sautes en un effroi que reconnue; et d'anxieux accords. (2003, 67–8)

> [Nature has taken place; it can't be added to, except for cities or railroads or other inventions where we change the form, but not the fact, of material.
>
> The one available act, forever and alone, is to understand the relations, in the meantime, few or many: according to some interior state that one wishes to extend, in order to simplify the world.
>
> Equal to creating: except that the notion of object, escaping, is lacking.
>
> Some such occupation suffices, to compare aspects and count their number as it touches our intelligence, so often brushed aside: arousing, like a décor, the ambiguity of a few beautiful figures, at the intersections. The total arabesque, which ties them together, has dizzying leaps into known fears, and anxious chords. (2007, 187–88)]

Mallarmé begins with a realist axiom, insisting that nature *takes place*. This axiom resonates with what the preceding paragraph called a 'formule absolue': 'n'est que ce qui est' (2003, 67) ['only what is, is' (187)], and with the 'rien au-delà' (234) ['nothing beyond' (236)] we encountered in 'Le Mystère dans les lettres'. Next, he explains how we can come to terms with reality by an act of capture ('saisir les rapports') through which we calibrate this outside world according to some interior state ('d'après quelque état intérieur'). Mallarmé presents this activity as a creative act that transcends our consciousness ('créer: la notion d'un objet, échappant' (67) ['creating: except that the notion of object, escaping, is lacking' (187)]).[6] Finally, the last paragraph gives a clear sense of the complexity of this creative practice: we must search for nodal points between the internal and external universe, for the complex and beautiful 'figures', the sudden leaps. We do this in order to establish the overall pattern: 'la totale arabesque'.

Throughout the paragraph, Mallarmé describes this creative entanglement in the world with metaphors that draw heavily upon the arts ('décor', 'accords') and often cut across various artistic forms: 'arabesque' and 'figures', for instance, are terms from the worlds of music, linguistics, ballet, and the visual arts. It is therefore possible to hear echoes both of Mallarmé's descriptions of dance performances by Loïe Fuller and others, and of typical Mallarméan metaphors for the artistic process: constellations, fireworks, lacework, and the idea of the poet as a spider, spinning complex webs. The task is to map the universe, and mapping is a creative act that allows the mapmaker to engage intimately with the world, blurring relations between inner and outer in order to achieve a form of equilibrium which Mallarmé describes as a simplification of the world ('simplifier le monde').

Many other texts could allow us to further set out Mallarmé's assemblage, his DIY aesthetic. Somewhat like musical scores, his poems require a careful, creative appropriation; and, in both his poetry and prose, syntax plays a crucial role in this step-by-step assemblage. To concretize further, I will turn to one of the most hands-on expressions

---

6   Again, Mallarmé is returning to ideas presented in the previous paragraph, where he celebrated our capacity to invent fictions that transcend our own understanding: 'je vénère comment, par une supercherie, on projette, à quelque élévation défendue et de foudre! le conscient manque chez nous de ce qui là-haut éclate' (67) ['I admire how, by means of a trick, we project, to a great, forbidden, thunderous height, our conscious lack of what, up there, gleams' (187)].

of his creativity: the playful and meticulously crafted reading machines that Mallarmé produced for the students in his English classes at the Lycée Condorcet in Paris.

L'Anglais récréatif (displayed at the Musée départemental Stéphane Mallarmé in a 2014 exhibition) is a small, brochure-like project focusing on twelve different aspects of the English language (Marchal and Pouly, 2014). Page ten, for instance, is dedicated to the learning of prepositions. Mallarmé has drawn a beautiful flower on a small stand. A piece of string connects the centre of the flower to a hand-painted piece of cardboard shaped like a butterfly. On the page, we find a series of prepositions in French and English, according to which the butterfly can be moved. It can for instance be placed 'over' the flower or 'below' it; it can remain 'far' from the flower or go 'into' it. It is easy to imagine the exercises one could perform with this page – and one might also allow the students to invent games of their own.

Other pages in *L'Anglais récréatif* have pull systems, strings, or loose pieces that can be used to cover sections of the page as in a game of bingo. Via small movements and interactions with the page, Mallarmé clearly hopes that his students will play their way to an understanding of English numbers, verb structures, adjectives, and so on. The wider conclusions that can be drawn from this pedagogical work have to do with the invention of new reading practices. As Arnar suggests, with these games Mallarmé leaves linearity behind and points towards the more spatially complex reading practice that is required for *Un coup de dés*, and for the many poems and prose texts in which he plays with syntax (Arnar, 2010, 165). We can also note how the various ways of animating the page, the complex relations between text and colour images, and the layering and superimpositions resonate with nascent media forms such as cinema (Wall-Romana, 2013). We thus sense how *L'Anglais récréatif* offers links between practice, play, science and aesthetics that recall the ones we found in Baudelaire's 'Morale du joujou' and in our analysis of colour perception as an exercise in mutual specification (see Chapter 5). The key point is that *L'Anglais récréatif* brings together ideas about the book, instruments, play, and enlightenment. The project thereby reminds us of the etymological link between instruments and instruction: 'instrument' comes from the Latin *instruere*, 'to build upon, assemble'. This etymology links to ideas of education as a process of formation, a step-by-step practice which aims at enlightenment. As we have already seen, this is precisely what reading and writing were for Mallarmé, not least if we push this process to the point where education is no longer simply a question of moulding and enlightening individual human beings, but also a less anthropocentric endeavour which allows ideas to manifest themselves in the universe: 'les preuves nuptiales de l'Idée' (234) ['nuptial proofs of the Idea' (236)]. In this way, the pedagogical book becomes a small-scale example of the book-event.

It is important to emphasize that Mallarmé's system of reverberations between man, page, and sky makes it very difficult to say exactly who does what. To further explore this issue of distributed agency, I will now return to the writings of Gilbert Simondon. In Chapter 1, I presented Simondon's philosophy of individuation, which invited us to rethink the human being as an 'individu-milieu', and to consider agency as a continuous process of unfolding in which this 'individu-milieu' is just one part of a larger assemblage. We shall now see how Simondon theorizes instruments (or rather, technical objects[7]) as participants in the assemblage, and how this puts Mallarmé's idea of the 'spiritual instrument' in a new light.

The Production of the *Individu-Livre*

Let us begin with the notion of the technical object. In an interview from 1965, Simondon explains that he introduced this notion (featured in the title of his 1958 dissertation *Du mode d'existence des objets techniques*) in the hope that it would resonate with the more well-known terms 'objets esthétiques' and 'objets sacrés' (2014b, 400). This move indicates that he sees technical objects as far more than utilitarian; he is keen to place them in relation to art and religion – thereby establishing the exact same triangular relation we find in Mallarmé's title 'Le Livre, instrument spirituel'. Part of the relation to art has to do with technical objects being *invented*, and therefore, Simondon insists, containing a human element.[8] Many scholars in the humanities forget this human dimension of the

---

7   Simondon has a much more fine-grained vocabulary for instruments, machines, and technical objects (open and closed) than Mallarmé. I am unable to present these differences here. See Simondon, 2005.

8   In these years of 'the nonhuman turn', at a time when so many cultural theorists are drawing on Simondon, it is worth saying that he has no ambition to be nonhuman. His ontology may be non-anthropocentric (he looks at life forms that are nonorganic, biological, and technical), but he never seeks to escape the human being.

technical, and *Du mode d'existence des objets techniques* therefore opens with a polemic against the 'facile humanisme' that has established itself through its opposition to technical reality: 'Nous voudrions montrer que la culture ignore dans la réalité technique une réalité humaine, et que, pour jouer son rôle complet, la culture doit incorporer les êtres techniques sous forme de connaissance et de sens des valeurs' (2012, 9) ['We would like to show that culture ignores a human reality within technical reality and that, in order to fully play its role, culture must incorporate beings in the form of knowledge and in the form of a sense of values' (2017, 15)]. Fundamentally, Simondon continues, 'l'opposition dressée entre la culture et la technique, entre l'homme et la machine, est fausse et sans fondement; elle ne recouvre qu'ignorance ou ressentiment' (9) ['the opposition drawn between culture and technics, between man and machine, is false and has no foundation; it is merely a sign of ignorance or resentment' (16)].

Even if the idea of the technical object is useful for drawing technics closer to the sacred and the aesthetic, Simondon's use of the term 'object' is also misleading. In fact, Simondon is interested in technics as a process, a life form, a matter of evolution. A cornerstone of his thinking is that the human being and technics interact in ways that allow both parties – *and* their shared environments – to co-evolve. In the slightly later text on 'Culture et technique' (1965), he therefore describes technics as an activity through which we become entangled in the world, an ecological practice:

> Il ne s'agit donc plus ici d'une technique comme moyen, mais plutôt comme acte, comme phase d'une activité de relation entre l'homme et son milieu; au cours de cette phase, l'homme stimule son milieu en introduisant en lui une modification; cette modification se développe, et le milieu modifié propose à l'homme un nouveau champ d'action, exigeant une nouvelle adaptation, suscitant de nouveaux besoins; l'énergie du geste technique, ayant cheminé dans le milieu, revient sur l'homme et lui permet de se modifier, d'évoluer. (2014b, 320)

> [It is no longer a question, here, of technics as means, but rather as act, as a phase in the relational activity between man and his environment; through this phase, man stimulates his environment by introducing a modification; as this modification develops, the modified environment offers man a new field of action, demanding a new adaptation and arousing new needs. The energy of the technical gesture, having passed through the environment, returns to man and allows him to modify himself and evolve. (2015, 19)]

This passage can also be used to elucidate Mallarmé's idea of the book as spiritual instrument. In both cases, the technical object (or book) facilitates a practice that mediates between human being and universe in 'une activité de relation' ['relational activity'], as Simondon put it. The interplay (or feedback loop) between humans, technical objects/books, and universe is dynamic: all three components are modified in this process, all three are implicated in a process of co-evolution.

In the third and most speculative part of *Du mode d'existence des objets techniques*, the philosopher further probes this relation between art, technics, and religion. Breaking with the sober approach found in the rest of his text, he tells a story about the development of human culture. This story begins in a magical universe where humankind and world were in direct communication. Simondon writes about 'la première structure de l'univers, à savoir la réticulation des points-clefs, médiation directe entre l'homme et le monde' (2012, 251) ['the first structure of the universe, in other words the reticulation of key-points, which is the direct mediation between man and the world' (2017, 194)]. Eventually, this magic universe split into a religious universe and what he calls a 'closed' technical universe, and the risk now is that the original structure will remain forever lost.[9] This is where art steps in:

> Or, l'activité esthétique préserve précisément cette structure de réticu-lation. Elle ne peut la préserver réellement dans le monde, puisqu'elle ne peut se substituer aux techniques et à la religion, ce qui serait recréer la magie. Mais elle la préserve en construisant un monde dans lequel elle peut continuer à exister, et qui est à la fois technique et religieux; il est technique parce qu'il est construit au lieu d'être naturel [...]; il est religieux en ce sens que ce monde incorpore les forces, les qualités, les caractères de fond que les techniques laissent de côté [...], la pensée esthétique [...] fait ainsi la réalité esthétique, nouvelle médiation entre l'homme et le monde, monde intermédiaire entre l'homme et le monde. (2012, 251–52)

> [And aesthetic activity preserves precisely this structure of reticulation. It cannot really preserve it in the world, since it cannot substitute itself for

9   Simondon's focus on technical processes does not mean that he overlooks how instruments and machines can produce alienation and reification. He distin-guishes between 'open' and 'closed' technical objects, the first being processual and allowing a mediation between humankind and environment, the second being non-processual, utilitarian, and separating us from world. See, for instance, Simondon, 2014b, 319–22.

technics and religion, which would be to recreate magic. But it preserves it by constructing a world in which it can continue to exist, and which is at once technical and religious; it is technical because it is constructed rather than natural [...]; it is religious in the sense that this world incorporates the forces, the qualities, the characteristics of ground that technics leave out; [...] aesthetic thought [...] thus makes the aesthetic reality, which is a new mediation between man and the world, an intermediate world between man and the world. (2017, 194)]

This passage presents the contours of what we might call the aesthetic rescue operation of the intimate relation between human beings and universe. Despite the potentially nostalgic ring to the passage, Simondon has no illusions about how the magical unity between humans and universe could return *in reality*. Instead, the passage makes clear that art offers a way of bringing the religious and the technical together *in a work of fiction*. Art is technical, it is constructed or invented, it relies on craft. But art is also religious insofar as it addresses and relates to those fundamental forces ('les forces, les qualités, les caractères de fond') that closed technologies cannot reach. In this manner, artworks draw on technics and religion to reinvent a relation to foundational elements, creating a fiction-assemblage situated between human beings and world. Art becomes a mediating event – neither subjective nor objective, but rather, as with Mallarmé's ambition to 'saisir les rapports' ['understand the relations'], an ecological practice.

When Mallarmé engages with the place and instrument he calls 'le Livre', we witness an exchange between universe, book, and writer/reader that brings to mind Simondon's writings on technicity and individuation. In this exchange, human beings (whether readers or writers) take part in a creative practice of mapping, and through this process understand themselves as part of an environment. Borrowing from Simondon's ideas about the 'individu-milieu' (see Chapter 1), we can call this the production of the *individu-Livre*. For this *individu-Livre*, action – reading and writing, for instance – is conceived as taking part in a process of 'réticulation': it is about establishing 'des relations entre tout' ['relations among everything'] with a view to creating a book-event, and it is about how we ourselves are integral to that process (like the spider making a web). Beauty is the proof that this event has been successful, it has turned towards the public.

This connection between Mallarmé and Simondon is also made in Bernard Stiegler and Ars Industrialis's *Réenchanter le monde: La valeur esprit contre le populisme industriel* (2006).[10] This volume presents an analysis of how electronic media undermine social structures, generate political and mental health crises, and eventually, the authors presciently predicted, will bring about an economic crisis too. To resist this entropic development, Stiegler and Ars Industrialis recommend that we rethink our pharmacological media (Internet, television…). They call for a state- and EU-sponsored media politics to ensure that new media are not just left in the hands of those looking for a quick return on investment; these media must instead be used for an increase in what they – borrowing from Valéry – call 'esprit'.

A strategically important role in this argument is played by Mallarmé's 'Le Livre, instrument spirituel' and Simondon's individuation. Stiegler and Ars Industrialis argue that our media are 'instruments spirituels': 'La radio, la télévision, les ordinateurs, le réseau internet sont de nouvelles formes d'"instruments spirituels", comme Mallarmé le disait du livre' (2006, 20) ['Radio, television, computers, and the internet are new forms of "spiritual instruments," as Mallarmé said of the book' (2014, 6)]. These instruments help to shape our psychic and collective life: 'Dans *Ars Industrialis*, nous pensons que l'esprit, qui suppose *toujours* des techniques ou des technologies de l'esprit, des "instruments spirituels", est une modalité de ce que nous appelons, après le philosophe Gilbert Simondon, *l'individuation psychique et collective*' (21) ['At *Ars industrialis*, we believe that spirit, which *always* presupposes techniques or technologies of spirit, or "spiritual instruments," is a modality of what we call *psychic and individual individuation* following the philosopher Gilbert Simondon' (7)]. The significance of Mallarmé's 'Livre' is that it constitutes an ideal for contemporary spiritual instruments. This does not mean that Stiegler and Ars Industrialis are aiming to revive Mallarmé's project (although, such a revival probably would not hurt); it instead means that we can rethink contemporary media with Mallarmé's example in mind.

It is hardly surprising that the most important idea Stiegler and Ars Industrialis take from Mallarmé concerns the collaborative nature of the 'Livre'. Spiritual instruments must be participatory and dialogical. In 2006, Wikipedia and open-source software are cited as examples

10   The organization Ars Industrialis – whose full name 'Ars Industrialis, association internationale pour une politique industrielle des technologies de l'esprit' gives a good idea of its ambitions – was founded by Georges Collins, Marc Crépon, Catherine Perret, Bernard Stiegler, and Caroline Stiegler in 2005.

of such media. This is what the authors write about the *practice* of Linux:

> les 'utilisateurs' des logiciels en sont par principe des *practiciens* [...] ils contribuent à l'individuation des logiciels (car il y a une individuation technique comme il y a une individuation psychique et une individuation sociale): leurs pratiques sont ce qui fait évoluer les logiciels eux-mêmes, dans la mesure où les praticiens des logiciels en sont aussi les développeurs: ils mettent en œuvre un savoir qu'ils forment par ces pratiques mêmes. (53)

> [the 'users' of [Linux] are in principle the *practitioners*, [...] they contribute to the individuation of software (because there is a technical individuation as there is a psychic individuation and a social individuation): their practices are what bring about the evolution of software itself, to the extent that the practitioners of the software are also the developers – they put to work a knowledge that they form by these very practices. (36)]

Also worth emphasizing is the 'ex-centric' nature of such individuating collaborations. Because Stiegler and Ars Industrialis build from Simondon, individuation unfolds as the mediation of a pre-individual environment that is both social and more broadly ecological in a process that is always incomplete. In other words, no individual is closed off, no individual will exhaust the pre-individual milieu: 'S'individuer, c'est se transformer: la trans-formation des modes de vie est la loi de la forme de vie humaine – de l'*existence*. L'homme ne fait pas que sub-sister: il ex-iste, et cela signifie qu'il se trans-forme' (40) ['To individuate is to transform oneself; the trans-formation of ways of life is the law of human life forms – of *existence*. Man does not just sub-sist; he ex-sists, and that means he trans-forms himself' (30, translation modified)].

It should be noted that even if Stiegler and Ars Industrialis emphasize the prefixes 'ex-' and 'trans-', they are more concerned with subject-*constitution* than I have been here.[11] It can also be argued that the various

---

11   See for instance: 'le locuteur *s*'individue, c'est-à-dire *se* trans-forme et devient ce qu'*il* est, par les énoncés qu'il produit (aussi bien que par ceux qu'il reçoit, mais qu'il est ne reçoit *en effet* que pour autant qu'il y répond par d'autres énoncés: tel est le *dialogisme* de la langue)' (49) ['the speaker individuates *himself*, that is, trans-forms *himself* and becomes who *he* is by the utterances that he produces (as well as by those that he receives, but which *in effect* he does not receive but to the extent that he responds to them with other utterances: such is the *dialogism* of language)' (34)].

milieux prioritized by Stiegler and Ars Industrialis are more anthropocentric than those I found in Verlaine, Baudelaire, and Mallarmé. For instance, *Réenchanter le monde* mentions how we keep becoming through historical mediations (inheriting and adopting from previous societies), intercultural mediations (adopting from foreign cultures), and linguistic practices: 'Le locuteur est celui qui *pratique* sa langue, et non celui qui l'"utilise": on n'emploie pas et on n'utilise pas sa langue: on est *constitué* par elle' (49) ['The speaker is he who *practices* his language, not he who "uses" or "employs" it. One neither employs nor uses a language: one is *constituted* by it' (34, slightly modified)]. Stiegler and Ars Industrialis focus on human individuation in human environments. My interest in *Réenchanter le monde* has to do with its clear focus on the role of 'spiritual instruments' in these always ongoing individuations. The volume demonstrates how the practice of spiritual instruments turns us outwards, produces ecological awareness, emphasizes relationality, and increases our psychic energy, whereas other instruments close us off, exhaust us, lead to entropy and burn-outs. To reuse the terms of the volume's subtitle: some instruments enhance 'la valeur esprit', others feed 'le populisme industriel'. Mallarmé belongs in the first category, and he articulates this very beautifully when he explains what 'l'art littéraire' is capable of:

> Son sortilège, à lui, si ce n'est libérer, hors d'une poignée de poussière ou réalité sans l'enclore, au livre, même comme texte, la dispersion volatile soit l'esprit, qui n'a que faire de rien outre la musicalité de tout. (2003, 65)

> [The literary charm, if it's not to liberate, outside of a fistful of dust or reality without enclosing it, in the book, even as a text, the volatile dispersal of the spirit, which has to do with nothing but the musicality of everything. (2007, 184–85)]

This complicated description of literature's sorcery appears first in *La Musique et les lettres* and is then (self-)quoted by Mallarmé in 'Crise de vers'. In the preceding sentence, the poet distances himself from those who want to describe or represent nature, instead insisting on the importance of 'suggestion' and 'allusion'.[12] In the sentence cited above,

---

12　An important dimension of Mallarmé's critique of representation (and his preference for suggestion and allusion) is political. The political can be understood in (at least) two complementary ways. As we have already seen, when Mallarmé advocates suggestion and allusion he seeks to empower readers: we become more active, we participate in (and are given a chance to individuate through) the spiritual

Mallarmé then institutes a complicated play between liberation and enclosure. Literature is not an act of capturing reality. It is rather an act of liberating the musicality of everything by using the book. If literature is enchanting, it is because it allows the world to become musical and free by exploding 'the real'. Like Stiegler and Ars Industrialis, Mallarmé presents literature as a reenchantment of the world. But it is also clear that when Mallarmé speaks about 'esprit', this 'dispersion volatile', is not just 'human spirit'. The 'esprit', what literature releases through 'textualisation', is a musicality that belongs to the world – an 'humble antienne' ['humble refrain'] (Verlaine), a 'symphonie' (Baudelaire), 'la musicalité de tout' ['the musicality of everything'] (Mallarmé). In the next chapter, I shall further explore this 'esprit', comparing it to the notion of 'mind' found in the anthropology of Gregory Bateson.[13]

On this basis, we can now return to the complex question of agency. Earlier, I asked: who does the recruiting when the human is 'chargé de voir divinement' ['charged with divine sight']? Does the initiative lie with the book, the writer, nature, language, or the reader? As we saw, Barthes answered that Mallarmé's poetics consists in overthrowing the author in order to empower the reader. Famous passages from Mallarmé's writing corroborate this reading, but we also found sentences that describe how nature recruits 'certain lovers of hers…', and how 'the book' takes place by itself. My view is not that Mallarmé is changing his mind or contradicting himself. Rather, the point is that the spiritual instrument cannot be captured in the subject–object relations that questions of agency frequently presuppose; Mallarmé's thinking is difficult to contain within a dialectical, anthropocentric framework. The logic of emergence that Mallarmé associates with the 'Livre' is one of *co*-emergence. Instead of

instrument. But it is also worth saying that, according to Mallarmé, the language of representation – *l'universel reportage* – relies on an economic logic. It relies on a logic of equivalence, where the value of words is determined by their ability to represent. This is why Mallarmé compares the conventional use of language to the act of 'mettre dans la main d'autrui en silence une pièce de monnaie' (2003, 212) ['put[ting] into someone else's hand in silence a coin' (2007, 210)]. To move beyond representation is therefore also to move beyond an economy of equivalence.

13   Interestingly, Stiegler and Ars Industrialis specify that their word 'esprit' should be taken in the sense of the English word 'mind' (2006, 27). However, they associate 'mind' with Hannah Arendt's *The Life of the Mind* (1981), not with the work of Bateson. As we shall see, Bateson's notion of mind is less tied to the human being than that of Arendt, Stiegler, and Ars Industrialis (and in my view, it is therefore closer to the poets studied here).

trying to reduce the issue of agency, it is more appropriate to say that the book takes place in and as a constellation; it modulates readers, writers, and their associated milieus, and is itself modulated in that process. It is these movements that Mallarmé terms 'spirituel[s]', and it is these movements that contemporary Mallarmé criticism has tended to marginalize (see Chapter 6).

Mallarmé is thus a poet with an ecological conception of individuation. This is one of the ways in which his poetry resonates with twenty-first-century thought: with theories about our Anthropocene condition, and with philosophies about our technologically mediated processes of individuation. He understands the human being as profoundly caught up in the structures of the world, and the book as an instrument for producing this condition, understanding it, and navigating it. Mallarmé's key metaphors (constellations, fireworks, spiderwebs, lacework, etc.) all highlight the relational nature of poetic work. This is why he so frequently writes about 'relations' and 'rapports'; and when he insists on the importance of syntax – 'il faut une garantie — La Syntaxe —' (2003, 232–33) ['We need a guarantee — Syntax —' (2007, 234–35)][14] – this Greek word must similarly be understood in its etymological sense of arranging, combining, composing. Mallarmé's emphasis on the relational work of the poet is so strong that when his 1893 letter to Edmund Gosse presents the etymology of another Greek keyword ('Musique') he almost manages to make it synonymous with 'syntaxe': 'Employez Musique dans le sens grec, au fond signifiant Idée ou rythme entre des rapports' (Mallarmé, 1995a, 614) ['Use the term Music in the Greek sense, meaning truly the Idea or rhythm between connections'].[15] Let us not forget either that Mallarmé is an author who took the unusual step of naming a key character after a conjunctive adverb (igitur), i.e. a word that mediates and connects between two different thoughts. With all these metaphors and concepts, Mallarmé is looking to link up, to tune; not to invent ex nihilo. (We shall return to relational work in the sixth chapter, where we will also consider some of the risks it involves.)

Among the many Mallarméan metaphors associated with relationality and 'poetry as patterned absence' (Pearson, 1996, 268) – fireworks,

---

14 Mallarmé introduces a double line-break before and after 'La Syntaxe —', visually communicating that syntax plays a pivotal role (the word 'pivot' is in Mallarmé's text).

15 A more conventional etymology would note that 'musique' refers to the art of the muses, and that the word 'muse' is linked to literary art in particular.

chandeliers, lacework, spiderwebs, fountains, etc. – constellations occupy a particularly important position (appearing in key texts such as 'Ses purs ongles…' and *Un coup de dés*). Why? Because no metaphor better expresses this idea of relationality. In some ways constellations are like colours, they are neither subjective nor objective (neither eggs nor chickens, as Rosch, Thompson, and Varela put it in Chapter 4). It is tempting to say they do not 'exist': when we look at the night sky there are no constellations, there is only a chaotic sea of stars. But constellations are obviously not subjective projections either, the stars are there in the sky. The act of naming is magical, it creates, it makes the constellation exist as a constellation. By 'naming well' we may become poets. When Mallarmé compares poems to constellations he therefore distances himself from the idea of poetry as representation and drives home the idea of performativity. In this manner, naming (or making poems) can be understood as an act through which world and poet create each other.[16]

Many scholars worry about the process-relational conceptions of individuation found in the work of philosophers like Whitehead and Simondon, and associated with Mallarmé, Verlaine, and Baudelaire here. They worry that if we understand ourselves as mediators who are being mediated as we mediate, we lose all individual human agency. But these ideas about our embeddedness in the world do not rob human beings of agency, and they certainly do not clear us of responsibility. Quite the contrary. As N. Katherine Hayles points out in the previously mentioned *Unthought*, which examines how certain forms of cognition are shared by humans and their technological inventions (see Chapter 2), it remains true that:

> the largest transformative forces on the planet today are undoubtedly human agency and human interventions, the effects of which are being

16   In *Pragmatism* (1907) William James is interested in constellations too. First, he makes an argument about our ability to order: 'We carve out groups of stars in the heavens, and call them constellations, and the stars patiently suffer us to do so – tho if they knew what we were doing, some of them might feel much surprised at the partners we had given them' (James, 2019, 91). Next, he wonders about the 'aesthetics' of ordering: 'Suppose a universe composed of seven stars, and nothing else but three human witnesses and their critic. One witness names the stars "Great Bear"; one calls them "Charles's Wain"; one calls them the "Dipper." Which human addition has made the best universe of the given stellar material?' (93) James does not leave his question fully unanswered: via a humorous anecdote he suggests that 'a culinary utensil' (92) certainly does not cut it; in other words, like Mallarmé he suggests that aesthetics and beauty are key criteria when human beings and the world come together to make sense.

registered in climate change, the worldwide loss of habitat for nonhuman animals, the idea of the Anthropocene, and in the reality that human actions are unleashing forces far beyond our ability to control them. (2017, 83)

In this situation we must search for 'inflection points at which systemic dynamics can be decisively transformed' (203). In other words, some of the (generally collective) modulations that the process-relational thinkers theorize can be highly significant, with a profound impact. Hayles thereby follows Félix Guattari, who argued in *Les Trois écologies* that precise, local interventions can effect wide-ranging, systemic change; 'micropolitics' is not minor politics (Guattari, 1989).

When it comes to the interpretation of Mallarmé's writings, the questions are: does Mallarmé distribute agency liberally across book-instruments, readers, writers, nature, and language? Does he present individuation as a radically ecological practice? Is the *individu-Livre* an appropriate way to describe the figure emerging from the poetic lacework? I have argued that Mallarmé's conceptualization of the book as spiritual instrument guides us to an affirmative answer to all of these questions, and that his imagination is therefore at once more wildly idealist and more practically *bricoleuse* than is often assumed. For Mallarmé, instrumentality has no necessary link to reification and objectification; on the contrary, the practice of (or play with) the instrumental, spiritual book produces an *individu-Livre* that can still inspire readers as we advance into the twenty-first century. Mallarmé is exploring key contemporary questions about what it means to be an environment, which forms of individuation are facilitated by our different instruments, and – going back to the issue of agency – how an 'action restreinte', a micropolitics, may help produce new constellations. He is challenging the idea of the liberal, humanist individual, thinking instead in terms of what contemporary critics call assemblages. In our next chapter we shall develop these ideas further, by placing them in the context of both mid-twentieth-century theories of information and communication (cybernetics, in particular) and early-twenty-first-century media studies. First of all, the sixth chapter will demonstrate that Mallarmé's idealism goes hand in hand with a more dystopian reading of subjective mediation and of individuation.

CHAPTER SIX

Mallarmé's Demonic Media Theory

Continuing the examination of how Mallarmé's writings relate to the present, the first and longest part of this final chapter will focus on the early prose poem 'Le Démon de l'analogie'. With a slight hyperbole, it could be said that this poem is so contemporary that only today do we have the vocabulary to understand it. This vocabulary is found in twenty-first-century media studies. The first argument of the chapter will be that 'Le Démon de l'analogie' explores what it is like to be modulated by code. In doing so, the poem (like previously studied texts by Verlaine and Baudelaire) operates with a process-relational understanding of human subjectivity, which the current chapter analyses with the help of texts by Mark Hansen, Steven Shaviro, and Eugene Thacker. Whereas Chapter 5 mainly looked at the optimistic aspects of the *individu-Livre*, the first two-thirds of the current chapter will bring out a more dystopian story. The last third will then place Mallarmé's writings in relation to cybernetics, and in the process it will aim to balance the relationship between Mallarmé's utopian and more dystopian tendencies. This section argues that Mallarmé's work hosts ambiguities that have continued to characterize twentieth- and twenty-first-century relations to media and technology.

Demonic Modulations

'Le Démon de l'analogie' was first published in 1874 under the title 'La Pénultième'. The moment of its conception has been debated, with some critics suggesting it was written as early as 1864 (see Lyu, 1998). However, as Roger Pearson and others have noted, there is 'no clear evidence that any version existed before Mallarmé sent one to Villiers de l'Isle-Adam in 1867' (1996, 74). The text immediately became a *succès de scandale* in the fairly narrow Parisian circles that read Mallarmé's poetry. In *Symbolistes et décadents* (1902), Gustave Kahn describes how '[l]a presse [...] avait accueilli d'un déferlement de rires la *Pénultième*' (1977, 16) ['the press [...] welcomed *The Penultimate* with a tidal wave of mockery']. In an oft-quoted sentence, he goes on to explain that the poem 'était alors le *nec plus ultra* de l'incompréhensible, le Chimborazo de l'infranchissable, et le casse-tête chinois' (138) ['was the last word in impenetrability, the pinnacle of unfathomability, and the ultimate conundrum']. The poem quickly acquired the status of a challenge: come figure me out, if you can!

This is hardly surprising, given that the poem opens by taunting the reader: 'Des paroles inconnues chantèrent-elles aussi sur vos levres?' (Mallarmé, 2003, 86) ['Have unknown words ever played about your lips [...]?' (2007, 17)] With this question Mallarmé inscribes himself in the tradition of Baudelaire's *Au Lecteur* ('hypocrite lecteur, – mon semblable, – mon frère!' [1975, 6], ['hypocritical reader, – my kindred spirit, – my brother!' (2008, 7)]), placing the reader between two equally unenticing positions. In Baudelaire's poem, we can accept the friend- liness of the narratorial voice, but must then also admit to the charge of hypocrisy, or we can distance ourselves from hypocrisy, but then lose the brotherly relation to the poet. In Mallarmé's poem, we can move close to the poetic voice, but must then also accept the 'paroles inconnues' ['unknown words'], or we can take on the hermeneutic challenge and begin to separate ourselves from the poetic voice by analysing the words. In both poems, the ambiguous address therefore floats somewhere between challenge and complicity – and this serves to heighten the stakes of the challenge and limit the sense of complicity: we are in the realm of the uncanny.

Multiple twentieth-century critics have taken on the challenge, seeking to explain the ambiguities. In one of the most famous readings of the text, Barbara Johnson highlights this aspect of the poem's reception, arguing that no matter how critics interpret the poem they are themselves in the grip of the demon: 'ils se servent tous de l'analogie comme d'un instrument interprétatif' (1979, 197) ['they all use analogy as an interpretative tool']. The poem is contagious.

LE DÉMON DE L'ANALOGIE

Des paroles inconnues chantèrent-elles sur vos lèvres, lambeaux maudits d'une phrase absurde?

Je sortis de mon appartement avec la sensation propre d'une aile glissant sur les cordes d'un instrument, traînante et légère, que remplaça une voix prononçant les mots sur un ton descendant: 'La Pénultième est morte', de façon que

> *La Pénultième*

finit le vers et

> *Est morte*

se détacha de la suspension fatidique plus inutilement en le vide de signification. Je fis des pas dans la rue et reconnus en le son *nul* la corde tendue de l'instrument de musique, qui était oublié et que le glorieux Souvenir certainement venait de visiter de son aile ou d'une palme et, le doigt sur l'artifice du mystère, je souris et implorai de vœux intellectuels une spéculation différente. La phrase revint, virtuelle, dégagée d'une chute antérieure de plume ou de rameau, dorénavant à travers la voix entendue, jusqu'à ce qu'enfin elle s'articula seule, vivant de sa personnalité. J'allais (ne me contentant plus d'une perception) la lisant en fin de vers, et, une fois, comme un essai, l'adaptant à mon parler; bientôt la prononçant avec un silence après 'Pénultième' dans lequel je trouvais une pénible jouissance: 'La Pénultième' puis la corde de l'instrument, si tendue en l'oubli sur le son *nul*, cassait sans doute et j'ajoutais en matière d'oraison: 'Est morte'. Je ne discontinuai pas de tenter un retour à des pensées de prédilection, alléguant, pour me calmer, que, certes, pénultième est le terme du lexique qui signifie l'avant-dernière syllabe des vocables, et son apparition, le reste mal abjuré d'un labeur de linguistique par lequel quotidiennement sanglote de s'interrompre ma noble faculté poétique: la sonorité même et l'air de mensonge assumé par la hâte de la facile affirmation étaient une cause de tourment. Harcelé, je résolus de laisser les mots de triste nature errer eux-mêmes sur ma bouche, et j'allai murmurant avec l'intonation susceptible de condoléance: 'La Pénultième est morte, elle est morte, bien morte, la désespérée Pénultième', croyant par là satisfaire l'inquiétude, et non sans le secret espoir de l'ensevelir en l'amplification de la psalmodie quand, effroi! — d'une magie aisément déductible et nerveuse — je sentis que j'avais, ma main réfléchie par un vitrage de boutique y faisant le geste d'une caresse qui descend sur quelque chose, la voix même (la première, qui indubitablement avait été l'unique).

> Mais où s'installe l'irrécusable intervention du surnaturel, et le commencement de l'angoisse sous laquelle agonise mon esprit naguère seigneur c'est quand je vis, levant les yeux, dans la rue des antiquaires instinctivement suivie, que j'étais devant la boutique d'un luthier vendeur de vieux instruments pendus au mur, et, à terre, des palmes jaunes et les ailes enfouies en l'ombre, d'oiseaux anciens. Je m'enfuis, bizarre, personne condamnée à porter probablement le deuil de l'inexplicable Pénultième.

Unlike most of Mallarmé's later writings, the hermeticism of 'Le Démon de l'analogie' does not begin at the syntactical level. In later texts, as we saw in the previous chapter, the poet – 'profondément et scrupuleusement syntaxier' (Mallarmé, 1995b, 95) ['profoundly and scrupulously syntactician'] – asks his readers to work carefully with the complicated syntax of the sentences, to determine how subjects, objects, and verbs relate. In 'Le Démon de l'analogie', the syntax is more straightforward and the difficulty of the poem lies less in what it *says* than in what it *means*. The strange facts in the case of 'Le Démon de l'analogie' can therefore be paraphrased.

After the opening question, a man leaves his apartment feeling the sensation of a wing gliding down the strings of an instrument. The poem begins with a sensation, with a narrator being played like an instrument. Before the end of the second sentence, this sensation gives way to a mysterious refrain: 'La Pénultième est morte' ['The Penultimate is dead']. The main part of the text then recounts how the narrator tries to get to grips with this haunting sentence.

He first describes – and the poem graphically shows – how the sentence appears 'sur un ton descendant' ['with a downward intonation' (17)], with a line-break after the first two words ('La Pénultième [—] est morte'). This break directs our attention to the syllable 'nul', which has now become the penultimate syllable before the line-break.[1] As the narrator remarks, the break thereby doubly suspends the sentence 'en le vide de la signification' ['in the absence of signification' (17)]: read with a pause in the middle, the verse not only speaks *about* negation, it also formally puts emphasis on the negative (*nul*). Having detected this play between semantics and form, the narrator concludes that he has understood the trick of the sentence ('le doigt sur le mystère' ['my finger on the secret behind the mystery's artifice' (17)]) and aims to move on: 'je souris et implorai de vœux intellectuels une spéculation différente'

---

1 See Lyu, 1998, 572, n. 21 for debates about versification in the key sentence.

['I smiled and pleaded, with all my intellectual wishes, for a different speculation' (17)].

But the sentence comes back, autonomous: 'elle s'articula seule, vivant de sa personnalité' ['it articulated itself all alone, animated by its own personality' (17)]. The narrator then engages in a play with the signifiers. However, this play offers no reprieve. Instead, he is once again pulled back to the syllable 'nul'. He imagines that the string of the instrument snaps and then he gives gravitas to the pronunciation of 'est morte' ['is dead']. He claims to be adapting the sentence to his own way of speaking ('l'adaptant à mon parler' ['making it fit my speech' (17)]), appropriating it, but he seems to overestimate himself: this is rather a case of the narrator adjusting to the sentence, coming under its spell.

The third attempt at mastering the refrain is *lexical*. The narrator seeks out the dictionary definition of 'pénultième' in the hope that it will calm him. He explains that this approach links to his daily practice as a poet, but he nevertheless feels that the detour by way of the dictionary is a form of cheating. The attempt therefore backfires: the threat of the sentence increases, as if nourished by 'la hâte de la facile affirmation' ['the haste and facility of the affirmation' (18)] of the lexical meaning of 'la pénultième' ('certes, pénultième est le terme du lexique qui signifie l'avant-dernière syllabe des vocables' ['of course "penultimate" is a lexical term signifying the next-to-last syllable of a word' (18)]).

The final attempt sees the poet–narrator revert to his playful signifier-based modulations. Again, the relation between sentence and poet is ambiguous. Previously, he claimed to adapt the sentence to his own speech; now he decides to let 'les mots de triste nature errer eux-mêmes sur ma bouche' ['the sad words just wander on my lips' (18)]. Clearly, we have returned to the poem's opening question. At the same time, he acknowledges his 'secret espoir' ['secret hope' (18)] to allay his anxiety via these modulations. Overall, no progress has been made: the poet still hopes to control the sentence, but he remains unable to move beyond the threat it seemingly carries.

At this point, reality breaks in – in two stages. The narrator suddenly discovers his own reflection in a shop window and sees that his hand is gliding down 'quelque chose': the instrument he has been referring to throughout. He recognizes that the voice that pursued him was his own. We thus have a mirror-scene that allows for a brief moment of self-recognition. But then he looks through the shop window and discovers that he is standing in front of an instrument-maker. On display are string instruments adorned with feathers from old birds.

The poem previously evoked feathers and instruments, and it therefore seems as though the various associations generated by the mysterious sentence have materialized before the eyes of the narrator. Terrified, he ends the poem with a sentence that both speaks about and performs the confusion that overwhelms him: 'Je m'enfuis, bizarre, personne condamnée à porter probablement le deuil de l'inexplicable Pénultième' ['I fled, strange person [bizarre], probably condemned forever to wear mourning for the inexplicable Penultimate' (18)]. Here, the unresolved nature of the anecdote is expressed by the narrator's impression of being forever stuck in a labour of mourning. But rather than offering a clear conclusion on the impossibility of concluding, the sentence resolves to an awkward 'probablement' and the white-flag word 'bizarre': is he calling himself bizarre? Is he describing the incident as bizarre? Is he speaking to himself? This forces the insecurity onto the readers, who are left to establish their own way of relating to 'l'inexplicable' – the term that, as many critics have noted, becomes the penultimate word in the poem.

The paraphrase above has presented the struggles of the narrator in four phases. In truth, these phases are difficult to separate. 'Le Démon de l'analogie' is a poem about flows and modulations. We go from a circum-scribed space (the apartment within which the sensation arises), possibly down a set of stairs (in *Igitur*, this is explicitly stated; in 'Le Démon de l'analogie', Mallarmé instead writes about the mysterious sentence being expressed 'sur un ton descendant' ['with a downward intonation'] whilst employing a mise-en-page that visualizes this downwards movement), and into the street where the sentence begins to drift, exactly like our narrator–flâneur. Towards the end of the poem, the narrator briefly stops, before realising he is condemned to perpetual unrest. Throughout the poem, it is suggested that all spaces are at the same time physical, mental, and textual. 'Le Démon de l'analogie' is thus a poem about a man walking through the streets…, a man walking a sentence through his mind…, a sentence walking across the lips of a man…, a sentence taking a man and his mind for a walk…, a man getting lost in a sentence, getting lost in his mind, getting lost in the streets of a city (which we assume to be Paris).

It is helpful to point back to the previous chapter and emphasize that when the narrator is playing (and being played by) the mysterious sentence, he is practising on a demonic, spiritual instrument. When the words run over his lips, they inform the process of individuation, reshaping our narrator. Already in 1868, when sending the 'Sonnet allégorique de lui-même' to Henri Cazalis, Mallarmé suggested that poetry can modulate subjectivities: '[e]n se laissant aller à le [le sonnet]

murmurer plusieurs fois on éprouve une sensation assez cabalistique'
(1998, 731) ['if you allow yourself to murmur it several times, you will
experience a rather cabalistic sensation']; and many years later, in *La
Musique et les lettres* (1894), he more explicitly commented on the
links between modulation, rhythm, and psyche, defining *le vers libre*
as a 'modulation (dis-je, souvent) individuelle, parce que toute âme est
un nœud rythmique' (2003, 64) ['an individual modulation (as I say
frequently), because every soul is a rhythmic tangle' (2007, 184)].

At this point, two paths open up for the reader. We can part ways
with the narrator and try to explain the mysterious sentence-event. This
is what most readers have done – thereby (often implicitly) working
their way to a negative answer to the opening question ('Des paroles
inconnues chantèrent-elles sur vos lèvres [...]?' [76], ['Have unknown
words ever played about your lips [...]?' (17)]), positioning themselves as
being wiser than the narrator. An example of this approach can be found
in Yves Bonnefoy's short book on the poem, *Le Secret de la Pénultième*
(2005). As the title suggests, Bonnefoy reads the text like a detective
story. He draws on psychoanalysis, discovers a sexual dimension in
the various elements in the shop window; and when he has finished his
work of translation, he concludes that the poem expresses Mallarmé's
semi-ironic regret about inventing a radically new and post-romantic
form of poetry. The last sentence in Bonnefoy's book very emphatically
concludes that 'Le Démon de l'analogie' 'c'est déjà toute son œuvre
à venir, et une clef pour déchiffrer son destin' (51) ['is already all of
his future works, and a key to deciphering his destiny']. Secrets, keys,
deciphering, and the perfect anticipation and explanation of everything
that was to come – nothing remains 'inexplicable' in this reading.

I would like to take a different approach to the poem, staying close
to the narrator and his confusion. I will – perhaps disappointingly
– already now conclude that the sentence is 'inexplicable' and the
experience 'bizarre'. From its opening question, the poem puts the reader
in the position of the protagonist: we are struggling to understand the
sentence. At the end of the poem, we have come no further. 'Le Démon
de l'analogie' thereby becomes a poem about the inadequacies of textual
analysis. In fact, it explicitly thematizes the impotence of some of our
best-known interpretative frameworks.

Most obviously, it singles out the limitations of lexical analysis.
When the poet seeks help in the dictionary definition of 'la pénultième',
he only sinks deeper into the quicksand of the sentence. As Barthes
reminded Picard in *Critique et vérité*, words are polysemic, dictionaries

do not simply stabilize meaning (1999, 18–19). Rather the poem is demonstrating the demonic derailment of analogical thinking and its concomitant categorizations. Other textual approaches prove equally impotent. For reasons that will become obvious shortly, it is particularly interesting to observe that the poem puts a conventional phenomenological framework under pressure. In his first attempt at coming to terms with the sentence, the narrator moves smoothly from sense-perception ('la sensation propre' ['the distinct sensation' (17)]) to a structure of meaning ('le doigt sur l'artifice du mystère' ['putting my finger on the secret' (17)]) and an accompanying sense of subjectivity, self-certainty ('je souris et implorai […] une spéculation différente' ['I smiled and pleaded […] for a different speculation' (17)]). However, it soon appears that something was lost in this process – something has escaped the narrator and the smile disappears. The poet therefore gives up on phenomenology and its prioritization of perception ('ne me contentant plus d'une perception' ['no longer contenting myself with mere perception' (17)]) and instead tries other, equally unsuccessful approaches.

Most prominent among these are the more performative, signifier-based plays on the sentence, which the narrator resorts to on two occasions. The poem clearly warns us against this practice too. We may be able to play around with the words, but this engagement with the matter of language allows for no taming of the sentence. Rather, the modulations turn out to be risky practices in which the poet gets caught up in a process he cannot control.

The ending to the poem makes the inadequacy of these various strategies of textual analysis evident. When the narrator finally stands in front of the shop window, we may hope for self-consciousness and self-identity, but this hope quickly gives way to the poet's fall into the bizarre and never-to-be-claimed. But at the same time – and this is obviously crucial – *the sentence works*. Mediation takes place. The poem brings us from the sensation-sentence to the materialization of the sensation: the shop window, the wings, the instruments. In the end, this is exactly why the words are so disturbing. The sentence produces reality, but the narrator and reader find themselves looped out of this effective mediation between text and reality, 'looped out' and at the same time influenced by the experience. In other words, the experience of the narrator is one of being incapable of accessing what nevertheless influences him. It is this paradoxical 'experience', and its implications for our understanding of individuation, which we shall now attempt to analyse in the next section.

Mallarméan Individuation and Twenty-First-Century Media

To understand and describe the experience of the narrator (and the reader), let us turn to the work of media scholar Mark Hansen and, in particular, to his 2015 monograph *Feed-Forward: On the Future of Twenty-First-Century Media*. As its title indicates, this book is not a text about Mallarmé (or poetry) and our borrowings will therefore be selective.

At the most foundational level, the grounds for this foray into media theory are that Mallarmé's poem shares with Hansen and other contemporary media theorists the following idea: we are living in an all-encompassing data ecology. We are, as one of Hansen's previous monographs put it, *Bodies in Code* (2006). What status do we have in this data ecology? We are formed in – and of – it; we are part of it, but we are not prioritized. Hansen's recent writings are inspired by philosophers such as Alfred North Whitehead and Gilbert Simondon. His examination of how we (continuously) come to be – of individuation – therefore begins with the environment, and not with the individual. In *Feed-Forward*, Hansen theorizes with Whitehead.

Hansen explains that Whitehead's 'entire speculative scheme is predicated precisely on the notion that consciousness *is* the function of hosting, that consciousness itself is nothing other than the hosting of other entities that act through it' (2015, x). In this scheme, 'we know ourselves as a function of unification of a plurality of things *which are other than ourselves*. Cognition discloses an event as being an activity, organizing a real togetherness *of alien things*' (x). This is why Whitehead calls the 'subject' a 'society': 'a certain organization of other, more elemental processes, *all of which are subjective in their own right*' (3).

But we are not only hosts, we are also being hosted – we are part of a bigger society. In Whitehead's ontology, the 'universe' is '*an entity (the supreme society) that necessarily includes (or as I prefer to say, implicates) humans within it and within each and every element comprising it*' (16). Since these two societies – consciousness and the universe – necessarily operate together, we understand that Whitehead presents a 'radically environmental perspective on agency: [...] every actual occasion implicates *the entirety of the universe*' (10). Hansen builds on this ontology when he theorizes individuation in our contemporary data environments.

As Hansen notes, most of the traffic on the Internet today is between computers and only thereafter, and indirectly, does it involve human beings. Storage is no longer primarily carried out directly by and for humans, but rather by computers, to allow them to communicate as smoothly as possible. In the present media ecology, human beings are not privileged.[2] And even if we are profoundly 'implicated', a substantial part of this communication escapes the human sensorial apparatus. Traditional phenomenology, with its focus on the *human* perception, is therefore under pressure, as the gap between experience and perception is opening:

> Human experience is currently undergoing a fundamental transformation caused by the complex entanglement of humans within networks of media technologies that operate predominantly, if not almost entirely, outside the scope of human modes of awareness (consciousness, attention, sense perception, etc.) (5)

In other words, we are largely unaware of the hosting we do. One of Hansen's aims with *Feed-Forward* is therefore to develop a twenty-first-century phenomenology that is commensurate with contemporary media ecologies. His book is therefore not arguing for a deprioritization of the human (his philosophy is not 'nonhuman'); rather, his optimistic project is to 'remake consciousness so that it can continue to be a crucial resource for human experience' (25). In order to do so, Hansen is interested in the bionic technologies that give access to that which 'largely evades the grasp of perception' (151), to the form of 'sensibility that is prior to the division of the subject from the world' (24). He calls this pre-perceptual region 'worldly sensibility' and describes 'human sensibility as a particular mode of such self-sensing' (30).[3] Drawing on Jan Patočka and Gilbert Simondon, as well as Whitehead (and anticipating the systematization of N. Katherine Hayles [see Chapter 2]), Hansen therefore presents an understanding of 'subjectivity' which recognizes higher-order cognitive functions, but also sees us as collective, processual, and ecological becomings:

2   When surfing on the Internet we are frequently reminded that we are not alone: we have to tick the box 'I am not a robot', and sometimes pass a small test to prove our humanness. (The fact that most of us occasionally fail this test speaks about the state in which we usually do our surfing, about the effects of technological individuation.)

3   As suggested in Chapter 2, when the poetic voice in Verlaine's 'C'est l'extase langoureuse' hesitantly speaks about an 'humble antienne' that could be 'la nôtre', 'peut-être', I think he is anticipating what Hansen here calls 'worldly sensibility'.

we humans can be 'collectives' composed of higher-order agencies functioning in operational overlap with more primordial processes of worldly sensibility impacting us both bodily and environmentally, but in some crucial sense prior to the very division of subject and world that informs the higher-order processes and that typically qualifies our status as human subjects. From this perspective, we are emphatically not distinct, substantial subjects that exist independently from the sensory confound with which we are at every moment in contact, but are rather heterogeneous compositions in ongoing and highly complex individuation with and within this confound. (2015, 69)

As suggested by these references to early-twentieth- (Whitehead) and mid-twentieth-century philosophers (Simondon), the ontology that Hansen presents is not new, but in twentieth-century literary and cultural studies it has been largely neglected. If Whitehead and Simondon have emerged as key thinkers over the last fifteen years, it is not only (as I have previously argued) because they invite us to think individuation in a manner that we would today call 'Anthropocene', but also because they (and Simondon in particular) prompt us to think our relation to technology in a similarly ecological way. In this sense, Hansen is not describing a new situation, but rather a situation that is becoming increasingly clear: 'Life in twenty-first-century media networks reveals something that has perhaps always been the case, but that has never been so insistently manifest: agency is *resolutely not* the prerogative of privileged individual actors' (2).[4] My argument is that in the second half of the nineteenth century, Mallarmé's writings detect the same situation – sometimes, as in 'Le Démon de l'analogie', offering a less optimistic diagnosis.

As already mentioned, Mallarmé's poem shares with Hansen the view that the data world is all encompassing. The experience of the narrator in 'Le Démon de l'analogie' is precisely one of being superseded by text, or code, of being a very limited part of a larger data ecology, and of becoming a channel (an instrument) for the sentence. The narrator struggles to come to terms with this situation and during his struggles

---

4   We thus see that Hansen argues both that 'Human experience is currently undergoing a fundamental transformation' (5) and that 'Life in twenty-first-century media networks reveals something that has perhaps always been the case...' (2). I agree with both of these positions, and this is exactly why I argue that Mallarmé's writings (like those of Verlaine and Baudelaire) can tell us something about where we are today.

he experiences the insufficiency of his perceptual apparatus, that of twentieth-century phenomenology. He also discovers that cognitive ('je souris et implorai de vœux intellectuels' ['I smiled, and pleaded with all my intellectual wishes' (17)]) and lexical ('pénultième est le terme du lexique qui signifie...' ['"penultimate" is a lexical term signifying...' (18)]) attempts at controlling the sentence are inadequate. Mallarmé's narrator is thus caught in code, struggling to understand 'his' experience and to emerge from the sentence-encounter as a coherent subject. Ultimately, he fails. On the way to this failure, Mallarmé has written out a conception of individuation that looks very much like a nightmare version of the ecological individuation theorized by Hansen. Here, distinctions between the mental, the environmental, and the linguistic are broken down in such a way that the sentence dismantles the subject, who is clearly incapable of 'organising a real togetherness *of alien things*', as Hansen put it.

The narrator's attempts at playing with the sentence (and thereby limiting his unease) deserve further consideration. I called this play 'modulation', which allows me to draw on Steven Shaviro's usage of the term in *Post-Cinematic Affect* (2010). Shaviro proposes that contemporary digital media (film, music videos, and video games) operate according to a logic of modulation. The digital signal consists of os and 1s that can be combined in an infinite number of ways. A code will determine the nature of these variations and it is impossible for the signal itself to break the code. On this basis, Shaviro distinguishes between *metamorphosis* and *modulation*: metamorphosis allows for change, for the invention of new codes, for the unexpected; modulation, on the other hand, prevents anything truly new and surprising from happening. One of Shaviro's key arguments is that the digital logic of modulation also characterizes contemporary capitalism. Capitalism is full of modulations: in fact, it largely depends on the kind of modulations we call fashions. But despite its apparent openness and malleability – or rather, *through* this apparent openness and malleability – capitalism prevents a systemic shift, the invention of a new code (Shaviro, 2010, 11–34).

It is precisely in Shaviro's sense of the word that the narrator *modulates* – and is *modulated* by – 'la pénultième est morte'. Of course, the sentence speaks about the death of the penultimate, about how certain norms of versification are being exploded, about the pressure on fixed forms. It also hints at the invention of new forms such as free verse; the text is itself a prose poem. Bonnefoy, in the analysis mentioned above, is not wrong to read the poem as Mallarmé's way of negotiating his place in literary history: this is also a poem about new media being haunted by (un)dead media. But unlike what happens in later prose texts such as *La Musique et les lettres* (1894) and 'Crise de vers' (1897), 'Le Démon de l'analogie' plays these themes in a minor key. It speaks from a vacuum, from an uncanny interregnum. There is no productive dialectic between sentence and narrator (who and where is the Demon? Everywhere?), no radical rupture, only an intricate interplay in which boundaries between sentence, narrator, and reality fall away. The sensation produced by this blurring stays entirely within the realm of the uncanny. The sentence's stickiness prevents escape.[5] If 'Le Démon de l'analogie' offers a more dystopian version of human–sentence entanglements, it is because it is a poem about demonic modulations.

This brings us to a third dimension in this *rapprochement* between contemporary media theory and Mallarmé's exploration of the processes of (dis)individuation. It is important to highlight that the sentence materializes at the end of the poem – mediation does happen. Mallarmé's poem thereby provides an example of what Eugene Thacker calls 'dark mediation'. Like Hansen and Shaviro, Thacker is interested in a form of mediation that exceeds conventional human views on information and communication. Presenting his key concept, Thacker writes:

> Dark media have, as their aim, the mediation of that which is unavailable or inaccessible to the senses, and thus that of which we are normally 'in the dark' about. But beyond this, dark media have, as another aim, the investigation into the ways in which all mediation harbors within itself this blind spot, the minimal distance that persists in any instance of mediation, however successful or complete it may be. Dark media inhabit this twofold movement – seeing something in nothing (e.g., the animate images appearing on the screen or the alchemical glass), and finding nothing in each something (the paradoxical absence of presence of the 'demon' behind each thing). (2014, 85)

5 Shaviro added a political dimension by arguing that the digital logic is also that of capitalism. To my knowledge, the question of politics has rarely been raised in relation to 'Le Démon de l'analogie' but, reading the poem alongside Shaviro's text, it is worth noticing that the narrator's modulations leave him in front of a shop window. This suggests a relation between consumerism and the impasse of the narrator. One may hypothesize that if 'Le Démon de l'analogie' had been a poem by Baudelaire, readers would have been more alert to this link between uncanny hauntings and consumer culture, which they might have linked to Marxist ideas of commodity fetishism.

In this passage, Thacker first underlines that some media operate beyond the human perspective, describing these as 'dark media'. In a second argument, he notes that dark media make evident that there is a 'blind spot' in all mediation. Mediation is demonic because there is a hole in it. In the subsequent pages, he clarifies that this has nothing to do with dark mediation being imperfect. On the contrary, Thacker is theorizing the 'instances in which media work "too well," that is, instances in which media and mediation seem to operate beyond the pale of human capacity or comprehension' (90).

Thacker draws on an eclectic corpus of medieval mysticism, negative theology, fantastic literature, and Japanese horror films (frequently using Mallarméan keywords such as 'démon' and 'grimoire') in order to stage situations where 'we get more than we bargained for, as specters turn up in our photos, the dead appear on our computer screens, and that videotape, well, you probably shouldn't watch that' (102).[6] In those instances, mediation is no longer epistemological: it is not about transmitting knowledge. Rather, mediation is ontological: we are in a logic of appearance, of the occult (including the 'blind spot') becoming manifest.

Both of Thacker's observations about dark media can inform a reading of Mallarmé's poem. 'Le Démon de l'analogie' is clearly a poem about mediation 'beyond the pale of human capacity or comprehension'. When the narrator stands in front of the objects in the shop window, he 'get[s] more than [h]e bargained for'. This radically unsettles him. At the same time, it can be argued that the appearance is partially unreal, that the mediation reveals a hole, a kind of spectrality. The experience at the shop window is not simply one of 'presence' and 'appearance': the objects on display are at a distance, behind glass and strangely absent.

6   The videotape that 'you probably shouldn't watch' belongs in Hideo Nakata's horror hit *The Ring* (1998). In this modern ghost story, watching a video cassette releases a deadly curse that can only be deflected by inviting someone else to watch the tape. Does 'Le Démon de l'analogie' reproduce this logic? We may read the narrator's decision to communicate his (ungraspable) experience to the reader as an attempt to pass on the curse. This adds a performative and thoroughly demonic dimension to the opening question: 'Des paroles inconnues chantèrent-elles sur vos lèvres, lambeaux maudits d'une phrase absurde?' ['Have unknown words ever played about your lips, the haunting and accursed fragments of an absurd sentence?' (17)] Barbara Johnson's remark about how all readers tend to approach the poem through analogies seems to suggest that Mallarmé's narrator has successfully passed on the curse.

Mallarmé's poem contains a word for this kind of presence–absence: *virtual*. The poem uses the term to describe the mode in which the sentence haunts the narrator ('[l]a phrase revint, virtuelle' ['the sentence came back, a virtual reality' (17)]), but virtuality floods all aspects of the poem, dislodging the narrator from an experience that never fully becomes 'his'.

Thacker's text can therefore be used to drive home the point that 'Le Démon de l'analogie' ties into contemporary debates about the weird mediations of what lies outside the scope of human perception but nevertheless remains influential. We are back in the territory we visited with Hansen: 'If there is a lesson to be learned from Scholastic demonology or medieval mysticism, it is that our ideas of media and mediation are, perhaps, all-too-human' (Thacker, 2014, 138). Similarly, Mallarmé's text is concerned with mediation beyond the human perspective and the impact this has on the narrator. Indeed, this is what it means to be haunted by 'le démon de l'analogie'.

We have thus seen that the narrator's experience is that of not being able to appropriate an experience in which he is nevertheless deeply implicated. To express this, the poem relies on a thoroughly ecological but also uncanny conception of individuation. Such a view of individuation resonates with the one contemporary media theorists find in our heavily digitized and networked societies. Of course, this does not mean that there are no differences between Mallarmé's poem and the ways in which media scholars engage with technological individuation. For instance, whereas Hansen writes about 'media technologies that operate predominantly, if not almost entirely, outside the scope of human modes of awareness' (2015, 5), Mallarmé's narrator is at least semi-aware of being 'looped out', even if he remains unable to respond. He is therefore placed somewhere between the twenty-first-century sensibilities described by Hansen and Hansen himself, the media theorist who responds critically to the new situation. Nevertheless, Mallarmé's poem anticipates contemporary analyses of how it feels to be modulated by code in a digital society, by proposing a media ecology in which distinctions between text, environment, and subject largely fall away.

Mallarmé and Cybernetics

As we saw in the previous chapter, the demonic logic does not dominate all of Mallarmé's writing. When Mallarmé writes about 'le Livre', he imagines a harmonious alignment between human and universe via the text (in Simondonian terms, he imagines a *réticulation*). The dream of this ideal man–world–text alignment often culminates in what Mallarmé figures as a moment of illumination: a constellation can be seen against the black sky when man, text, and universe fall into place; a firework lights up when the world becomes book. This does not mean that Mallarmé is an idealist author in the sense that the illumination is the sign of a power originating in anything other than a man-made fiction, but it does mean that fiction ('le Livre') becomes both an *instrument* (musical and technical) that can help human beings find their place in the best world possible *and* the name of this *world* in which we may live harmoniously.

An anachronistic way to formulate this idea is to suggest that Mallarmé was 'pre-haunted' by a dream of cybernetics. Interestingly, there is a small and exclusive tradition of thinking Mallarmé's instrument-Livre in terms of cybernetics (in the more humanistic version of this diverse tradition). As early as 1958 – when Gilbert Simondon, Raymond Ruyer, and others were (critically) importing cybernetics to France – Jean Hyppolite offered a cybernetics-inspired reading of *Un coup de dés* (1991, 977–84).[7] And twenty-two years later, Jeffrey Mehlman followed in Hyppolite's footsteps, again reading *Un coup de dés* with cybernetics (1980, 374–80). Here too, I would like to spend time with the comparison between Mallarmé's work and the heterogeneous tradition(s) of cybernetics.[8] There are at least three good reasons for doing this. The first has to do with the wide-ranging ambitions of this discipline.

Associated with the Austrian mathematician Norbert Wiener, cybernetics grew out of research into anti-aircraft artillery during World War Two. The challenge for Wiener and other researchers working for the American military was to develop an anti-aircraft system that would be able to register an enemy airplane, determine its position, velocity, and direction, and calculate where to shoot, *whilst adjusting* for the distance the aircraft had crossed since it first registered. This challenge prompted research into feedback loops and invited researchers to consider shooter and machine as a singular unit.

---

7   Simondon's 600-page dissertation on *L'individuation à la lumière des notions de forme et d'information* was written under the supervision of Jean Hyppolite (and defended in 1958).

8   Cybernetics has gone through several phases and developments since the 1940s. Today we speak of fourth-generation cybernetics.

As Thomas Rid (2016) explains in his popular history of cybernetics, following World War Two Wiener went on to theorize the links between three different ideas that make up the foundation of cybernetics. The first was the idea of homeostasis, of an equilibrium between organisms and environments, like a body adjusting its temperature in relation to its surroundings. Maintaining homeostasis was a question of *control*. The second central idea was that the effort to maintain homeostasis (the struggle against entropy) would happen through feedback loops. For instance, such feedback loops are a central feature of the thermostat, which regulates between a heating unit and its surroundings. This second element had to do with *communication*. The final idea was the establishment of a very tight relation between human being and machine (or instrument), between organic and inorganic systems: thermostats work like a human body, machines can function like human beings. These different dimensions were neatly summed up in the title of Wiener's ground-breaking 1947 volume *Cybernetics: Or Control and Communication in the Animal and the Machine*. The neologism 'cybernetics' was derived from the Greek word 'cyber-', meaning steersman or pilot ('Maître' in Mallarméan), thus establishing cybernetics as an art of navigation, a science of control and communication, of interactions between man, machine, and environment.

From its very inception, cybernetics reached beyond mathematics and computer science towards psychology, artificial intelligence, biology, and the social sciences. Wiener played a key role in the expansion of cybernetics, as he wrote about the ethical, social, and philosophical implications of his work, collaborating extensively with thinkers from diverse disciplines, fostering one of the most mythical interdisciplinary communities in twentieth-century research culture (the Macy Conferences). It can be said that cybernetics was aiming to be a kind of meta-science, integrating and bridging many other scientific disciplines. Cybernetics is a theory of systems, and, as we shall soon see, aesthetics plays an important role too.

This immoderate ambition – the desire to understand the unity of everything, how everything connects – is one we find in Mallarmé's work too. It is an ambition that has been downplayed in many recent writings on Mallarmé. Since the heyday of post-structuralism, we have seen a turn to historically oriented Mallarmé criticism, a desire to anchor the poet in his time. This has been productive, and in studies such as Bertrand Marchal's *La Religion de Mallarmé* (1988) and Jacques Rancière's *Mallarmé: La Politique de la sirène* (1996) the historical grounding took nothing away from the speculative and metaphysical dimensions of Mallarmé's texts. However, since the late 1990s many books have been so keen on anchoring Mallarmé in day-to-day life that the extraordinary nature – the madness (to use a term Mallarmé was happy to use about himself) – of his speculations has been drowned out. Instead, the poet has ended up looking almost like a contemporary academic: a person who goes to the theatre, is interested in arts, music, and literature, thinks about his time, and writes about it. The fact that he also wanted to understand how everything connects, that he wanted to prove to the world that literature can make sense of everything by creating balance and harmony, meaning that literature has to be placed at the heart of any social construction..., the fact that he not only speculated but worked, systematically, to realize these immoderate ideals has been pushed into the background. The comparison with cybernetics brings this speculative utopianism to the forefront again, highlighting that Mallarmé's sense of wonder (like Baudelaire's) in no way respects the distinctions between sciences, social sciences, and humanities.

But it is not just the ambition of bringing everything together in an overarching system that Mallarmé shares with cyberneticians, it is also the nature of his systematizations that invite the parallel. Cybernetics is about (constructing) machines, about feedback loops, about looking at the world as a self-regulating system (in which the human beings aren't necessarily privileged). In the late 1960s and throughout the 1970s, optimistic cybernetics-inspired writers such as Stewart Brand (the editor of *The Whole Earth Catalog*) imagined a man–machine (*homme-Livre*) interaction that would work as a dynamic, self-regulating system, eventually paving the way for a harmonious society. This would be a system built on a feedback-loop that allowed for the gradual perfection of the all-embracing machine-*Livre*.[9] Many of these ideas were inspired

9   The parallel between Mallarmé and the hippie cybernetics of Stewart Brand is no doubt a stretch. Nevertheless, reading works such as Fred Turner's *From Counterculture to Cyberculture: Stewart Brand, the Whole Earth Network, and the Digital Utopianism* (2006) and Rid's already mentioned *Rise of the Machines* (2016), the resemblances between Brand's ambitions for *The Whole Earth Catalog* and Mallarmé's ambitions for 'le Livre' are striking. As Rid puts it: 'Brand's vision was to turn the catalog itself into a tool. The CATALOG – he usually spelled it in capital letters – was to form a feedback loop. He wanted it to be a communication device that connected the far-flung community he cared so much about. He wanted the catalog to be part of something that would create an equilibrium. The catalog was part of a whole system, a dynamic and self-regulating system. Brand would

by the work of the biologist Gregory Bateson, whose most famous volumes – *Steps to an Ecology of Mind* (1972) and *Mind and Nature* (1979) – are therefore worth a short mention. The recurring titular word, 'Mind', is a good place to begin.

In *Mind and Nature* Bateson explains that his ambition is to find 'the pattern which connects all the living creatures' (2002, 7). This overall pattern, immanent in the system of human beings and environment, is precisely what Bateson calls 'Mind'. Bateson can therefore formulate his ambition in the following terms: 'the immediate task of this book is to construct a picture of how the world is joined together in its mental aspects' (18). Bateson distinguishes between minds and Mind, seeing the larger Mind as made up by more individual minds. Each individual mind is a cybernetic system (2000, 465), and the larger Mind appears through the 'comparing of comparisons' (2002, 81), the establishment of an overall system. In this theory all is relation, there is no essence or substance. We can therefore already now sense how Bateson's theorizations resonate with Mallarmé's insistence on relation, but to give a more precise idea of Bateson's Mind, we need to follow him a bit further.

In 'Form, Substance, and Difference', Bateson specifies what he sees as his own contribution to the field of evolutionary biology. He explains 'that Darwinian evolutionary theory contained a very great error in its identification of the unit of survival under natural selection' (2000, 456). In Darwinian theory, the essential motor for evolution was believed to be 'either the breeding individual or the family line or the subspecies of some similar homogeneous set of conspecifics' (457). This theory has required two important adjustments. First, geneticists challenged the idea of 'the breeding individual or the family line', demonstrating that heterogeneous families (species with great internal variation) and flexible organisms had better chances of survival, being more capable of responding to change. Today, Bateson explains, a second change is needed: the environment must be introduced into the evolutionary theory. With an expression that recalls Simondon's *individu-milieu*, Bateson argues that the basic 'unit of survival is a flexible organism-in-its-environment' (457). So, whereas Darwin began with the idea of a singular species, Bateson focuses on relations between organisms and

collect the crucial negative feedback in the supplement every few months and loop it back to the land by mail, to the readers [...]. His publications, as he saw it, were part of an adaptive machine [...]. The catalog itself, with its supplements and its community, *was the learning mechanism*' (172).

environment, a system of feedback loops that needs a kind of co-tuning (i.e. a homeostasis) of organism and environment. For 'if an organism or aggregate of organisms sets to work with a focus on its own survival and thinks that is the way to select its adaptive moves, its "progress" ends up with a destroyed environment' (457), and, as we should all know by now in this era of the Anthropocene, 'the organism which destroys its environment destroys itself' (457).

Cybernetics is, then, about thinking the Mind, the system and its internal relations. Bateson insists heavily on the fact that this Mind is immanent, but he also writes that when it occasionally shows up, it shows up as aesthetic. At this point he references the harmonious, poetic system of Johan Sebastian Bach (but he could just as well have referred to Mallarmé's constellations). Bateson suggests that poets and artists have been particularly good at thinking relations, whereas 'the rest of us have gone astray into all sorts of false reifications of the "self" and separations between the "self" and "experience"' (469). Rather than getting stuck in such reifications, rather than thinking of the 'self' as an independent unit and of experiences as something this unit has, Bateson is advocating for an entirely new way of thinking about ourselves and our place in the world as 'organisms-in-their-environment'.

As we have seen, Mallarmé believes 'le monde est fait pour aboutir à un beau livre' (2003, 702) ['the world is made to end up as a beautiful book'], and he suggests that this beauty results from the links between 'des relations entre tout' (224) ['relations among everything' (2007, 226)]. A very direct link between Mallarmé and Bateson can then be established if we suggest that what the poet calls 'Livre' is similar to what the biologist calls 'Mind' (which again is synonymous with the idea of music, as we encountered in our previous chapter: 'Employez Musique dans le sens grec, au fond signifiant Idée ou rythme entre des rapports' [Mallarmé, 1995a, 614], ['Use the term Music in the Greek sense, meaning truly the Idea or rhythm between connections']). Livre is immanent in nature, it is about relations (and relations between relations), and it shows up as aesthetics. It is a system to which we may all contribute with our personal minds/poems, which is why it is so important for Mallarmé that we participate in the creative process. Likewise, in Bateson's theory, working towards the realization of Mind is about finding oneself at home on earth, being part of nature.[10]

---

10   A similar idea is expressed by Whitehead, who famously suggested that 'The teleology of the universe is directed towards the production of beauty' (1967, 265).

We are getting close here to the idea of religion (in the non-clerical sense in which Bertrand Marchal uses the term). Bateson explicitly addresses this issue:

> The individual mind is immanent, but not only in the body. It is immanent also in pathways and messages outside the body; and there is a larger Mind of which the individual mind is a subsystem. This larger Mind is comparable to God and is perhaps what some people mean by 'God,' but it is still immanent in the total interconnected social system and planetary ecology. (2000, 467)

My second reason for staying with cybernetics is therefore this parallel between Mallarmé's Livre and Bateson's *Mind in Nature*.[11]

At this point we may pause to ask: does it really make sense to suggest that Mallarmé is offering a poetic 'systems theory' *avant la lettre*? Is it not fanciful to insist on the links between the machinic and the biological? Many critics prefer to think of Mallarmé's 'instrument' as musical only, but if we remember how widespread the fascination for (textual) machines was in late-nineteenth- and early-twentieth-century French avant-garde circles, it may alleviate some reservations. As Madeleine Chalmers (2021) has demonstrated, the interest in machines (and text-machines) is typical of Mallarmé's time. We can mention Didier de Chousy's forgotten epic *Ignis* (1883), the multiple machinic inventions of Charles Cros and Villiers de l'Isle-Adam (including Villiers's 'La Machine à gloire' from *Contes Cruels*, a text dedicated to Mallarmé), Alfred Jarry's machinic surmâle, the mannequin at the end of Rachilde's *Monsieur Vénus*, not to mention the many futurist, surrealist, and Rousselien machines that we find in the early twentieth century.[12]

Furthermore, paying attention to Mallarmé's vocabulary it is clear that technology, engineering, and industry infuse his work. Just think of his most famous poetic summary statement from *La Musique et les lettres* (2003, 67). Here the poet initially places himself in competition with industry ('Ainsi toute industrie a-t-elle failli à la fabrication du bonheur' [67], ['industry has failed to make happiness' (186–87)]). And when the next sentences explain Mallarmé's own poetic ideals, the technical vocabulary continues to dominate. The text now considers 'le

---

11   We thus see that Bateson too would have been happy with Mallarmé's idea, inspired by 'The Impressionists and Édouard Manet', that nature draws on certain lovers of hers (the artists) in order to express herself.

12   On most of these see Chalmers, 2021.

mécanisme littéraire' (67); Mallarmé claims that he will not 'opérer en public le démontage impie de la fiction' (67) ['take apart impiously, in public, the fiction' (187)]; he will not reveal its 'moteur' (but he is doing precisely this, showing how fiction runs on the kind of nothingness that religions call the '*au-delà*'). As soon as he has finished presenting his ideal of fiction, he goes back to what he calls our *matériel*, noting that 'La Nature a lieu, on n'y ajoutera pas; que des cités, les voies ferrées et plusieurs inventions formant notre matériel' (67) ['Nature has taken place; it can't be added to, except for cities or railroads or other inventions where we change form, but not the fact, of material' (187)]. This brings Mallarmé to the proto-Batesonian conclusion that 'Tout l'acte disponible, à jamais et seulement, reste de saisir les rapports' (68) ['The one available act, forever and alone, is to understand the relations' (187)].

This passage is by no means extraordinary in Mallarmé's work, but the role given to industry, machinery, and technology is rarely mentioned by Mallarmé scholars. Indeed, railways, urban developments, and other inventions frequently make their way into the Mallarméan text, reminding us that his time too was marked by intense network-binding. Not of the digital kind we see today, but of the industrial kind, also known as telegraphs, telephones, photography, cinema, etc. All these different inventions made the world smaller, tighter. Mallarmé hoped to produce a text-machine that could help his contemporaries explore their minds and thereby the more general Mind – a machine that made of everyone a signatory of 'le Livre'.[13]

The third and final reason for considering the relationship between Mallarmé and cybernetics concerns the considerable hermeneutic potential of a cybernetics-inspired approach to Mallarmé. I cannot pursue this point in great detail, but I want to give a few brief indications of how such an approach to Mallarmé connects to some of his texts and their readers. For instance, a cybernetics-inspired approach allows us to make (some) sense of 'Les Notes en vue du "Livre"'. One of the first things the reader notices when confronted with these notes is how little they reveal about the content of the various readings and publications

13   When Roger Pearson reads *Un coup de dés*, he similarly brings out the interdisciplinary character of the poem, emphasizing not only its multiple connections to music and the visual arts, but also those to 'theology, law, mathematics and the natural sciences' (1996, 279), arguing that 'the poem displays at once a chemical event, a botanical specimen, and a physical phenomenon' (282).

that would make up the Livre (what is 'le Livre' *about?*). Instead, the notes are full of calculations and thoughts on the interaction between text and public. But if we approach the fragments as notes towards the invention of a new apparatus (or instrument), this begins to make sense. Mallarmé is concerned with designing a creative environment in which text and reader/spectator can evolve together. He is not concerned with content yet – we might even suggest that content could vary. It is as if Mallarmé is inventing some new medium. He considers how to involve people in the performance, how many copies to print, how many sessions to host, and what role the 'opérateur' (a term that makes perfect sense) should have. 'Les Notes en vue du "Livre"' are about machinic design (and not yet about what he called the 'anecdote').

As briefly suggested, a poem like *Un coup de dés jamais n'abolira le hasard* can also benefit from this approach (in addition to the more traditional textual analysis). This is another textual machine. Beginning and ending with the same four words ('un coup de dés'), the poem has been designed to draw the reader into a loop by means of which meaning gradually settles. More specifically, this machine aims for a reticulation of the relationship between the stars in the sky and the struggle in the waves; on the last page of the poem, the celestial throw of the dice falls into place, bringing out the light, making text and mind coincide – until a new game begins. It is this mathematical, coded, cosmic, and metaphysical dimension that explains why it has been picked up by cybernetics-inspired readers. The overarching ideas about the poem as a place where cognitive, ontological, and existential dimensions gradually align bring the poem close to cybernetics.

The more arithmetic approaches to *Un coup de dés* by Mitsou Ronat and Tibor Papp (1980), Roger Pearson (1996), and Quentin Meillassoux (2011) among others therefore also deserve our careful attention. These critics see *Un coup de dés* as coded: they believe that Mallarmé has wanted to put something like a key to the universe into the text. We can try to break the code, find 'l'unique Nombre qui ne peut pas être un autre' (Mallarmé, 1998, 372–73) ['the unique Number which cannot be another' (2001, 34–35)], like Ronat (no. 12) and Meillassoux (no. 707) aim to do, but we can also (as I would prefer to do) focus on the machinic design, and rethink Mallarmé as a media or game designer. Media here should be taken in the very broad sense that W.J.T. Mitchell and Mark Hansen give the word when they write about the design of (textual) spaces, of textual ecologies. Media is about mediation, and mediation is about relationality. For Mitchell and Hansen, therefore, 'media studies can and should designate the study of our fundamental relationality, of the irreducible role of mediation in the history of human being' (Mitchell and Hansen, 2010, xii) – media is 'a general environment for the living' (xiii). *Un coup de dés*, 'Le Livre', and Mallarmé's other texts aim to be such an environment.

Paul Valéry's famous texts about Mallarmé point in a similar direction. For Valéry, Mallarmé is almost a scientist – although a most curious scientist who did not take a very profound interest in the sciences, but instead isolated himself and worked out a kind of arithmetics of literature all by himself.[14] It is Mallarmé's universalizing ambitions, his desire to understand the deepest structures of the universe, that Valéry associates with Mallarméan mathematics. In Valéry's view, this is what Mallarmé calls 'le Livre': 'Il est venu à vouloir donner à l'art d'écrire un sens universel, *une valeur d'univers*, et [...] il a reconnu que le suprême objet du monde et la justification de son existence [...] ne pouvait être qu'un *Livre*' (1924, 201) ['So it was that he came to dream of giving the art of writing a *universal* meaning, a universal value, and [...] to acknowledge that the supreme object of the world and the justification of its existence [...] could only be a Book' (1972, 244)]. The role of this 'Livre', then, was to fulfil what Valéry calls the destiny of the universe: '[Mallarmé] ne voyait à l'univers d'autre destinée concevable que d'être finalement *exprimé*' (173) ['He could see no other conceivable destiny for the universe than to be finally *expressed*' (331)]. This brings us to Valéry's famous account of his encounter with *Un coup de dés*. Mallarmé first read the text in a sober, monotonous diction. Then he revealed the mise-en-page, describing the design as his 'démence' (180) ['madness' (310)]. The effect on the 25-year-old Valéry was overwhelming. But it was only really in the evening, when Mallarmé walked his guest to the station under a starlit sky, that Valéry understood that the poem was an attempt at the ultimate upload, 'la figure d'une pensée, pour la première fois placée dans notre espace' (178) ['I was looking at the form and pattern of a thought, placed for the first time in finite space' (309)]. Here is the perfect alignment between thought, page, night sky, and cosmos:

---

14   See: 'Il est extrêmement remarquable qu'il soit arrivé, par l'étude approfondie de son art, et sans connaissances scientifiques, à une conception si abstraite et si proche des spéculations les plus élevées de certaines sciences' (1924, 188) ['He had no scientific training, and yet it is most remarkable that a thorough study of his art should have led him to such an abstract conception and one so close to the final speculations of certain sciences' (1972, 326)].

'Il a essayé, pensais-je, *d'élever enfin une page à la puissance du ciel étoilé!*' (181) ['*He has undertaken*, I thought, *finally to raise a printed page to the power of the midnight sky*' (312)].

The Livre and the Anti-Livre

If we compare 'Le Démon de l'analogie' to the mature poetics of 'le Livre', we can read the prose poem as the nightmare version of Mallarmé's dream. 'Le Démon de l'analogie' also presents a text–world alignment – mediation happens – in this case between a single sentence and the world. But in the prose poem, the text does not facilitate a process whereby 'L'Homme, puis son authentique séjour terrestre, échangent une réciprocité de preuves' (2003, 158) ['Man and his authentic stay on earth exchange a reciprocity of proofs' (2007, 112)]; as demonstrated, it serves instead to shut out the narrator and derail the process of individuation. Unlike other Mallarmé texts, 'Le Démon de l'analogie' therefore presents no final illumination in the sky, no projections from a refreshing fountain, no perfect spider web, no beautiful lacework, but only a confused, haunted consciousness and body, caught in a nightmarish web, struggling to host an experience which it cannot comprehend. In this sense, 'Le Démon de l'analogie' is an anti-'Livre', and the ground on which this dichotomy between 'Livre' and anti-'Livre' rests is the ecological, networked conception of individuation that I have presented with references to Whitehead, Simondon, cybernetics, and twenty-first-century media studies.

But no sooner has this distinction between the utopian and dystopian versions of world–text alignments been established than we need to let go of it and recognize that tensions and ambiguities mark Mallarmé's writings throughout. His trajectory has often been presented as a movement from early spleen-haunted idealism, through the crisis years (1866–71), and finally leading to a more optimistic, mature Mallarmé capable of seeing the 'Néant' as a positive precondition for the work of Fiction. In this account, we go from the unfinished prose of *Igitur* and the tormented verse of 'Hérodiade' to the illuminations of *La Musique et les lettres* and the brilliant playful eroticism of a poem such as 'Billet à Whistler'. There is truth to this presentation, but the narrative is too neat. Even if Mallarmé moves from the anguish of the early texts to the playfulness of sonnets like 'Billet' and 'Salut', he remains haunted by the demon.

This can be seen in a mature poem such as 'Prose — pour des Esseintes' (1885). It is difficult to feel at home in this fantastical poem about a magical – and perhaps non-existent (or virtual) – island where 'de lis multiples la tige/ Grandissait trop pour nos raisons' (1998, 29) ['The stem of multiple lilies grew/ Too large to be contained by reason' (1994, 47)]. Here, mediation is happening at an ontological rather than an epistemological level and the narrator is unable to map the situation. The reader feels uneasy too, desperately trying to decipher the poème–grimoire. Similarly, when reading key texts of illumination such as 'Ses purs ongles…' and *Un coup de dés* it is worth remembering that the world–text alignments happen either while 'le maître est allé puiser des pleurs au Styx' (1998, 37) ['the Master has gone to draw tears from the Styx' (1994, 69)], or when he is lying shipwrecked in the waves, clutching a pair of dice (*Un coup de dés*).

Complementing the more positive, cybernetics-inspired reading of *Un coup de dés* suggested above (the idea that the poem offers a positive feedback loop), we may therefore do wisely to remember that the submerged 'Master' is taking advice from 'l'ultérieur démon immémorial' (1998, 374) ['the ulterior immemorial demon' (2001, 36)]. This paradoxical temporal structure places the demon firmly outside human temporality – at the same time already far into the past and far into the future, making these 'ends' meet and, in the process, cutting off human beings and their temporality. (Note also that 'ulterior' precedes 'immemorial'.) This suggests a looped structure like the one we encountered in 'Le Démon de l'analogie'. *Un coup de dés* then drives this point home by situating the démon in 'de contrées nulles' (374) ['nonexistent regions' (36)]. Still operative and influential from this virtual space, the demon seemingly pushes the Maître to throw the dice. But this act remains covered under a 'voile d'illusion' (374) ['veil of illusion' (36)] and therefore appears only as 'le fantôme d'un geste' (374) ['the phantom of a gesture' (36)], a virtual gesture never really appropriated by the Master. While recognizing the multiplicity of readings this poem offers, and without denying that at the end the celestial throw of dice falls into place and illuminates the sky (generating a new game), it seems clear that in 1897 the ghostly hauntings of demons and the fear of being excluded from the process of mediation have still not been eradicated.[15]

15 For a different and more detailed account of the relation between 'Le Démon de l'analogie' and *Un coup de dés*, see Dornbush (1980).

It can therefore be argued that Mallarmé's work brings together two tendencies that have also marked media studies since their inception. On the one hand, there is the optimistic, cybernetic dream of a self-regulating man-instrument ('homme-Livre') environment: a process capable of paving the way for harmonious co-existence, a technophile vision optimistically embraced in *The Whole Earth Catalog* (Californian for 'le Livre'?) and in later ideas about the Internet saving democracy and the world. On the other hand, there is the nightmare explored by science-fiction films such as Alex Garland's *Ex Machina* (2014), in which the machine adapts so well that it/she eventually dispenses with its/her maker and continues its/her exploration of the world without interference. But what Mallarmé's texts – from 'Le Démon de l'analogie' to *Un coup de dés* and the 'Notes en vue du "Livre"' – all invite us to conclude is that agency is distributed so evenly across textual, physical, and mental environments that these distinctions only partly make sense. His work brings out the potential of a truly participatory technological environment. When networks are co-constituted, when readers participate, there is a chance that technologies (like the book) can lead to collective illumination. But Mallarmé also knows that a large crowd doesn't guarantee a participatory aesthetic (this is his critique of Wagner), and he knows that participatory aesthetics can be upset by the presence of a demon. Today, we remain suspended in front of the pharmacological nature of contemporary technology.

Coda: Is Mallarmé Digital?

In two closely related books from the 1980s – *Into the Universe of Technical Images* (1985) and *Does Writing have a Future?* (1987) – the Czech media theorist Vilém Flusser tried to understand how the increasingly technologically mediated nature of modern society impacted both individual and social life. To do so, Flusser offered some very broad systematizations, dividing world history into three large periods. First, he posited a prehistorical period in which human beings mediated their relation to the world through images such as the ones discovered on the walls of caves – images which human beings produced by 'step[ping] back from their surroundings to observe and depict' (2011a, 170). Then came a second period, where a culture of writing took over, and with it a linear organization of information that Flusser describes as the 'time of history'. This period has now come to a close and writing no longer has a future (something Flusser regrets); we have entered the universe of technical images, Flusser's third period. Technical images 'are models that give form to a world and a consciousness that has disintegrated' (2011a, 170). They are not concerned with the representation of an external world. Instead, the digital is associated with the gathering and assembling of data, with becoming part of assemblages; its images are 'projective'. They function in a feedback loop with their consumers: 'people pattern their behaviour according to the images, and images pick up on their behaviour to function better and better as models' (2011a, 170).

It is important to understand that, for Flusser, the digital revolution is therefore *not* about the invention and dominance of digital technologies and apparatuses. Rather, the digital revolution results from early-twentieth-century scientific inventions and discoveries – particularly with regard to the fields of quantum mechanics and Einstein's theory of relativity. With the quantum revolution, we discovered that matter is multi-layered, relationally constituted, and that we are inextricably caught up in the world. For instance, our thinking results from the movements of electrons and protons, and when we try to understand our thinking by considering these electrons and protons, we cannot help but interfere in this system. The new technologies that we use to navigate in the digital world did not create this reality. They may contribute to the way in which this reality develops, but they are responsive; they are tools invented for our quantum reality.

The function of art and poetry changes in this new world. The world is no longer out there to be represented. Instead, the world is a sea of data (in which we participate, at a sub-molecular level) and the role of poets (and 'makers' in general) is to assemble images that give directions. The poet is a steersman, a cybernetician, an 'information designer' (2011b, 75). And Flusser goes on:

> Such an informatic approach to poetry has long been in preparation. In Mallarmé, for example, this attitude finds theoretical, nearly informatic expression; and the cool, calculating, exact, even mechanical dimension of poetry is clearly visible in the precision of many of Shakespeare's sonnets. [...] All our conceptions of poets favored by the muse must yield to a conception of the poet as a language technician. Poetry will be desanctified. (2011b, 75)

Flusser adds two modifying comments to his analysis. First, he notes that similar remarks about the 'technologizing and desanctifying of poetry' were made when alphabetic poetry replaced oral poetry (with Homer); secondly, he specifies that the new informatic poet 'is gripped by a creative delirium no less intense than the one a writing poet felt in his struggle with language' (2011b, 75).

Flusser's account is provocative (and stimulating) – partly because of the very broad generalizations, and partly because of its technical nature. If we consider his analysis in relation to Mallarmé, three observations are possible. First, as suggested throughout the last two chapters, I am willing to follow Flusser quite a long way into this conception of Mallarme's poetry as systems and game design; Mallarmé is a poet of the quantum age.[16] If this reading seems provocative, it is no doubt partly because most of us (poetry readers and scholars in the humanities) have bought into at least some aspects of what Simondon called the 'facile humanism' that has constructed itself by opposition to a reductive image of technology – an image which overlooks that there is creativity and humanity in technology too. As we have seen, this image of technology is a far cry from Baudelaire's 'Morale du joujou' and from Mallarmé's *L'Anglais récréatif*. I am therefore happy to see Mallarmé as a game designer ('A quoi sert cela — A un jeu' [2003, 67], ['What is this good for — For a game' (2007, 187)]), not least if we remember that such games simultaneously impact their players, their designers, and the world more widely.

Secondly, I would stress the importance of the second self-corrective remark in Flusser's text. It is important to see the game developer as someone who can be in a state of 'creative delirium'. The delirium points to our senses, to a Rimbaldian 'immense et raisonné *dérèglement* de *tous les sens*' (Rimbaud, 2005, 376) ['gigantic and rational *derangement* of *all the senses*' (377)], and therefore to the body. We must avoid the error frequently associated with first-generation cybernetics (and frequently found in Mallarmé criticism too), which consists of overlooking the body. As mentioned, the *individu-Livre* is a body-in-code. Mallarmé

16 Reading popular science books on quantum mechanics, I am struck by the number of Mallarméan formulations they contain. I take from books such as those by Carlo Rovelli the idea that reality is granular; 'a dense web of interactions' (Rovelli, 2021, 68); it is 'relational' – and not just in the vague sense that independent elements interact, but in the strong sense that reality is nothing but such interactions (2017, 115); therefore 'the world is made of events, not things' (2019, 85), it lights up, Mallarmé might say, as constellations; and Rovelli adds that '[o]ur discourse on reality is itself part of that reality. *Relations* make up our 'I', as our society, our cultural, spiritual and political life' (2021, 166).

does not ignore the body – when we consider his frequent play with the homonym between 'Maître' and 'mètre', and his view that Victor Hugo 'était le vers personellement' (2003, 205) ['was verse personnified' (2007, 202)], neither must we.

Finally, I believe that approaching Mallarmé texts through information theory – thinking of the effect that his poetry has had since it was thrown into the social world of the late nineteenth century – provides us with a very good illustration of how an 'action restreinte' can work. Mallarmé altered our conception of what poetry is. He (and others) largely cut the link to the lyrical tradition, largely cut the link to representation also, and instead went on to produce poetic games which allowed his gamers to understand poetry, ourselves, and the world differently, seeing ourselves as *individus-Livres*. A poem (or 'carte de visite' [1998, 789], as he put it) is a micropolitical intervention, and Mallarmé has arguably managed to 'prouver' (67) the efficiency of such micro-machines. Throughout the twentieth century, Mallarméan webs have spread and infiltrated art, philosophy, and the minds of thousands of readers, making sure the work of this so-called ivory-tower poet has registered in ways that far exceed the boundaries of anything that can be summed up in the name 'Stéphane Mallarmé'.

Conclusion

Over six chapters, I have studied how the writings of Verlaine, Baudelaire, and Mallarmé relate to our present. My focus has been on the subject position established in a selection of poems, prose poems, essays, and articles chosen among many other texts precisely because I think these specific texts present – and produce – an understanding of the human being that can still inspire today. By way of conclusion, I will first offer a partial summary of my main argument, before turning to a theme that has played a big role in debates about modernist poetry, that of depersonalization, in order to clarify its relation to the theme of non-anthropocentricity.

In the opening chapters on Verlaine, I compared some of his most famous poetry with the haiku as theorized by Roland Barthes. Two aspects of the haiku were particularly important: on the one hand, haikus are *ecological*. They are deictic, tied to the time of the day or the season, and very strongly embedded in a specific setting. On the other hand, the reading of haikus constitutes a *practice*. To read a haiku is a spiritual exercise aimed at experiencing the transience of the universe and approaching *kenosis*. These two dimensions can be brought together in the idea that the Barthesian haiku is a practice generating awareness of ecological becoming. I argued that this could be said of the selected Verlaine poems also. They are exercises in becoming part of the environment, in letting the environment become part of us – in sensing that we were always already part of the environment. They frequently have an image-like character ('images' being understood as in Simondon's 'image-cycle', as processes and what he called 'quasi-organisms') and operate through musical patterns, subtle rhythms and repetitions, almost imperceptibly pulling us into an 'humble antienne'. Some of the poems retain a dialogical aspect ('c'est la nôtre, n'est-ce pas?'), thereby making the experience of becoming-song communal;

all of them invite us to think ourselves as what Simondon calls 'individual-environments'. As mind and matter entwine, 'anthropocentricity is cast into doubt' (as Scott put it [1988, 238]), and Verlaine emerges both as an affect-poet and as a poet of our Anthropocene condition.

In the chapters on Baudelaire, subjectivities were again drawn into and taken up by their environments, realising in that process that they had always been individual-environments. These environments, or atmospheres, could be threatening, enticing, or both; they were frequently more intense, dramatic, and electric than the ones encountered in Verlaine's poetry. Re-establishing the chronology, we might therefore say that Verlaine's haiku-poetry (and *not* all his writings) distils an affective understanding of subjectivity which is already present in Baudelaire's work. I also found in Baudelaire's work (most explicitly in the 'Morale du joujou') a reflection on art and poetry (along with science) as forms of individuation, as practices through which we experience our entanglement in the world. Whereas many critics have paid attention to how these often-bewildering experiences of entanglement play out in urban life, I turned to Baudelaire's art historical writings on colour to find a less anthropocentric and more explicitly vitalistic experience of entanglement. Baudelaire's universe is alive in a way that makes it difficult to map, and difficult to capture with terms like 'alienation' and 'reification'. This is not to say that such themes have no place in an analysis of Baudelaire, but in many critical texts the urban angle has proven too restricted to capture the intricacies of Baudelaire's entanglements. Going through the art historical writings (as Rancière also did), we see that Baudelaire's texts overflow in such a manner that they unsettle social hierarchies, political dichotomies, and many of the systematizations that Baudelaire criticism has established – including those which separate the urban from the pastoral, the social world from nature, the modernist from the romanticist. In this manner, Baudelaire troubles what Latour calls the 'modern constitution' – allowing me to suggest that in a Latourian sense Baudelaire was never modern. If Verlaine offered the possibility of becoming-song, Baudelaire explored the potential of being-in-colour: poetry, world, and reader form each other in a process of mutual specification.

Finally, the chapters on Mallarmé presented perhaps the most hands-on version of the idea of *poetry as practice* (as Anatole France only semi-ironically said: 'Je savais bien que Mallarmé est de nous tous l'esprit le plus pratique' [in Steinmetz, 1998, 396], ['I always knew that

Mallarmé would be the most practically minded among us']).[1] I argued that for Mallarmé writing is not unlike game design. This is true for the pedagogical material published as *L'Anglais récréatif*, but also for the gamble called *Un coup de dés*, and for the major unfinished project published as 'Notes en vue du "Livre"'. Even more generally, Mallarmé's syntax – in both poetry and prose – is a game. It is a friendly challenge to the reader to establish 'des relations entre tout' (2003, 272) ['Relations among everything' (226)], therefore relying on a granular understanding of reality. Through such creative games we learn how to make sense of ourselves and the universe. Mallarmé's art machines are therefore both hands-on and tremendously idealistic. Writing for 'plus tard ou jamais' (1998, 789) ['later or never'], Mallarmé hopes that his 'actions restreintes' can help generate a new society. This society must be modelled on the media machine he calls 'le Livre', in which all components (transmitter, code, reader, world...) co-evolve. There is no guarantee of success: games can go wrong and media can become haunted. But Mallarmé puts his faith in collective and open-ended creation, positioning Beauty as a guiding principle.

My answer to the question of how the various poetic texts speak to the present has thus emphasized that they operate with the subject position theorized in Chapter 1 with reference to Simondon's notion of the individual-environment. Here, life is shared among text, nature, environments, and human beings. This subject position can be more or less harmonious, more or less vibrant, and it exists in organic, machinic, urban, and pastoral versions, but it always encourages us to think carefully about ourselves as dynamic mediations of our environments. And the poets do even more than that. They do something that Anthropocene theory rarely manages (or tries) to do: they make the experience of entanglement available to us as readers; they make us sense the intensity of being individual-environment. If we pick up their volumes and play, the 'humble antienne' can become ours too. Tying the key concepts of this study together, we can therefore say that the three writers all present poetry as *practice*. This practice is an exercise in *individuation*; in the most successful instances, the readers are opened to the wider environment, participating in processes of becoming that make of us environments-in-song.

---

1   France's remark was made in relation to Mallarmé's indeed very practical project of redistributing the publishing income from literary classics to benefit young authors (see 'Le Fonds littéraire' [Mallarmé, 2003, 322]).

On our way through these arguments (and others, such as rethinking phenomenology so that we no longer overestimate perception and thereby underestimate the amount of hosting we do – or *are*), we occasionally bumped into the classical idea of depersonalization. For instance, we saw that Verlaine aimed for a 'lyrisme impersonnel' and that he dreamt about a collection entirely without human beings. Similarly, Ross Chambers argues that Baudelaire's 'agency' goes through impersonality and effacement, that it stems from actively giving himself over to the social situation ('a kind of denial of self by means of an actively *assumed* anonymity' [2015, 132]); Baudelaire himself highlighted this anonymity in the work and life of Constantin Guys. Finally, Mallarmé has of course long been considered the *emblematic figure of deperson-alization* (if that isn't too paradoxical), the poet who recommended 'la disparition élocutoire du poète' (2003, 211) ['the disappearance of the poet speaking' (2007, 208)], and who proudly proclaimed: 'je suis maintenant impersonnel, et non plus Stéphane que tu as connu – mais une aptitude qu'a l'Univers Spirituel à se voir et à se développer, à travers ce qui fut moi' (1998, 714) ['I am now impersonal and no longer the Stéphane that you knew, – but a capacity possessed by the spiritual Universe to see itself and develop itself, through what was once me' (Mallarmé, 1988, 74)].

The argument about depersonalization is a classic theme in the critical literature about modern poetry. Hugo Friedrich's *Die Struktur der modernen Lyrik* (1956) tells one version of this well-known story. According to Friedrich, poetry – like painting – became abstract in the mid-nineteenth century. From this moment on, language would no longer be tasked with conveying personal emotions; instead, formal innovation took centre stage. Language was made strange and self-reflexive while at the same time magical and mathematical, with poets offering what Friedrich calls 'impassive inwardness in lieu of feelings' (1974, 22). Edgar Allan Poe played a key role in this development, pushing both the mathematical and esoteric tendencies to their extremes. In the French context, Baudelaire became the inaugural figure. Friedrich quotes Baudelaire's 'La sensibilité de cœur n'est pas absolument favorable au travail poétique' (Baudelaire, 1976, 116) ['the sensibility of the heart is not entirely favourable to poetic work'], and cites the poet's various claims concerning the rigorous, mathematical composition of *Les Fleurs du mal*. Turning to Mallarmé, Friedrich takes Hérodiade's 'du reste je ne veux rien d'humain' (Mallarmé, 1998, 20) ['besides, I want nothing human'] to speak for Mallarmé's poetry more widely, before concluding that 'Mallarmé's poetry embodies total solitude. It has no desire for Christian, humanistic, or literary tradition. It refuses to interfere with the present. It rebuffs the reader and imposes inhumanity upon itself' (Friedrich, 1974, 106).

It is precisely this kind of reading that late-twentieth- and early-twenty-first-century critics have sought to oppose – not least the readers of Mallarmé. In studies by critics such as Bertrand Marchal, Jacques Rancière, and many others, emphasis has instead been placed on the multiple ways in which the poet situated himself in late-nineteenth-century society and culture and how he lived, to take the eloquent title of Jean-Luc Steinmetz's 1998 biography, *L'Absolu au jour le jour*.[2]

This volume has not entered into debate over this dichotomy between the depersonalized Mallarmé and the historically grounded (or historically contextualized) Mallarmé. It has instead tried to open up the idea of what constitutes relevant context, so that our present time can play a fuller role. This said, it is obvious that these poets all engage with their contemporary societies; for instance, when they write to their many friends, in multiple letters and texts that build social relations and tie networks, that can then be mapped by historicist scholars. On the other hand, there is no doubt that depersonalization is a recurring theme in the writings of these poets, including in those very letters. There is not only an anti-psychological strand in many texts by Verlaine, Baudelaire, and Mallarmé, there is also, as I have sought to emphasize, a speculative dimension that aims to set free poems (and colours) so they can assume a life of their own, do work on their own.

In my opinion, both the focus on depersonalization and the version of historicism we find in many recent, critical texts are too intent on keeping the poetry within an anthropocentric horizon. Both positions get in the way of what we – inspired by Cézanne – could call *convex reading*. As Cézanne explained, only when he realized that the shadow of the Sainte-Victoire was convex rather concave did he manage to

2   The theme of depersonalization has sometimes been traced back to Valéry, Blanchot, and their post-structuralist readers, with this tradition being taken to task for overlooking history and context (see for instance Bakken, 2018). In some cases, this claim seems to me misleading (think of the historical richness presented in Julia Kristeva's *La Révolution du langage poétique* [1974]); in other cases, it seems the debate is really about what is recognized as 'historical context'. If we include Nietzsche, Marx, Freud, and the anarchist movement in the idea of context (why wouldn't we?), most post-structuralist readings are contextualizing too.

capture how the mountain's fiery, granite rocks take off toward the sun, participate in the world. Only then did his paintings 'spin in the air'. Similarly, we must allow the work of these writers to overflow and animate their surroundings (and their logical contexts), bringing their readers with them in the process. John Dewey writes that art is a chance 'to be set on fire' (2009, 68); sitting by his fireplace, Mallarmé likens the theatre and the hearth ('théâtre' and 'âtre' [2003, 162]); and Baudelaire's writings on colour (like Cézanne's, Merleau-Ponty's, and Deleuze's) clearly demonstrate how this fire can open up readers and viewers, and blur distinctions between landscapes and hands, rivers and blood vessels. As we saw in chapters 3 and 4, such openings have both a social dimension, allowing for non-hierarchical relations between human beings (as in Mallarmé's exposition of the democratic pixelation politics in Manet's 'Le Linge' ['The Laundry', 1875] and in Rancière's reading of Baudelaire's 'goût infini de la république' [Rancière, 2014a, 94–112], ['infinite taste of the republic']), and a more general ontological dimension, opening human beings up to the world. To communicate this experience to a reader or viewer requires careful organization of the gathered forces, and few poets have been more aware of the necessity of this formal work (inventing new poetic forms such as the 'rêverie' that Rancière highlighted) than the three poets studied here. The work of art, then, is a spiritual instrument through which we mediate our relation to the world. When these instruments are well constructed, they heighten our experience of the world, intensifying the 'vibratory continuum'. They require bodies to host the intensities, and, through the process of hosting, these bodies travel elsewhere.

I have used the term 'spiritual materialism' in an attempt to avoid the dichotomies between depersonalization and historicism, the abstract and the concrete, the mind and the body. The poets in question are both more speculative and more embedded than is often argued. This claim is similar to the double insistence on the non-subjective and the embedded that we encountered in the work of Mark Hansen. Borrowing from Hansen, and distancing ourselves from many author-centred readings, we can therefore say that on the one hand this poetry – with its affects, atmospheres, electricity, networks, and constellations – communicates 'something that has perhaps always been the case, but that has never been so insistently manifest: agency is *resolutely not* the prerogative of privileged individual actors' (Hansen, 2015, 2). And borrowing from Hansen again, and distancing ourselves from Friedrich's abstractions, we can also say that the poetry demonstrates – through exactly the same affects, atmospheres, electricity, networks, and constellations – that we are more thoroughly 'implicated' than we ever thought we were.[3] The selected texts thereby familiarize us with the idea that action is a collective (or assembled) activity – even when it's carried out by something that looks like an individual; and that its effects are felt in places we might not even suspect.

As mentioned, the body is of central importance in this double insistence on depersonalization and implication. The body is the site where this doubleness plays out – at once personal and impersonal. This is a view shared by the 25-year-old 'depersonalized' Mallarmé. It is therefore not contradictory when, two weeks after declaring himself 'une aptitude qu'a l'Univers Spirituel à se voir et à se dévélopper, à travers ce qui fut moi' (1998, 714) ['a capacity possessed by the spiritual universe to see itself and develop itself, through what was once me' (1988, 74)], Mallarmé turns to the body to specify the role it plays when the universe thinks itself. Warning against being overly cerebral, he explains to his friend Eugène Lefébure how nature sings – and thinks – the body electric:

> Je crois que pour être bien l'homme, la nature se pensant, il faut penser de tout son corps — ce qui donne une pensée pleine et à l'unisson comme ces cordes du violon vibrant immédiatement avec sa boîte de bois creux. Les pensées partant du seul cerveau (dont j'ai tant abusé l'été dernier et une partie de cet hiver) me font maintenant l'effet d'airs joués sur la partie aiguë de la chanterelle dont le son ne réconforte pas dans la boîte — qui passent et s'en vont sans se *créer*, sans laisser de trace d'elles. (1998, 720)

> [I think that to be truly a man, to be nature capable of thought, one must think with one's entire body, which creates a full, harmonious thought, like those violin strings vibrating directly on their hollow wooden box. Thoughts produced by the brain alone (which I so abused last summer and of this winter) now appear to me like airs played on the high part of the E-string without being strengthened by the box, — which pass through and disappear without creating themselves, without leaving a trace of themselves. (1988, 80, translation modified)]

Eager to move away from mind–body dualisms, Mallarmé here presents himself as a creative instrument – a violin.[4] In the first sentence of the

---

3 As Hansen wrote in his exposition of Whitehead's radically ecological ontology: 'every actual occasion implicates *the entirety of the universe*' (2015, 10).

4 I alluded to this letter in my third chapter. As mentioned, it was written on the day that Lefébure wrote to Mallarmé about the links between Spinoza, Poe,

citation, Mallarmé wants out of what Barthes calls 'l'Individuel (bloc classique de la personne)' (2003, 78) ['the Individual (the traditional unit of the human being)' (2011, 43)]; instead, he combines impersonality, body, and non-anthropocentricity in his version of spiritual materialism. This is his way of participating in the vibratory continuum, just as Baudelaire gave us the chance to reverberate in the 'hymne compliqué [qui] s'appelle la couleur' ['complicated hymn called colour'] and Verlaine in the 'humble antienne' ['humble refrain'].

In addition to becoming-violin, the letter proposes another and related way in which the human being can become 'nature se pensant' ['nature capable of thought']: Mallarmé presents the option of becoming-cricket. He comes to this animal through Baudelaire's sonnet 'Bohémiens en voyage' ['Travelling Gypsies']. There, the cricket sets up a verse in which the goddess Cybele animates and intensifies nature for the travelling gypsies. When Mallarmé first read the poem, he had only heard the English cricket, and it struck him as rather inadequate ('maigre' [721]) in the context of the poem. Now in Besançon, walking on country roads, he experiences the powerful 'singing' of the French cricket, and he understands why Baudelaire trusted this little animal to inspire Cybele, so that she could put the world in motion:

> Du fond de son réduit sablonneux, le grillon,
> les regardant passer, redouble sa chanson;
> Cybèle, qui les aime, augmente ses verdures
>
> Fait couler le rocher et fleurir le désert.[5]

The first two lines cited here read almost like a haiku; strongly deictic, they carve out an *oikos*, giving the snapshot of a micro-event which

and Baudelaire. Mallarmé is in similar Spinozist territory here when he presents his body as the site where nature thinks itself. Merleau-Ponty is in this territory too. He defines painting as 'nature naturante', and explains that 'elle donne ce que la nature veut dire et ne dit pas: le "principe générateur" qui fait être les choses et le monde' (1996, 56) ['it gives us what nature means and does not say: the "generative principle" which makes things and the world be'].

5   Here are two published translations – by Roy Campbell: 'Out of his hole the cricket sees them pass/ And sings the louder. Greener grows the grass/ Because Cybele loves them, and has made// The barren rock to gush, the sands to flower' (Baudelaire, 1952, 19) – and by James McGowan: 'The cricket, as he sees them pass along,/ Deep in his lair redoubles his shrill song;/ Cybele, their friend, augments her greenery,// Turns rocks to springs, brings flowers from the sand' (Baudelaire, 2008, 33).

then (in the following lines) takes on a cosmic significance. Operating through condensation ('réduit') and intensification ('redouble'), the cricket is an animal whose body 'sings' the surroundings into movement: the world 'tourne dans l'air'. Mallarmé concludes his letter with an enthusiastic exclamation: 'Tout le bonheur qu'a la terre de ne pas être décomposée en matière et en esprit était dans ce son *unique* du grillon!' (721) ['All the happiness the earth possesses in not being broken down into matter and spirit was contained in the unique sound of the cricket' (1988, 81)]. The letter thereby communicates Mallarmé's desire that the coherence of the universe may express itself through a mediating body that vibrates, intensifies, and makes song available to all; taking inspiration from Baudelaire, Mallarmé proposes the ideal of the individual-environment-in-song.

Bibliography

Baudelaire, Mallarmé, and Verlaine

Charles Baudelaire, *Poems of Baudelaire*, trans. by Roy Campbell (London: The Harvill Press, 1952).

Charles Baudelaire, *Paris Spleen*, trans. by Louise Varèse (New York: New Directions, 1970).

Charles Baudelaire, *Œuvres complètes vol. 1*, texte établi, présenté et annoté par C. Pichois (Paris: Gallimard, 1975).

Charles Baudelaire, *Œuvres complètes vol. 2*, texte établi, présenté et annoté par C. Pichois (Paris: Gallimard, 1976).

Charles Baudelaire, *The Prose Poems and La Fanfarlo*, trans. and intro. by Rosemary Lloyd (Oxford: Oxford University Press, 1991).

Charles Baudelaire, *Flowers of Evil and Other Works: A Dual-Language Book*, ed. and trans. by Wallace Fowlie (New York: Dover Publications, 1992a).

Charles Baudelaire, *Selected Writings on Art and Literature*, trans. and intro. by P.E. Charvet (London: Penguin, 1992b [1972]).

Charles Baudelaire, *The Flowers of Evil*, trans. by James McGowan (Oxford: Oxford University Press, 2008).

Charles Baudelaire, 'The philosophy of Toys', in K. Gross, *On Dolls* (London: Notting Hill Editions Ltd, 2012).

Charles Baudelaire, *The Flowers of Evil 1868*, trans. by John E. Tidball (2018).

Stéphane Mallarmé, *Selected Letters of Stéphane Mallarmé*, trans. by Rosemary Lloyd (Chicago, IL: University of Chicago Press, 1988).

Stéphane Mallarmé, *Collected Poems: A Bilingual Edition*, trans. by Henry Weinfield (Berkeley and London: University of California Press, 1994).

Stéphane Mallarmé, *Correspondance complète 1862–1871* suivi de *Lettres sur la poésie 1972–1898* (Paris: Gallimard, 1995a).

Stéphane Mallarmé, *Les Interviews de Mallarmé*, textes présentés et annotés par Dieter Schwarz (Neuchâtel: Ides et Calendes, 1995b).

Stéphane Mallarmé, *Œuvres complètes I*, édition présentée, établie et annotée par Bertrand Marchal, Bibliothèque de La Pléiade, 2 vols (Paris: Gallimard, 1998).

Stéphane Mallarmé, 'A Throw of Dice Not Ever Will Abolish Chance (1897)', in *Manifesto: A Century of Isms*, ed. by Mary Ann Caws, trans. by Tom Csaszar (Lincoln, NE: University of Nebraska Press, 2001), 27–49.

Stéphane Mallarmé, *Œuvres complètes II*, édition présentée, établie et annotée par Bertrand Marchal, Bibliothèque de La Pléiade, 2 vols (Paris: Gallimard, 2003).

Stéphane Mallarmé, *Divagations*, trans. by Barbara Johnson (Cambridge, MA: Harvard University Press, 2007).

Paul Verlaine, *Œuvres poétiques complètes*, texte établi, présenté et annoté par Y.-G. Le Dantec, édition révisée, complétée et présentée par Jacques Borel (Paris: Gallimard, 1962).

Paul Verlaine, *Œuvres en prose complètes*, texte établi, présenté et annoté par Jacques Borel (Paris: Gallimard, 1972).

Paul Verlaine, *Correspondance générale vol. 1*, établie et annotée par Michael Pakenham (Paris: Fayard, 2005).

Paul Verlaine, *Romances sans paroles*, édition critique de Steve Murphy (Paris: Honoré Champion, 2012).

Critical literature

Joseph Acquisto, *The Fall out of Redemption: Writing and Thinking beyond Salvation in Baudelaire, Cioran, Fondane, Agamben, and Nancy* (London: Bloomsbury, 2016).

Theodor W. Adorno and Walter Benjamin, *The Complete Correspondence 1928–40* (London: Polity Press, 1999).

Éric Alliez (ed.), *Gilles Deleuze, une vie philosophique* (Le Plessis-Robinson: Institut Synthélabo, 1998).

Hannah Arendt, *The Life of the Mind: One-volume edition* (New York: Harcourt Brace Jovanovich, 1981).

Anna Arnar, *The Book as Instrument: Stéphane Mallarmé, the Artist's Book, and the Transformation of Print Culture* (Chicago, IL: University of Chicago Press, 2010).

Antonin Artaud, *Œuvres* (Paris: Gallimard, 2004).

Gaston Bachelard, *La Poétique de l'espace* (Paris: PUF, 2012 [1957]).

Gaston Bachelard, *The Poetics of Space* (Boston, MA: Beacon Press, 1994).

Arild Michel Bakken, *La Présence de Mallarmé* (Paris: Honoré Champion, 2018).

Roland Barthes, *Writing Degree Zero*, trans. Annette Lavers and Colin Smith (London: Jonathan Cape, 1967).

Roland Barthes, *S/Z* (Paris: Seuil, 1970).

Roland Barthes, *Le Degré zéro de l'écriture (suivi de Nouveaux essais critiques)* (Paris: Seuil, 1972).

Roland Barthes, *Fragments d'un discours amoureux* (Paris: Seuil, 1977a).

Roland Barthes, *Image, Music, Text* (London: Fontana, 1977b).

Roland Barthes, *Leçon* (Paris: Seuil, 1978).

Roland Barthes, *Camera Lucida: Reflections on Photography* (New York: Hill and Wang, 1981).

Roland Barthes, *On Racine* (New York: Performing Arts Journal Publication, 1983a).

Roland Barthes, *The Empire of Signs* (London: Cape, 1983b).

Roland Barthes, *Le Bruissement de la langue* (Paris: Seuil, 1984).

Roland Barthes, *Œuvres complètes, vol. 1: 1942–1965* (Paris: Seuil, 1993).

Roland Barthes, *Critique et vérité* (Paris: Seuil, 1999).

Roland Barthes, *Œuvres complètes vol. III* (Paris: Seuil, 2002a).

Roland Barthes, *Œuvres complètes vol. IV* (Paris: Seuil, 2002b).

Roland Barthes, *Le Neutre: Notes de cours au Collège de France, 1977–1978*, texte établi par Thomas Clerc (Paris: Seuil-IMEC, 2002c).

Roland Barthes, *La Préparation du roman I et II, cours et séminaires au Collège de France (1978–79 et 1979–80)*, texte établi, annoté et présenté par Nathalie Léger (Paris: Seuil-IMEC, 2003).

Roland Barthes, *L'Empire des signes* (Paris: Seuil, 2005).

Roland Barthes, *Criticism and Truth* (Minneapolis, MN: University of Minnesota Press, 2007).

Roland Barthes, *The Preparation of the Novel: Lecture Courses and Seminars at the Collège de France, 1978–1979 and 1979–1980* (New York: Columbia University Press, 2011).

Roland Barthes, *La Chambre claire, Note sur la photographie* (Paris: Cahiers du cinéma, Gallimard, Seuil, 2012).

Georges Bataille, *Manet, a biographical and critical study* (Geneva: Éditions d'art Albert Skira, 1955).

Georges Bataille, *Manet* (Geneva: Éditions d'art Albert Skira, 1994).

Gregory Bateson, *Steps to an Ecology of Mind* (Chicago, IL: University of Chicago Press, 2000).

Gregory Bateson, *Mind and Nature* (Cresskills, NJ: Hampton Press, 2002).

Walter Benjamin, *Charles Baudelaire, Un poète lyrique à l'apogée du capitalisme* (Paris: Payot, 1979).

Jane Bennett, 'De Rerum Natura', *Strategies vol. 13–1* (2000), pp. 9–22.

Jane Bennett, *Vibrant Matter: A Political Ecology of Things* (Durham, NC: Duke University Press, 2010).

Marshall Berman, *All That Is Solid Melts into Air: The Experience of Modernity* (London: Verso, 2010).

Arnaud Bernadet, *L'Exil et l'utopie, politiques de Verlaine* (Saint-Etienne: Publications de l'Université de Saint-Etienne, 2007).

Arnaud Bernadet, *Poétique de Verlaine* (Paris: Classiques Garnier, 2014).

Leo Bersani, *Homos* (Cambridge, MA: Harvard University Press, 1996).

Miguel de Bestegui, 'Science and Ontology: From Merleau-Ponty's "Reduction" to Simondon's "Transduction"', *Gilbert Simondon: Being and Technology*, ed. by Arne de Boever, Alex Murray, Jon Roffe, and Ashley Woodward (Edinburgh: Edinburgh University Press, 2013), pp. 154–75.

Yves Bonnefoy, *Le Secret de la Pénultième* (Paris: Abstème & Bobance, 2005).

Pierre Bourdieu, *Les Règles de l'art* (Paris: Éditions du Seuil, 1992).

Rosi Braidotti, *The Posthuman* (Cambridge: Polity Press, 2013).

Rosi Braidotti, *Posthuman Knowledge* (Cambridge: Polity Press, 2019).

Mauro Carbone, *La Chair des images* (Paris: Vrin, 2011).

Mauro Carbone, *The Flesh of Images: Merleau-Ponty between Painting and Cinema* (Albany, NY: SUNY Press, 2015).

Madeleine Chalmers, *Unruly Technics in the French Literary Avant-Garde: Technological Writings of the Third Republic and their Afterlives in Contemporary Thought* (PhD dissertation, 2021, University of Oxford).

Ross Chambers, *An Atmospherics of the City: Baudelaire and the Poetics of Noise* (New York: Fordham University Press, 2015).

Timothy Clark, *Ecocriticism on the Edge* (London: Bloomsbury, 2015).

Robert Greer Cohn, *L'Œuvre de Mallarmé: Un coup de dés* (Paris: Librairie les lettres, 1951).

Gilles Deleuze, *Logique du sens* (Paris: Éditions de Minuit, 1969).

Gilles Deleuze, *Francis Bacon: Logique de la sensation* (Paris: Éditions de la différence, 1994).

Gilles Deleuze, *Cinéma 2: L'image-temps* (Paris: Éditions de Minuit, 2002).

Gilles Deleuze, *Francis Bacon* (London: Continuum, 2006).

Gilles Deleuze and Félix Guattari, *Mille Plateaux* (Paris: Seuil, 1980).

Gilles Deleuze and Félix Guattari, *A Thousand Plateaus* (London: Continuum, 1987).

Jacques Derrida, *La Dissémination* (Paris: Seuil, 1972).

John Dewey, *The Public and Its Problems* (Pennsylvania State University Press, 2012 [1927]).

John Dewey, *Art as Experience* (New York: Perigee Books, 2009 [1934]).

Jean Dornbush, 'The Death of the Penultimate: Paradox in Mallarmé's "Le Démon de l'analogie"', *French Forum* 5:3 (1980), pp. 239–60.

Ruth Felski, *The Limits of Critique* (Chicago, IL: University of Chicago Press, 2015).

Stanley Fish, *Is There a Text in This Class?* (Cambridge, MA: Harvard University Press, 1980).

Vilém Flusser, *Into the Universe of Technical Images* (Minneapolis, MN: University of Minnesota Press, 2011a).

Vilém Flusser, *Does Writing Have a Future?* (Minneapolis, MN: University of Minnesota Press, 2011b).

Hugo Friedrich, *The Structure of Modern Poetry: From the Mid-Nineteenth to the Mid-Twentieth Century* (Evanston, IL: Northwestern University Press, 1974).

Joachim Gasquet, *Cézanne: A Memoir with Conversations* (London: Thames & Hudson, 1991).

Joachim Gasquet, *Cézanne* (Paris: Les Belles Lettres, 2012).

Marit Grøtta, *Baudelaire's Media Aesthetics: The Gaze of the Flâneur and Nineteenth-Century Media* (London: Bloomsbury, 2015).

Richard Grusin, *The Nonhuman Turn* (Minneapolis, MN: University of Minnesota Press, 2015).

Félix Guattari, *Les Trois écologies* (Paris: Gallilée, 1989).

Mark Hansen, *Bodies in Code: Interfaces with Digital Media* (London: Routledge, 2006).

Mark Hansen, *Feed-Forward: On the Future of Twenty-First-Century Media* (Chicago, IL: University of Chicago Press, 2015).

Susan Harrow, *Colourworks* (London: Bloomsbury, 2021).

Arnold Hauser, *The Social History of Art 4* (London: Routledge, 1989).

N. Katherine Hayles, *Unthought: The Power of the Cognitive Nonconscious* (Chicago, IL: University of Chicago Press, 2017).

Erich Hörl (ed.), w. James Burton, *General Ecology: The New Ecological Paradigm* (London: Bloomsbury, 2017).

Bernard Howells, *Baudelaire, Individualism, Dandyism and the Philosophy of History* (Oxford: Legenda, 1996).

Jules Huret, *Enquête sur l'évolution littéraire* (Paris: José Corti, 1999).

Jean Hyppolite, *Figures de la pensée philosophique vol. 2* (Paris: Presses Universitaires de France, 1991).

William James, *Pragmatism, Meaning of Truth and The Varieties of Religious Experience* (Hayesville, NC: AJBT Classics, 2019).

Barbara Johnson, *Défigurations du langage poétique* (Paris: Flammarion, 1979).

Adrian Johnston, *Adventures in Transcendental Materialism* (Edinburgh: Edinburgh University Press, 2014).

Gustave Kahn, *Symbolistes et décadents* (Geneva: Slatkine Reprints, 1977).

Russell S. King, 'Verlaine's "Romances sans paroles": The Inscription of Gender', *Nineteenth-Century French Studies*, Fall–Winter 1998–99, Vol. 27, No. 1–2, pp. 117–31.

Julia Kristeva, *La Révolution du langage poétique* (Paris: Seuil, 1974).

Henri Laborit, *L'Homme et la ville* (Paris: Flammarion, 2011).

Bruno Latour, *Nous n'avons jamais été modernes* (Paris: La Découverte, 1991).

Jacques Le Rider, 'Ligne et couleur: Histoire d'un différend', *Revue Germanique Internationale*, No. 10 (1998), pp. 173–84.

Frédéric Lenoir, *Le Miracle Spinoza* (Paris: Fayard, 2017).

Rosemary Lloyd, *Mallarmé: The Poet and His Circle* (Ithaca, NY: Cornell University Press, 1999).

Nikolaj Lübecker, *Le Sacrifice de la sirène, La poétique de Mallarmé et « Un coup de dés »* (Copenhagen: Museum Tusculanum, 2002).

Nikolaj Lübecker, *Community, Myth and Recognition in Twentieth-Century French Literature and Thought* (London: Continuum, 2009).

Claire Lyu, 'The Poetics of the Penult: Mallarmé, Death, and Syntax', *Modern Language Notes* German Issue 113:3 (1998), pp. 561–87.

Bertrand Marchal, *La Religion de Mallarmé* (Paris: José Corti, 1988).

Bertrand Marchal, *Lire le symbolisme* (Paris: Dunod, 1993).

Bertrand Marchal and Marie-Pierre Pouly, *Mallarmé et l'anglais récréatif: le poète pédagogue* (Paris: Cohen & Cohen, 2014).

Gyorgy Markus, 'Walter Benjamin or the Commodity as Phantasmagoria', *New German Critique* 83 (2001), pp. 3–42.

Brian Massumi, *Parables for the Virtual* (Durham, NC: Duke University Press, 2002).

Brian Massumi, '"Technical Mentality" Revisited: Brian Massumi on Gilbert Simondon', in *Gilbert Simondon: Being and Technology*, eds. Arne de Boever, Alex Murray, Jon Roffe, and Ashley Woodward (Edinburgh: Edinburgh University Press, 2013).

Brian Massumi, *What Animals Teach Us about Politics* (Durham, NC: Duke University Press, 2014).

Brian Massumi, *The Power at the End of Economy* (Durham, NC: Duke University Press, 2015a).

Brian Massumi, *Politics of Affect* (London: Polity Press, 2015b).

Patrick McGuinness, *Poetry and Radical Politics in Fin de Siècle France* (Oxford: Oxford University Press, 2015).

Patrick McGuinness, 'Existe-t-il une politique du symbolisme?', *Communications*, No. 99, 2016, pp. 41–54.

Marshall McLuhan, *Understanding Media* (London: Routledge, 2001).

Jeffrey Mehlman, 'Mallarmé/Maxwell: Elements', *Romanic Review* 71:4 (1980), pp. 374–80.

Quentin Meillassoux, *Le Nombre et la sirène: Un déchiffrage du Coup de dés de Mallarmé* (Paris: Fayard, 2011).

Françoise Meltzer, *Seeing Double: Baudelaire's Modernity* (Chicago: University of Chicago Press, 2011).

Maurice Merleau-Ponty, *The Merleau-Ponty Aesthetics Reader: Philosophy and Painting*, ed. by Galen A. Johnson and Michael B. Smith (Evanston, IL: Northwestern Cenurity Press, 1993).

Maurice Merleau-Ponty, *Sens et non-sens* (Paris: Gallimard, 1996).

Maurice Merleau-Ponty, *L'Œil et l'Esprit* (Paris: Gallimard, 1997).

Maurice Merleau-Ponty, *Vie et individuation avec des inédits de Merleau-Ponty et Simondon*, eds. Renaud Barbaras, Mauro Carbone, Helen A. Fielding, and Leonard Lawlor (Paris: Vrin, 2005).

Maurice Merleau-Ponty, *Notes de cours, 1959–61* (Paris: Gallimard, 2019).

Stamos Metzidakis, '(Post-)Romantic Vision in *Le Spleen de Paris*', in C. Krueger (ed.), *Approaches to Teaching Baudelaire's Prose Poems* (New York: MLA, 2017), pp. 64–72.

W.J.T. Mitchell and Mark B.N. Hansen, *Critical Terms for Media Studies* (Chicago, IL: University of Chicago Press, 2010).

Henri Mondor, *Eugène Lefébure: Sa vie, ses lettres à Mallarmé* (Paris: Gallimard, 1951).

Ève Morisi, *Capital Letters: Hugo, Baudelaire, Camus, and the Death Penalty* (Evanston, IL: Northwestern University Press, 2020).

Roger Munier, *Haiku* (Paris: Fayard, 1978).

Antonio Negri, *Art & Multitude* (Cambridge: Polity Press, 2011).

Kevin Newmark, 'Now You See It, Now You Don't: Baudelaire's Modernité', *Nineteenth-Century French Studies*, Vol. 44, No. 1–2, 2015, pp. 1–24.

Friedrich Nietzsche, *On the Genealogy of Morality*, trans. by Maudemarie Clark and Alan J. Swensen (Indianapolis, IN: Hackett Publishing Company, 1998).

Friedrich Nietzsche, *The Birth of Tragedy: Out of the Spirit of Music* (London: Penguin Classics, 2003).

Roger Pearson, *Unfolding Mallarmé* (Oxford: Clarendon Press, 1996).

Roger Pearson, *Stéphane Mallarmé* (London: Reaktion Books, 2010).

Jennifer Phillips, 'Relative Color: Baudelaire, Chevreul, and the Reconsideration of Critical Methodology', *Nineteenth-Century French Studies*, Vol. 33, No. 2, 2005, pp. 342–57.

Raymond Picard, *Nouvelle critique ou nouvelle imposture* (Paris: J.-J. Pauvert, 1965).

Claude Pichois, 'Introduction', in Charles Baudelaire, *Les Fleurs du mal* (Paris: Poésie/Gallimard, 2005 [1972]), pp. 7–26.

Edgar Allan Poe, *Tales, Poems, Essays*, intro. by Laurence Meynell (London: Collins, 1952).

Laurence M. Porter, *The Crisis of French Symbolism* (Ithaca, NY: Cornell University Press, 1990).

Georges Poulet, *Les Métamorphoses du cercle* (Paris: Flammarion, 1979 [1961]).

Georges Poulet, *The Metamorphoses of the Circle* (Baltimore, MD: Johns Hopkins University Press, 1966).

Georges Poulet, 'Proust et la répétition', in *L'Arc: Proust* (Paris: Librairie Duponchelle, 1990), pp. 5–13.

Marcel Proust, 'Contre l'obscurité', *La Revue blanche* 11:2 (1896).

Jacques Rancière, *Mallarmé: La Politique de la sirène* (Paris: Hachette, 1996).

Jacques Rancière, *L'Espace des mots: De Mallarmé à Broodthaers* (Nantes: Musée des Beaux-Arts de Nantes, 2005).

Jacques Rancière, *Les Écarts du cinéma* (Paris: La fabrique, 2011).

Jacques Rancière, *Le Fil perdu – essais sur la fiction moderne* (Paris: La fabrique, 2014a).

Jacques Rancière, 'The Infinite Taste of the Republic', in *Yale French Studies*, No. 125/126 (2014), Time for Baudelaire (Poetry, Theory, History) (2014b), pp. 30–44.

Jean-Pierre Richard, *Poésie et profondeur* (Paris: Seuil, 1955).

Thomas Rid, *Rise of the Machines: The Lost History of Cybernetics* (Melbourne: Scribe, 2016).

Arthur Rimbaud, *Œuvres complètes*, édition établie, présentée et annotée par Antoine Adam, Bibliothèque de La Pléiade (Paris: Gallimard, 1972).

Arthur Rimbaud, *Complete Works, Selected Letters: A Bilingual Edition*, translated with an introduction and notes by Wallace Fowlie. Updated, revised, and with a foreword by Seth Whidden (Chicago: University of Chicago Press, 2005).

Mitsou Ronat and Tipor Papp, 'présentation', in Stéphane Mallarmé, *Un coup de dés jamais n'abolira le hasard* (Paris: Change Errant, 1980).

Carlo Rovelli, *Reality Is Not What It Seems: The Journey to Quantum Gravity* (London: Penguin, 2017).

Carlo Rovelli, *The Order of Time* (London: Penguin, 2019).

Carlo Rovelli, *Helgoland* (London: Penguin, 2021).

Debarati Sanyal, *The Violence of Modernity: Baudelaire, Irony, and the Politics of Form* (Baltimore, MD: Johns Hopkins University Press, 2006).

Jean-Paul Sartre, *Situations IX*, 10 vols (Paris: Gallimard, 1972).

Jean-Paul Sartre, *Situations III*, 10 vols (Paris: Gallimard, 2003).

Anne Sauvagnargues, 'Crystals and Membranes: Individuation and Temporality', in *Gilbert Simondon: Being and Technology*, eds. Arne de Boever, Alex Murray, Jon Roffe, and Ashley Woodward (Edinburgh: Edinburgh University Press, 2013), pp. 57–70.

Leon Ter Schure, *Bergson and History: Transforming the Modern Regime of Historicity* (Albany, NY: SUNY Press, 2019).

Clive Scott, *The Riches of Rhyme: Studies in French Verse* (Oxford: Clarendon Press, 1988).

Maria C. Scott, *Baudelaire's Le Spleen de Paris: Shifting Perspectives* (Aldershot: Ashgate, 2005).

Steven Shaviro, *Post-Cinematic Affect* (Winchester: Zero Books, 2010).

Gilbert Simondon, 'The Genesis of the Individual', in *Incorporations*, eds. Jonathan Crary and Sandford Kwinter (New York: Zone Books, 1992), pp. 297–319.

Gilbert Simondon, *L'Invention dans les techniques: cours et conférences* (Paris: Éditions du Seuil, 2005).

Gilbert Simondon, *Communication et information* (Paris: Presses universitaires de France, 2010).

Gilbert Simondon, *Du mode d'existence des objets techniques* (Paris: Aubier, 2012).

Gilbert Simondon, *L'Individuation à la lumière des notions de forme et d'information* (Grenoble: Million, 2013).

Gilbert Simondon, *Imagination et invention (1965–66)* (Paris: Presses universitaires de France, 2014a).

Gilbert Simondon, *Sur la technique* (Paris: Presses universitaires de France, 2014b).

Gilbert Simondon, 'Culture and Technics', in *Radical Philosophy* 189 (Jan/Feb 2015), pp. 17–23.

Gilbert Simondon, *On the Mode of Existence of Technical Objects* (Minneapolis, MN: Univocal, 2017).

Ann Kennedy Smith, *Painted Poetry: Colour in Baudelaire's Art Criticism* (Oxford: Peter Lang, 2011).

Philippe Sollers, *L'Écriture et l'expérience des limites* (Paris: Seuil, 1968).

Philippe Sollers, *Writing and the Experience of Limits* (New York: Columbia University Press, 1983).

Tom Sparrow, *Plastic Bodies: Rebuilding Sensation After Phenomenology* (London: Open University Press, 2015).

Baruch Spinoza, *Complete Works* (Indianapolis, IN: Hackett, 2002).

Jean-Luc Steinmetz, *Stéphane Mallarmé – L'Absolu au jour le jour* (Paris: Fayard, 1998).

Isabelle Stengers, 'Introductory Notes on an Ecology of Practices', *Cultural Studies* 11:1 (2005), pp. 183–96.

Bernard Stiegler and Ars Industrialis, *Réenchanter le monde: La valeur esprit contre le populisme industriel* (Paris: Flammarion, 2006).

Bernard Stiegler and Ars Industrialis, *The Re-Enchantment of the World: The Value of Spirit Against Industrial Capitalism* (London: Bloomsbury, 2014).

Eugene Thacker, in Alexander Galloway, Eugene Thacker, and McKenzie Wark, *Excommunication: Three Inquiries in Media and Mediation* (Chicago, IL: University of Chicago Press, 2014).

Tiqqun, *Théorie du Bloom* (Paris: La fabrique, 2004).

Fred Turner, *From Counterculture to Cyberculture: Stewart Brand, the Whole Earth Network, and the Digital Utopianism* (Chicago, IL: University of Chicago Press, 2006).

Alain Vaillant, *Baudelaire, Poète Comique* (Rennes: Presses Universitaires de Rennes, 2007).

Paul Valéry, *Variété II* (Paris: Gallimard, 1924).

Paul Valéry, *Collected Works, volume 8* (Princeton, NJ: Princeton University Press, 1972).

Francisco Varela, Evan Thompson, and Eleanor Rosch, *The Embodied Mind: Cognitive Science and Human Experience*, revised edition (Cambridge, MA: MIT Press, 2016).

Jean Wahl, *Vers le concret: Études d'histoire de la philosophie contemporaine, William James, Whitehead, Gabriel Marcel* (Paris: Vrin, 2010).

Christophe Wall-Romana, *Cinepoetry: Imaginary Cinemas in French Poetry* (New York: Fordham University Press, 2013).

Seth Whidden, *Leaving Parnassus: The Lyric Subject in Verlaine and Rimbaud* (Amsterdam: Rodopi, 2007).

Alfred North Whitehead, *Adventures of Ideas* (New York: The Free Press, 1967).

Norbert Wiener, *God & Golem, Inc* (Cambridge, MA: MIT Press, 1966).

Norbert Wiener, *Cybernetics: Or Control and Communication in the Animal and the Machine* (Cambridge, MA: MIT Press, 2013).

Jennifer Yee, '"La Beauté": Art and Dialogism in the Poetry of Baudelaire', in *Neophilologus* 102:1 (2018), pp. 1–14.

Slavoj Žižek, *In Defense of Lost Causes* (London: Verso, 2008).

Index